P9-CJK-167

Praise for *Saving Freedom*

Saving Freedom is a new Declaration of Independence, a call for the American people to reclaim America. Jim DeMint's passion for the cause of individual liberty and personal responsibility is evident in this manifesto. It needs to be read—and acted upon—by every citizen of this republic.

—**Newt Gingrich**, former Speaker of the U.S. House of Representatives

Once again, as we did in 1776, Americans must choose between freedom and oppression. In *Saving Freedom*, Jim DeMint describes the clear and present danger posed by big government—and what we must do to preserve individual liberty and personal responsibility. Every American needs to read this book.

—**Sean Hannity**, host of the *Sean Hannity Radio Show* and *Hannity's America* on FOX News Channel

It's comforting to know that someone like Jim DeMint is standing in the gap as we see so many of our nation's founding principles eroding. I view *Saving Freedom* as a blueprint for the effort that all concerned Americans must join to restore and protect the freedoms we depend on.

—**Steve Forbes**, president and chief executive officer of Forbes and editor-in-chief of *Forbes* magazine

In a book rich with details and examples, Jim DeMint has captured America's disturbing transformation from a nation built on individual freedom to one ruled by the kind of unchecked government against which our fathers and our father's fathers valiantly fought. His practical advice for taking action should be of interest to all Americans concerned about reversing this trend.

—**William J. Bennett**, Washington Fellow, The Claremont Institute

Conservatism comes in many flavors, but few of them are as tangy as Jim DeMint's, as readers will discover in this mince-no-words manifesto.

—**George F. Will**

Jim DeMint has delivered a "how to" plan for avoiding a future that we neither want nor deserve. For those of us who want to keep America the "land of the free and the home of the brave," *Saving Freedom* is a must read!

—**LtCol Oliver L. North**, USMC (Ret.) NYT best-selling author of
American Heroes

Senator DeMint and his ideas represent a fresh new spark that is the understanding of the origins of truth and freedom. It is my hope that with God's help, a wildfire will burn in the hearts of young Americans to be part of this still great nation's thriving future and the preservation of its bright shining liberty.

—**Stephen Baldwin**, actor and New York Times best-selling author
of *The Unusual Suspect*

Jim DeMint goes to work everyday and sees firsthand how America is slowly giving away its freedom. *Saving Freedom* is a battle plan to turn the tide and rescue our nation from the siren song of socialism.

—**Edwin J. Feulner, PhD**, president, The Heritage Foundation

Senator Jim DeMint has done all freedom-loving Americans a great service by writing *Saving Freedom*. In addition to providing a devastating critique of socialism and "big government," Senator DeMint explains the role Christian principles have played in the birth and the flourishing of our freedoms in America. Not content to just curse the darkness, Senator DeMint concludes *Saving Freedom* with action plans citizens can embrace to join the struggle to restore and maintain our God-given liberties in America.

— **Dr. Richard Land**, president, The Southern Baptist Convention's
Ethics & Religious Liberty Commission

Jim DeMint has been an effective and outspoken leader for free markets and conservative values on the floor of the Senate since his election in 2004 and before that in the House of Representatives. Now Senator DeMint lays out the bedrock principles that define conservatism in our time while sounding a crucial set of alarms about the direction of the new Congress and President Obama. In sharply written and completely documented chapters, Senator DeMint lays out why the slide toward statism has to be stopped and how to do it. Buy the book for yourself and a copy for a friend or relative who needs both a primer and a guide forward. This powerful book is part of the solution to what ails our economy and country, so spread it around.

　　　　　　—**Hugh Hewitt**, nationally syndicated talk radio host

Jim DeMint's new book, *Saving Freedom*, is a disturbing work. It is tough on both Republicans and Democrats. It tells the truth, frightening though it may be, and calls all Americans to account for the loss of freedom in our country. This hard-hitting exposé is a must read and will challenge all to a recognition of what is truly happening in America. While DeMint is an optimist and feels there is hope, I truly hope that the impact this book can make is not too late.

　　　　　　—**Dr. Frank S. Page**, Immediate Past President, Southern Baptist
Convention 2006–2008

With an engaging mix of facts, faith, wit, and wisdom, Jim DeMint's *Saving Freedom* serves as a crucial handbook for the everyday American tired of encroaching big government and ready to do something about it.

　　　　　　—**John Nolte**, editor-in-chief, *Big Hollywood*

Freedom matters and you can make a difference. This is the message that resonates from *Saving Freedom* by Senator Jim DeMint. Read it and be challenged. Read it and be prepared to do something!

　　　　　　—**Daniel Akin**, president,
Southeastern Baptist Theological Seminary

Jim DeMint has been a courageous voice in the U.S. Congress. In *Saving Freedom* he shows that he is wise as well. *Saving Freedom* is a wake-up call for Americans. It lays out a clear and persuasive case that the greatest threat Americans face today is socialist collectivism. Senator DeMint's book could not have come at a better or more urgent time.

—David Horowitz

Saving Freedom is a powerful book which should be read by all Americans regardless of political affiliation. Senator DeMint, in an easy to read primer on our history and our legacy, explains why we need to return to constitutional principles if the United States is to continue to be that "light on the hill."

—Bob Hamer, author of *The Last Undercover: The True Story of an FBI Agent's Dangerous Dance with Evil*

JIM DEMINT
U.S. SENATOR

SAVING FREEDOM

WE CAN STOP AMERICA'S SLIDE INTO SOCIALISM

FIDELIS
BOOKS

NASHVILLE, TENNESSEE

ISBN: 978-0-8054-4957-0

Fidelis Books, an imprint of B&H Publishing Group
Nashville, Tennessee

Dewey Decimal Classification: 323
Subject Heading: SOCIALISM—UNITED STATES \ FREEDOM \
GOVERNMENT OWNERSHIP

All Scripture quotations are taken from the Holman Christian Standard
Bible.® Copyright © 1999, 2000, 2002, 2003 by Holman Bible
Publishers. Used by permission. Holman Christian Standard Bible®,
Holman CSB®, and HCSB® are federally registered trademarks of
Holman Bible Publishers.

Scripture references marked NASB are taken from the New American
Standard Bible, copyright © the Lockman Foundation, 1960, 1962,
1963, 1968, 1971, 1972, 1973, 1975, 1977; used by permission.

Scripture references marked NIV are taken from the New International
Version, copyright © 1973, 1978, 1984 by International Bible Society.

Scripture references marked KJV are taken from the King James Version.

At time of printing, all Web sites were checked for accuracy.

1 2 3 4 5 6 7 8 9 10 • 13 12 11 10 09

Dedicated to my grandsons, Jimbo and Clark, and all their future brothers, sisters, cousins, and fellow Americans of the next generation.

Acknowledgments

My deepest gratitude goes to my wife Debbie, who only wanted some stability and predictability as the mother of our four children. Instead, God gave her me, a Don Quixote who wants to change the world. "How can you change the world when you can't even cut the grass?" Good question.

I am also grateful to the dedicated staff that God gave me in my Congressional and Senate offices. Their youthful energy and optimism inspired me to keep fighting even when I knew I was beaten. Their commitment to America and belief in freedom gave me the courage to "march into hell for a heavenly cause."

My greatest inspiration has come from my four children. They have shown me that God can use imperfect parents to raise up a generation of Americans who can rebuild our great nation and make it better than it has ever been.

Most of all I am thankful to Jesus who saved me and gave me freedom.

Contents

In CONGRESS, July 4, 1776.

The unanimous Declaration of the thirteen united States of America.

When in the Course of human events, it becomes necessary for one people to dissolve the political bands which have connected them with another, and to assume among the powers of the earth, the separate and equal station to which the Laws of Nature and of Nature's God entitle them, a decent respect to the opinions of mankind requires that they should declare the causes which impel them to the separation.

We hold these truths to be self-evident, that all men are created equal, that they are endowed by their Creator with certain unalienable Rights, that among these are Life, Liberty and the pursuit of Happiness.—That to secure these rights, Governments are instituted among Men, deriving their just powers from the consent of the governed,—That whenever any Form of Government becomes destructive of these ends, it is the Right of the People to alter or to abolish it, and to institute new Government, laying its foundation on such principles and organizing its powers in such form, as to them shall seem most likely to effect their Safety and Happiness. Prudence, indeed, will dictate that Governments long established should not be changed for light and transient causes; and accordingly all experience hath shewn, that mankind are more disposed to suffer, while evils are sufferable, than to right themselves by abolishing the forms to which they are accustomed. But when a long train of abuses and usurpations, pursuing invariably the same Object evinces a design to reduce them under absolute Despotism, it is their right, it is their duty, to throw off such Government, and to provide new Guards for their future security.—Such has been the patient sufferance of these Colonies; and such is now the necessity which constrains them to alter their former Systems of Government. The history of the present King of Great Britain is a history of repeated injuries and usurpations, all having in direct object the establishment of an absolute Tyranny over these States. To prove this, let Facts be submitted to a candid world.

He has refused his Assent to Laws, the most wholesome and necessary for the public good. He has forbidden his Governors to pass Laws of immediate and pressing importance, unless suspended in their operation till his Assent should be obtained; and when so suspended, he has utterly neglected to attend to them. He has refused to pass other Laws for the accommodation of large districts of people, unless those people would relinquish the right of Representation in the Legislature, a right inestimable to them and formidable to tyrants only. He has called together legislative bodies at places unusual, uncomfortable, and distant from the depository of their public Records, for the sole purpose of fatiguing them into compliance with his measures. He has dissolved Representative Houses repeatedly, for opposing with manly firmness his invasions on the rights of the people. He has refused for a long time, after such dissolutions, to cause others to be elected; whereby the Legislative powers, incapable of Annihilation, have returned to the People at large for their exercise; the State remaining in the mean time exposed to all the dangers of invasion from without, and convulsions within. He has endeavoured to prevent the population of these States; for that purpose obstructing the Laws for Naturalization of Foreigners; refusing to pass others to encourage their migrations hither, and raising the conditions of new Appropriations of Lands. He has obstructed the Administration of Justice, by refusing his Assent to Laws for establishing Judiciary powers. He has made Judges dependent on his Will alone, for the tenure of their offices, and the amount and payment of their salaries. He has erected a multitude of New Offices, and sent hither swarms of Officers to harrass our people, and eat out their substance. He has kept among us, in times of peace, Standing Armies without the Consent of our legislatures. He has affected to render the Military independent of and superior to the Civil power. He has combined with others to subject us to a jurisdiction foreign to our constitution, and unacknowledged by our laws; giving his Assent to their Acts of pretended Legislation: For Quartering large bodies of armed troops among us: For protecting them, by a mock Trial, from punishment for any Murders which they should commit on the Inhabitants of these States: For cutting off our Trade with all parts of the world: For imposing Taxes on us without our Consent: For depriving us in many cases, of the benefits of Trial by Jury: For transporting us beyond Seas to be tried for pretended offences For abolishing the free System of English Laws in a neighbouring Province, establishing therein an Arbitrary government, and enlarging its Boundaries so as to render it at once an example and fit instrument for introducing the same absolute rule into these Colonies: For taking away our Charters, abolishing our most valuable Laws, and altering fundamentally the Forms of our Governments: For suspending our own Legislatures, and declaring themselves invested with power to legislate for us in all cases whatsoever. He has abdicated Government here, by declaring us out of his Protection and waging War against us. He has plundered our seas, ravaged our Coasts, burnt our towns, and destroyed the lives of our people. He is at this time transporting large Armies of foreign Mercenaries to compleat the works of death, desolation and tyranny, already begun with circumstances of Cruelty & perfidy scarcely paralleled in the most barbarous ages, and totally unworthy the Head of a civilized nation. He has constrained our fellow Citizens taken Captive on the high Seas to bear Arms against their Country, to become the executioners of their friends and Brethren, or to fall themselves by their Hands. He has excited domestic insurrections amongst us, and has endeavoured to bring on the inhabitants of our frontiers, the merciless Indian Savages, whose known rule of warfare, is an undistinguished destruction of all ages, sexes and conditions.

In every stage of these Oppressions We have Petitioned for Redress in the most humble terms: Our repeated Petitions have been answered only by repeated injury. A Prince whose character is thus marked by every act which may define a Tyrant, is unfit to be the ruler of a free people.

Nor have We been wanting in attentions to our Brittish brethren. We have warned them from time to time of attempts by their legislature to extend an unwarrantable jurisdiction over us. We have reminded them of the circumstances of our emigration and settlement here. We have appealed to their native justice and magnanimity, and we have conjured them by the ties of our common kindred to disavow these usurpations, which, would inevitably interrupt our connections and correspondence. They too have been deaf to the voice of justice and of consanguinity. We must, therefore, acquiesce in the necessity, which denounces our Separation, and hold them, as we hold the rest of mankind, Enemies in War, in Peace Friends.

We, therefore, the Representatives of the united States of America, in General Congress, Assembled, appealing to the Supreme Judge of the world for the rectitude of our intentions, do, in the Name, and by Authority of the good People of these Colonies, solemnly publish and declare, That these United Colonies are, and of Right ought to be Free and Independent States; that they are Absolved from all Allegiance to the British Crown, and that all political connection between them and the State of Great Britain, is and ought to be totally dissolved; and that as Free and Independent States, they have full Power to levy War, conclude Peace, contract Alliances, establish Commerce, and to do all other Acts and Things which Independent States may of right do. And for the support of this Declaration, with a firm reliance on the protection of divine Providence, we mutually pledge to each other our Lives, our Fortunes and our sacred Honor.

Part I

THE RISE AND FALL OF FREEDOM IN AMERICA

If . . . My people who are called by My
name humble themselves, pray and seek My face,
and turn from their evil ways, then I will hear
from heaven, forgive their sin, and heal their land.
2 CHRONICLES 7:13–14

It may be that a free society . . . carries within itself the
forces of its own destruction, that once freedom
is achieved it is taken for granted and ceases to be
valued. . . . Does this mean that freedom is valued only
when it is lost, that the world must everywhere go through
a dark phase of socialist totalitarianism before the
forces of freedom can gather strength anew? It may
be so, but I hope it need not be.[1]
—Friedrich Hayek

Freedom and Socialism
The Gingerbread Man and the Fox

There was once a lonely old couple who had no children of their own.
One day when the woman was making some gingerbread, she used the leftover
dough to make a little Gingerbread Man. She made eyes, a nose, and a smiling
mouth using currants and placed more currants down his front to look like but-
tons. Then she laid him on a baking tray and put him into the oven.

After a little while, she heard something rattling at the oven door. She
opened it and out jumped the little Gingerbread Man. She tried to catch him
as he ran across the kitchen, but he slipped past her, calling as he ran: "Run,
run, as fast as you can. You can't catch me; I'm the Gingerbread Man!"

She chased him into the garden where her husband was digging. He put
down his spade and tried to catch him too, but as the Gingerbread Man sped
past the old man, he called over his shoulder, "Run, run, as fast as you can. You
can't catch me; I'm the Gingerbread Man!"

The Gingerbread Man ran through the town and soon had a whole host of
animals and people chasing him—a cow, a horse, and a large group of farmers

1

who had been bringing in a field of hay. The Gingerbread Man was too fast; no one could catch him. As he left the town and headed out into the country, he called out to the large group behind him: "Run, run, as fast as you can. You can't catch me; I'm the Gingerbread Man!"

But soon the Gingerbread Man came to a wide, deep, and swift-flowing river with no bridge to cross. The little man began to panic because the entire town was still in hot pursuit and close behind. As he considered his plight, a sly fox appeared and offered to give him a ride across the river. The Gingerbread Man was suspicious, but he wasn't sure he could make it across the river on his own.

The Gingerbread Man accepted the fox's offer but only on the condition that he could ride far down on the fox's back—as far from the fox's mouth as he could get. The fox agreed, so the Gingerbread Man jumped on his back. The fox began to swim, but as he reached deeper water, his back began to sink under the water. The Gingerbread Man howled, but the fox said, "The water is deep. You can move up to my neck to stay dry."

The fox then began to swim even deeper, and the water closed in around the increasingly nervous Gingerbread Man. The fox said, "Move to the top of my head, and you will be safe." The Gingerbread Man moved quickly to the fox's head because they were in the middle of the river and he had no where else to go.

Then, as the fox neared the opposite shore, his head began to go beneath the water. "Move to my nose to stay dry," said the fox. The Gingerbread Man reluctantly moved to the fox's nose, and as he did, the fox suddenly went snap! The Gingerbread Man disappeared into the fox's mouth and was never seen again.

There may be no better metaphor for America than the Gingerbread Man. When we came out of the oven in 1776, we were hot. We sent the British packing, formed a constitutional republic, and were soon off and running. America was fast and confident. Soon, no other country could even come close to the strength and speed of our military, our economy, or our culture.

Like the Gingerbread Man, Americans valued their freedom above all else. No nation in history had ever made freedom work so well. We truly became "The Shining City upon a Hill" that attracted admiration and immigrants from every country in the world. But in 1929 America "came to a wide, deep, and swift-flowing river with no bridge to cross." That river was the Great Depression. That's when the federal government became our "fox."

As Americans lost confidence in our free-enterprise economic system and our ability to cross this wide river on our own, the federal government came to our rescue. At first the expanding federal role seemed harmless enough, and the people were safely positioned far away from the fox's mouth. But as America endured one politically manufactured "crisis" after another, the fox has invited us to move ever closer to his mouth.

Today Americans, along with all our hopes and dreams, are perched on the tip of the fox's nose. We are in the middle of what seems like a deep river, and we're not sure we can swim. Now is the time for Americans to decide, once again, to fight for freedom.

Freedom Begins with Values

"Private values," said President Reagan in his 1986 state-of-the-union message, "must be at the heart of public policies."[2] Americans have always valued faith, character, hard work, personal responsibility, self-reliance, discipline, competition, charity, fairness, and achievement. Values originate from what people believe, especially what they believe about God.

Reagan won the hearts and votes of the American people by shifting the debate from a myriad of confusing political issues to values Americans recognized immediately as their own. By reminding Americans of our goodness and strengths, Reagan held up a mirror and helped us see ourselves at our very best. He made us believe we could get across any river on our own. Reagan convinced Americans that freedom would work for everyone and that the big-government welfare state was just a fox clothed in deceptive political promises.

Unfortunately the cause of freedom has had too few articulate champions since Ronald Reagan. Republican leaders have continued to embrace his policies rhetorically but have forgotten that the appeal of those policies was derived from their connection to the consensus values of the voters. They seem to have forgotten that America did not become the greatest country in the world because of the legislative process or even the people's right to vote. America became great because the people who voted had character, integrity, and strong values. They translated these personal values into principles and policies that protected freedom and allowed it to work.

Maintaining stability and strength in a diverse and dynamic nation like the United States requires leaders who can maintain a consensus among our citizens about faith, values, principles, and policies. There will always be tension because values conflict, even those values held by the same individual. Americans want to reduce wasteful spending and the size of government, but they also want to maintain costly social programs. They want to reduce costly farm subsidies but save the small farmer. They want to eliminate the welfare state but help the poor. They want to crack down on crime by throwing more criminals in jail, but they don't want to build more prisons (especially in their own backyards). They want everyone to have health care but do not want to pay more taxes for government-run health care.

Political leaders since Reagan have disconnected national policy from our core values by telling Americans we can have it all without making the difficult choices. Even Reagan, who championed the principles of free-market capitalism and peace-through-strength, failed to make some of the tough choices of leadership. In order to get his priorities through a Democrat Congress, he sacrificed his promise "to check and reverse the growth of government" and to reduce our dependence on foreign oil. He left the nation with large deficits and more dependent on foreign governments for our energy.[3]

While conservatives should not naively romanticize Reagan as the perfect leader, we can claim an important distinction between Reagan and other presidents of this generation: he made it clear the government was not the answer to our problems or the means to our prosperity. The you-can-have-it-all-and-the-government-will-guarantee-it political leaders since Reagan have fundamentally changed the American mind-set. Any interruption in our "having it all" elicits a knee-jerk response from federal politicians who promise to "bail us out" with more spending and debt.

The Fox: "You Can Have It All"

Washington politicians have told us we can have low taxes, a balanced budget, a strong military, and unlimited, "compassionate" federal spending. We have been told we can ban the development of America's energy resources and still have plenty of low-cost gas and electricity. We have been told the government can guarantee mortgages for low-income Americans without disrupting the financial markets.

We have been told we can tax, regulate, and sue our businesses more than any other country in the world and still be competitive in a global economy. We have been told the government can set health-care prices and heavily regulate health-care services and still have an efficient, affordable private health-care system. We have been told we can spend every dime in the Social Security and Medicare trust funds on unrelated programs and still keep our promises to seniors.

We have been told we can ban religion, prayer, and faith from schools, businesses, and public places and continue to be a strong and moral nation. We have been told we can educate our children in secular government schools and still have responsible, moral citizens. We have been told we can subsidize unwed births and teach "safe sex" to teenagers and still maintain strong families and a commitment to the institution of marriage. **We have been told what cannot possibly be!**

Now, as we end the first decade of the twenty-first century, the wheels have come off. The word *crisis* comes up as regularly as the sun. We have a crisis in the auto industry, the financial markets, education, health care, energy, housing, transportation, Social Security, Medicare, government spending, the national debt. There is almost no area of American life politicians and the media are not telling us is in crisis.

And who is to blame? The fox says the culprit is freedom. Politicians tell us capitalism and corporate greed are the problems, so we need to move closer to the fox's mouth. We need more government control and ownership of financial institutions. Big oil companies and speculators have created our energy crisis, so we must have tighter government controls. Greedy private doctors who refuse to treat seniors for the pittance paid by Medicare are the reason we need a national government-run, health-care system. School choice is the greatest threat to education, and the solution is yet more money for government schools.

Yes, not to worry; the government will save us—our economy, our prosperity, our jobs, our health care, our schools—and build a better America. We just need to jump onto the fox's nose. Every election brings more political promises, and each election Americans move closer to the fox's mouth, hoping that this time the promises will be kept. Andrew Bacevich, author of *The Limits of Power,* offers a cynical but hauntingly accurate perspective of the dilemma facing the eternally optimistic American voter:

> At four-year intervals, ceremonies conducted to install a president reaffirm this inclination. Once again, at the anointed hour, on the steps of the Capitol, it becomes "morning in America." The slate is wiped clean. The newly inaugurated president takes office, buoyed by expectations that history will soon be restored to its proper trajectory and the nation put back on track. There is something touching about these expectations, but also something pathetic, like the battered wife who expects that this time her husband will actually keep his oft-violated vow never again to raise his hand against her.
>
> For the abused wife, a condition of dependence condemns her to continuing torment. Salvation begins when she rejects that condition and asserts control over her life. Something of the same can be said of the American people.
>
> For the United States the pursuit of freedom, as defined in an age of consumerism, has induced a condition of dependence—on imported goods, on imported oil, and on credit. The chief desire of the American people, whether they admit it or not, is that nothing should disrupt their access to those goods, that oil, and that credit.

The chief aim of the U.S. government is to satisfy that desire, which it does in part through the distribution of largesse at home (with Congress taking a leading role) and in part through the pursuit of imperial ambitions abroad (largely the business of the executive branch).[4]

Bacevich's perspective ignores the most critical point and the central theme of this book: many Americans want out of this abusive marriage with the federal government, and they are willing to fight and sacrifice to end their dependence on empty political promises. As I've traveled this nation, thousands of Americans have confirmed this fact; many grabbing my arm, asking with passion and urgency, "How can I help?"

Americans will fight for their freedom, but we need leaders who will show the way. We need a clear vision and a pathway out of our dependency. We need to understand how to translate our values and principles into policies that will reduce the government stranglehold on our beliefs, our economy, and our lives. We must believe freedom will work for everyone. And we need to know the true enemy of freedom: socialism.

Sink or Swim: Americans Must Choose Freedom

Americans who have become increasingly dependent on the federal government in many areas of their lives must now make a difficult choice. As Ronald Reagan said, we must decide . . .

> whether we believe in our capacity for self-government or
> whether we abandon the American Revolution and confess
> that a little intellectual elite in a far-distant capital can plan our
> lives for us better than we can plan them ourselves. You and I
> are told increasingly that we have to choose between a left or
> right, but I would like to suggest there is no such thing as a left
> or right. There is only an up or down—up to man's old-aged
> dream, the ultimate in individual freedom consistent with law
> and order—or down to the ant heap of totalitarianism. And

regardless of their sincerity, their humanitarian motives, those who would trade our freedom for security have embarked on this downward course.[5]

Reagan knew our fight is against socialism. He knew every generation of Americans must make a choice between freedom and socialism. Today that choice confronts Americans more urgently than ever before. Government tentacles have reached deep into every area of our lives and have made it impossible for freedom to work. Now freedom stands accused of causing our problems. Freedom is now riding on the back of big-hearted, well-intended socialists who cannot see the destruction caused by their own philosophies and policies.

Socialists are now marching under the banner of a new secular-progressive style of freedom: the freedom from responsibility, the freedom to behave destructively without moral judgment, the freedom from risk and failure, the freedom from want, the freedom from religion, and the freedom to have material equality with those who work harder and accomplish more.

Traditional, hardworking, God-fearing, freedom-loving Americans want to know how they can fight back—how they can save real freedom. To fight well, we must first learn to recognize the difference between freedom and socialism. Freedom is tightly woven into the tapestry of America's consensus values. We must translate these values into the principles and policies that reflect our love of freedom. Then we will have the confidence to defend freedom against the "intellectual" liberal gibberish pervading politics, academics, and the media.

Reagan had a way of making the complex concept of freedom understandable to everyone. He once read a letter from a student on his national radio show that explained why freedom works better than socialism.[6] The letter recounted a class experiment where fifteen volunteers participated in a push-up contest. The first round was structured in socialist fashion where everyone shared equally in the prizes. No one could do more than thirty push-ups, and the total number of push-ups for the group was averaged.

Every student received one piece of candy for every five push-ups averaged by the group. In the first round four students did the maximum of thirty push-ups, and the average for the whole group was 16.2. Everyone received three pieces of candy.

There was just one change in the experiment on day two. A capitalist model was employed where individuals were rewarded for their own performance. The results were significantly better under the capitalist system. Seven students did the maximum of thirty push-ups, and the average for the group was 21.2, a 30 percent improvement over the socialist system. A large majority of the group received more candy than under the socialist system (an average of four pieces of candy per student), and only a few received less.

Socialists would say the capitalist model is not fair because some students were stronger or in better physical shape than others. Some students may have even had disabilities that inhibited their performance. "It is just not fair for seven students to receive six pieces of candy while some receive only one or two."

The capitalist would say everyone is better off under the capitalist system. The group produced 30 percent more wealth (candy) as a whole, a large majority is better off, and those who received fewer rewards have an incentive to improve their performance. The capitalist system also creates the wealth that allows many to share with those who are less able.

> The inherent vice of capitalism is the unequal sharing of blessings; the inherent virtue of socialism is the equal sharing of miseries.[7] —Winston Churchill

Freedom and Socialism Don't Mix

For more than fifty years American presidents and Congress have attempted to mix socialism with our capitalist system to make it fairer. We have taken a lot of the candy earned by top performers and created federal programs to distribute candy to those who didn't earn it. But socialism and capitalism don't work well together. Socialist policies dramatically increase government spending and debt, siphoning wealth and productivity from the private sector. Government intrusion into the free market has undermined personal responsibility, reduced incentives to work and save, and insulated people and businesses from the consequences of bad decisions.

It is actually quite amazing that there is any debate in America on the value of freedom versus socialism. The collapse of the Soviet Union was a definitive rejection of the principles of a socialized economy and culture. China and India were backward economies until capitalism began to raise the standard of living of their citizens. There is no example in the world or from any time in history where the principles of socialism actually worked.

My goal is to expose the historical failures of socialism and to help Americans see how socialistic policies have incrementally worked their way into all areas of American life. Socialism is truly a "fox in shepherd's clothes," and it is difficult to recognize it as a threat:

> Socialism is based on the idea that we should use the vast resources of society to meet people's needs. It seems so obvious—if people are hungry, they should be fed; if people are homeless, we should build homes for them; if people are sick, the best medical care should be available to them. A socialist society would take the immense wealth of the rich and use it to meet the basic needs of all society. The money wasted on weapons could be used to end poverty, homelessness, and all other forms of scarcity.[8]

How could such lofty and compassionate goals be so detrimental to our nation? They are not . . . unless we attempt to accomplish them through the force of government. One of the primary causes of the growth of socialism is the blurring of the lines between the role of government and the proper functions of a free society. Voters must distinguish between the role of voluntary charities and the proper role of local, state, and federal governments. I hope this book will help Americans reestablish these constitutional boundaries.

Freedom and Socialism

Few in America and in Congress would call themselves socialists. They believe they are liberals, progressives, Democrats, compassionate conservatives, moderate Republicans, or obedient religious adherents. They are good people with good intentions, and they would be deeply offended if anyone called them socialists. Yet they believe almost every need, cause, or activity should be supported, regulated, or controlled by the federal government. Their worldview is packaged with compassion, tolerance, fairness, and enough good intentions to pave the "road to serfdom."

While they would never admit it, most members of Congress lean toward socialist policies. They're not involved in a conspiracy, nor are they intent on destroying freedom. They are patriotic Americans who want the best for our country and our people, but they just don't understand how freedom works, and they don't understand the dangers of socialism. In fact, policies promoting freedom often seem to lack the compassion and certainty of immediate government solutions. Despite their good intentions, these politicians are more of a threat because of their ignorance than avowed socialists who openly attack freedom.

Please join me in discovering the history and future of freedom, what it is and how it works. It is my hope that this book will help Americans see and understand how creeping socialism is stealing our freedoms, our prosperity, and our way of life. This book is your plan and playbook for joining the fight to save freedom.

Saving Freedom is not an exhaustive academic analysis of history or of American politics, though I have referenced many highly respected authors to support my conclusions. Many direct quotes allow these authors to speak for themselves. To keep the book a reasonable length, I summarize and oversimplify many complex historical accounts and issues. The stories that begin each chapter are my attempts to simplify complex concepts so folks like me can understand them.

The fight to save freedom begins with you, not Washington. We must recruit an army of well-informed, freedom-loving Americans who will—one person at a time—win the fight for freedom.

> Our natural, unalienable rights are now considered to be a dispensation of government, and freedom has never been so fragile, so close to slipping from our grasp as it is at this moment. . . . You and I have a rendezvous with destiny. We will preserve for our children this, the last best hope of man on earth, or we'll sentence them to take the last step into a thousand years of darkness.[9] —President Ronald Reagan

Today, we need a nation of Minutemen, citizens who are not only prepared to take arms, but citizens who regard the preservation of freedom as the basic purpose of their daily lives and who are willing to consciously work and sacrifice for that freedom.[1]
—President John F. Kennedy

CHAPTER ONE

From Normal to Politician

How a Nice Guy like Me Ended Up in a Place like This

The timeless themes of humor, character, honesty, and wisdom have kept The Andy Griffith Show *in reruns since the 1960s. Sheriff Andy Taylor's calm wisdom provided a humorous contrast to Deputy Barney Fife's excitable, clumsy, and often foolish behavior. The television show remains popular fifty years later because of the attractive simplicity of the town of Mayberry, the country humor provided by the characters, and the positive moral lessons integrated into every show.*

In one episode Andy's son, Opie, developed a pattern of borrowing nickels from friends and family. Andy also noticed that Opie seemed dispirited. Barney decided to play detective, so he followed Opie one day—hiding behind trees, bushes, and parked cars in detective-like fashion. Opie, who was no more than eight years old, walked up to a bigger boy and with his eyes looking at the ground, handed the boy a nickel. The bigger boy shook his fist at Opie and demanded there be another nickel the next day.

Barney reported back to Andy that Opie was being bullied into collecting nickels for another boy. Barney demanded that Andy call the bully's father immediately. When Andy said "no," Barney then said he would teach Opie some of his karate moves so he could defend himself. Andy said he had a better idea.

The next day Andy took Opie fishing. Without revealing he knew anything about Opie's dilemma, Andy told a story about himself when he was Opie's age. A bully followed Andy to his favorite fishing hole and told him if he ever came back he would beat him up. Andy left in fear, but after several days he felt so ashamed of himself, he decided to go back and reclaim his fishing hole. When he arrived, the bully was there and hit Andy right in the eye. Andy told Opie he didn't even feel it and then went after the bully "like a windmill in a tornado." When Opie asked who eventually won fishing rights, Andy smiled and said, "Who's fishing here today?"

Without telling Andy, Opie decided to face down his own bully. Andy and Barney, knowing Opie made his decision, waited anxiously at the sheriff's office for the outcome. Suddenly Opie burst through the door with a black eye and torn clothes but smiling from ear to ear. Opie, brimming with pride, told Andy how he didn't even feel it when the bully hit him in the eye and that "he went after that bully like a windmill in a tornado."

Today Andy would likely be reported to the Department of Social Services for allowing his son to get into a fight resulting in cuts, bruises, and a black eye. But Andy understood a principle many have forgotten: character and self-esteem cannot be given; it has to be earned.

I was one of four children of divorced parents. Andy Griffith was my surrogate dad along with Ben Cartwright (Lorne Greene) from *Bonanza* and Matt Dillon (James Arnez) from *Gunsmoke*. My mother supported four children by running a ballroom dancing school in our home. She ran the place like a drill sergeant. There were typed duties for each of us everyday before and after school. We even had duties on Saturday morning and could not play with our friends until they were done.

Mom had a quick, succinct answer to our cries of "It's not fair" and

"Why can't we have what other kids have?" and "Other kids don't have duties." She would point her finger at us and say, "The world ain't fair, and no one owes you anything." It sounded cruel at the time, but it was a good dose of reality that has helped me throughout my life. I learned to expect more from myself and less from other people.

At age twelve I got a job delivering an afternoon paper route. Later I added a morning route. At sixteen I bagged groceries at a local Winn Dixie supermarket after school and earned a little extra money playing drums in a rock-and-roll band. During my summer breaks in college, I delivered and installed restaurant equipment and unloaded railcars in my spare time. Work was always a part of my life, and I developed confidence that I could do just about anything that needed to be done.

My college major was advertising, my first job after graduation was in sales, and I eventually worked my way through graduate school. With my MBA in hand, I landed a job in advertising and finally started my own marketing business at age thirty-two. My wife and I had three children when I started my business, and our fourth child was born a year later. It took a while for the business to generate enough income to live on, and there was always too much month left at the end of our money.

If there is a stereotypical American family, we were it. I ran a small business, volunteered in my church and community, and spent the rest of my time with family activities. My wife stayed home with our four children, led school field trips, served on the school board, and tried to manage the chaos. We had a modest income and lived in a modest home in a middle-class neighborhood.

My business allowed me to do consulting work with retailers, manufacturers, hospitals, colleges, public schools, and just about every type of business. As a strategic planner and marketing consultant for hundreds of companies, I became a real believer in America's free enterprise system. I knew what it took to start a business and make it grow. I saw how jobs were created and how profits led to more growth and higher salaries.

Like most small business owners, I served as a volunteer for many charitable and civic organizations. Civic responsibility and Christian duty compelled me and an army of volunteers to help those in need and improve the quality of life throughout the community. It was hardly sacrificial or drudgery. There were no lines between business activity, social events, charitable work, and volunteerism. A Rotary meeting could include a business contact, plans for weekend golf with a group of friends, appeals for volunteers to man posts at an upcoming fund-raiser, and a speech about how to improve our schools. A formal society ball was actually a fund-raiser for breast cancer research. There was no better way to make new business contacts than to serve as a board member of the United Way or other charity.

I saw how volunteerism provided the vision and backbone for our community. I also saw how many of the problems we faced as a community were the result of well-intended but misguided government policies. No government agency or program was ever as effective as a determined volunteer effort. It was impossible, however, to keep the unintended consequences of government from diminishing the good we were trying to accomplish. As my family and business grew and my involvement in the community increased, I began to see more clearly the role politics played in the quality of life we were trying to improve. I wasn't interested in politics, but it was increasingly apparent politics was interested in me. Government wanted more of my money and more control over my business, my family, my community—my life.

I never aspired to be in politics and didn't run for elected office until I was forty-seven years old. Until then I believed there were normal people, . . . and then there were politicians. My first close encounter with politics was as a volunteer strategist for a friend running for Congress. He was running against a popular incumbent, and no one gave him any chance to win. When he won, some called his victory one of the biggest political upsets in South Carolina history. I suddenly became a political genius. Actually, I probably had little to do with the victory, but the experience showed me that an unknown, nonpolitician could be elected to the big stage in Washington. The thought of running for office someday started percolating in my head.

From Normal to Politician

My only interest in politics was a desire to make government work better. It seemed to me government should allow freedom to work for everyone and not try to use problems as an excuse to replace freedom with more government. I was burdened that an increasing number of Americans were dependent on government for their income, health care, the education of their children, housing, food subsidies, and other government benefits. I saw firsthand how government dependency robbed people of their motivation to work, encouraged destructive behavior, and created a sense of entitlement and victimization.

My friend, the new congressman, promised to limit his time in office to no more than six years. After three years I began to write theoretical policy statements and campaign slogans. My whole focus was on *freedom*. I had seen freedom work. I witnessed how free enterprise expanded choices, improved quality, and created jobs. I saw how personal responsibility leads to self-respect, and I believed self-control was essential to self-government. I also saw how government welfare and entitlement programs robbed people of self-respect and freedom by making them dependent and by encouraging behaviors that led to poverty, crime, dropping out of school, and many other systemic societal problems.

Two years before the 1998 elections, I decided I would run for Congress. I ran as a Republican because their ideas of personal responsibility, limited government, and more freedom matched what I personally experienced as the reasons for America's greatness. My campaign slogan was "Bring Freedom Home." For me it was all about bringing dollars and decisions back to individuals, families, and communities.

My campaign platform was bold and naive. People should own their Social Security accounts, and the money they pay in Social Security taxes should be saved in a personal account the government can't spend. People should have the freedom to own a health insurance policy they can afford and keep from job to job. Parents should have many more choices of schools, and the money we spend on public education should follow the student and not be reserved solely for government-run schools. And finally, we should eliminate the personal income tax and the IRS and replace our tax code with a simple retail sales tax. *No one would even have to fill out a tax form.*

There were five challengers in the Republican primary, and on election day I placed a distant second behind a well-known state senator. Fortunately he didn't receive the required 51 percent to avoid a runoff. Two weeks later I surprised almost everyone (including myself) by winning the Republican nomination. In November I beat my Democrat opponent and headed to Washington for the new member orientation.

The campaign had been a painful, grueling process. It required thousands of fund-raising telephone calls, thousands of miles traveled, and thousands of hours away from my family and business. Two of my children were in high school, and two were in middle school, so my campaign put a lot of strain on my wife as she tried to pick up the slack. I had to downsize my business significantly during the campaign, and my income declined as my time shifted from making money to getting votes. By election day my business was hanging by a thread.

After announcing my candidacy, I was surprised by the subtle alienation I began to feel. Business clients were concerned that my political involvement might offend some of their employees and customers. My Rotary club told me they didn't allow political candidates to make announcements at our lunches. Some civic organizations suggested I no longer serve on their boards. Even good friends seemed to relate to me and my wife differently. I never imagined public life would be so isolating. As they say, "Not all that glitters is gold." I quickly learned there is little glamour and a lot of suspicion in politics.

My arrival in Washington was like the old Jimmy Stewart movie *Mr. Smith Goes to Washington.* I never served in the state legislature and only visited Washington once before my election, so just trying not to look foolish was my first goal. The election year 1998 had been bad for Republicans—our small majority got even smaller. There were only nineteen new Republicans in my freshman class.

I heard from a veteran congressman that every new class elects a president and other officers. The president of the class was allowed to meet with the Republican House leadership, which included the speaker. I wanted the opportunity to sell my agenda to the Republican leadership, so I decided to try to get myself elected president of the class. The class was disorganized, and everyone seemed to be waiting for someone to provide leadership. I stood up at one of our first meetings and announced that we were required to elect officers and report back to leadership. I also passed out an agenda that announced when elections would be held and outlined some ideas we should take to leadership. It worked! I was elected president of my freshman class.

I expected to meet with Speaker Newt Gingrich, but the poor election results and discontent in the party forced him to resign. Bob Livingston was in line to take his place, so at the big freshman class dinner at the Capitol, my wife and I sat at the table with outgoing Speaker Gingrich and (I thought) incoming Speaker Livingston. This was center stage at the big dance. I spent the evening bending Livingston's ear about freedom and the policy ideas I believed would inspire all Americans. He seemed really interested, but by the end of the week, he was forced to withdraw from the speaker's race. Republicans were in disarray.

The Republican Revolution and the great victories of 1994 were clearly hitting some speed bumps and losing momentum. My optimism and hope kept me from seeing the whole picture, but signs of deterioration were all around. Throughout the orientation program for new members, nothing was said about what we believed as Republicans, and there was no list of goals or any plans to move ahead with reforms. Most of the discussion was about how we should always vote with leadership and how important it was to start raising money immediately for our next election. The goal seemed to be to hold and grow our majority, not fight for bold reforms.

The problem became more apparent after months of working on my proposals for a drastically simplified tax code, personal savings for Social Security, and individual ownership of health insurance plans. My attempts to interest our leadership and other colleagues were met with indifference or excuses like, "I'm going to be in a tight election next year, so I can't put my name on anything controversial." My analytical business mind could not accept this kind of thinking. I once stood up at a Republican conference meeting and said our approach "was completely illogical." Someone from the back of the room yelled, "Don't worry, you'll get used to it." *I never did.*

There were notable exceptions of courageous Republicans who still believed in reform and were willing to take the risks necessary to continue the fight. Majority Leader Dick Armey turned out to be one of my heroes. He cosponsored my Social Security plan and called it the best plan he had ever seen. Whenever I heard someone mention the DeMint/Armey plan, it gave me hope we could save freedom. Armey's endorsement also validated me as a serious legislator and gave me the confidence to continue to take on the big issues.

The long odds of being elected to the House of Representatives, much less to the Senate, should give every member a sense of calling and providential purpose. For me the journey to the Senate still seems so unreal and miraculous that I am heavily burdened with the belief God has put me here for an important reason. After more than ten years in Congress, I am more convinced than ever that my reason for being here is to fight with everything I have in me to save freedom.

The keepers of the Washington status quo (often called the "old bulls") have sometimes bullied me around and even given me a few black eyes, but this country is my fishing hole, and I plan to keep swinging back "like a windmill in a tornado."

Perhaps the fact that we have seen millions voting themselves into complete dependence on a tyrant has made our generation understand that to choose one's government is not necessarily to secure freedom.[1]
—Friedrich Hayek

CHAPTER TWO

The Siren Song of Socialism

The Irresistible Temptation of More "Generous" Government

In Homer's Odyssey *written about 700 BC, Odysseus was warned not to sail his ship too close to an island inhabited by mythical winged women called sirens. The siren song was so wonderful and tempting that sailors could not resist. When passing sailors heard the siren song wafting over the waters, it was impossible for them not to turn their boats toward the island. Many sailors would even jump overboard in a desperate attempt to swim to the island. Once men were under their control, the sirens devoured them. None escaped.*

Odysseus was willing to risk his life to experience the sirens enchanting song. He filled the ears of his sailors with wax so they could not be tempted and then ordered them to tie him to the mast of his ship. When the ship passed the sirens' island, the sailors could hear nothing and kept the ship on course. Odysseus succumbed to the siren song and struggled to free himself. He ordered the sailors to untie him and to steer to the island, but they ignored him until the ship was well past the island.

It didn't take long for me to learn there are few things more tempting to politicians than using taxpayer money to buy votes at election time. The promises of more government solutions, more government programs, and more government spending are like the sirens' song to both politicians and voters. Even when voters know government programs seldom work (the sailors knew the sirens would kill them), they often succumb to the promise that government can solve their problems and make life better. This is the siren song of socialism, and it has proved irresistible for every democracy in history.

During My Lifetime

I frankly didn't think much about freedom or pay a lot of attention to politics until I was more than forty years old. Apparently most other Americans didn't either. Our government grew quickly while we were doing other things.

I was born in 1951 when Truman was still president. Before I was two years old, World War II General Dwight Eisenhower was elected president. Eisenhower created the U.S. Department of Transportation to build the interstate highway system. Although the interstate highway system has been essentially complete for many years, the USDOT continues to grow and now takes eighteen cents from every gallon of gasoline sold in America. Federal highways are now a small part of their role. The USDOT has become heavily involved with funding and regulating local and state road and mass transit projects throughout the nation. Congressmen and senators compete for funding for thousands of local projects or "earmarks" to prove they can "bring home the bacon."

In 1963 I was sitting in my sixth-grade class when an announcement was made that our thirty-fifth president, John F. Kennedy, had been shot. Vice President Johnson took over and created Medicare and expanded our welfare state. I was in college when President Nixon created the EPA (Environmental Protection Agency), implemented wage and price controls, and was then forced to resign in disgrace after the infamous Watergate scandal.

President Ford tried to heal the nation until Jimmy Carter brought his good intentions to Washington in 1976. President Carter created the

The Siren Song of Socialism

Department of Education, which greatly expanded the federal role in our schools. The quality of education for our nation as a whole has declined ever since. Carter also stopped the building of new nuclear plants and shut down the recycling of nuclear fuel. His good intentions for the environment backfired as America increased its use of coal while Europe reduced coal emissions with nuclear power. My wife and I had our first two children and bought our first house with interest rates above 15 percent during the Carter years.

We had two more children and started my business during the Reagan years. President Reagan's philosophy seemed to match the ideas I saw work in the real world. By lowering taxes and reducing regulations, he encouraged investments and lowered interest rates. By expanding the power of our economy and our military, he increased American prosperity, weakened our enemies, and promoted peace. His optimism and promotion of strong character encouraged work and personal responsibility. Reagan believed in freedom, and his policies proved that good government policies will allow freedom to work.

Reagan's economic policies and the emerging technology industry laid the foundation for two decades of growth. The first President Bush attempted to continue Reagan's legacy but undermined his own credibility and lost his reelection after allowing himself to be snookered into raising taxes by the Democrats. Bill Clinton defeated Bush and caught the wave of economic expansion created by Ronald Reagan. The massive Clinton tax increase of 1993 resulted in short-term increases in revenues to the government but eventually became an anchor that stopped economic growth. Clinton left the country on the brink of recession at the end of his second term in 2001.

The Republican Revolution of 1994 initially proved to be a good counterbalance to Clinton's attempts to expand government. The Republicans stopped Clinton's attempt to take over America's health-care system, forced him to sign a welfare reform plan (after two vetoes), and finally balanced the federal budget for the first time in decades.

The achievement of the balanced budget was short-lived (it was actually never even close to being balanced if you count what was being borrowed from the Social Security Trust Fund) and more the result of America's economic expansion than anything done by the Republicans or Clinton. Government spending and pork barrel earmarking expanded dramatically under Republican control. Republicans in Congress put up some resistance to Clinton's increases in spending, but when the second President Bush was elected, he expanded spending with very little Republican resistance.

Bill Clinton was president during my first two years in Congress. I enjoyed working with my conservative House colleagues trying to stop (with limited success) Clinton's attempts to grow government and increase spending. Republicans generally worked together in the House when Clinton was President, but Republicans in the Senate were willing to go along with higher levels of spending. Unfortunately the good economy and balanced budget created an excuse to increase spending dramatically.

The second President Bush had some good ideas, but he turned out to be a weak negotiator with the Democrats. Wasteful spending and earmarks expanded dramatically under Bush II and the Republican majority. The Bush tax cuts pulled the economy out of recession, but government spending and debt increased to historic levels. The number of Americans who were dependent on some government service reached the highest level in history.[2] I began to question if President Bush and the Republican leadership shared my sense of urgency to stop America's slide toward socialism.

After Bush was elected, I found myself fighting Republicans as often as Democrats. My first trip to the Bush White House came during the debate over Bush's No Child Left Behind (NCLB) education program. I was in hot water for deeming the legislation the "No Democrat Left Behind" bill after it was changed to accommodate Democrat demands. Initially some of Bush's proposal seemed to have some promise. I knew we couldn't improve education unless we were willing to measure the results. I also knew we wouldn't improve education if the federal government controlled our schools from Washington. The first draft of NCLB solved this problem for me by allowing states to opt out of the federal regime if they agreed to meet the new federal standards. This would work much like charter schools, only for whole states.

The Siren Song of Socialism

Before the NCLB legislation came up for a vote in the House, the state flexibility provision was stripped. Bush agreed to drop it in return for Democrat support of the bill. I filed an amendment to add the provision back to the bill. That's when I got a call from the White House. The president wanted to see me.

His staff ushered me into the Oval Office and sat me in one of those chairs next to the fireplace where we often see foreign dignitaries seated in media photos. I suspected the president would stop by, say "hello," and then turn me over to some junior staffer. The president entered through a door disguised as part of the curved wall. He was followed by Vice President Dick Cheney. The doors were closed, and to my surprise the only ones left in the room were the president, Cheney, and me. I was prepared for attempts to intimidate me into withdrawing my amendment. I wasn't prepared for the president to plead with me to help him avoid a "blood bath" over my amendment on the floor of the House. He was afraid that if my amendment passed, the Democrats would not support the final bill.

Had the president tried to pressure me to withdraw my amendment, it would have been easy for me say "no." But I'm a sucker for gentle persuasion. The president promised that if I withdrew my amendment, he would make sure the state flexibility provision would be added back at some point. I agreed to withdraw the amendment. The president said "trust me" when he promised the provision would be added back, but it never happened. The result of NCLB was more federal control of education and a lot more federal spending but no appreciable improvement in the quality of America's government-run education system.

Adding prescription drug coverage to Medicare followed the same pattern as NCLB. Only about 25 percent of seniors were without insurance for prescription drugs, but the Democrats insisted that any plan had to be universal; it had to cover everyone. Bush's initial proposal would give Americans the choice to keep their private health insurance after retirement, with Medicare helping pay for the cost of the premium. This would save the government money and give older Americans more choices of coverage. To get the Democrats on board, however, Bush gave up this provision and dramatically expanded the cost and size of the program. Medicare was already in financial trouble and the addition of universal drug coverage created a huge new unfunded liability. It was important to me that this bill be changed or stopped.

I was still in the House but running for the U.S. Senate during the Medicare prescription drug debate. After publicly expressing my opposition to the bill, I was once again invited to meet with the president along with several other conscientious objectors. In that meeting the president made it easy for me; he threatened me by telling the group, "Some of you have tough elections, and we are watching how you vote." And he looked straight at me when he said it. The White House political operatives contacted some of my top supporters in South Carolina and asked them to pressure me. One of my key supporters publicly switched his support to my top primary opponent after hearing from the White House. These tactics only strengthened my resolve to stop the bill. They also led me to question whether the president and I were on the same team.

On the night of the vote in the House, my team—the opponents of the bill—appeared to have won. But after keeping the vote open for more than three hours, the Republican leadership finally twisted enough arms (and promised enough "projects") to get the votes they needed to pass the bill. Today a large majority of senior citizens are dependent on the federal government for their health care and prescription medication, the Medicare program is trillions of dollars in debt, and because of exploding costs, Medicare often pays physicians less than their cost to treat senior citizens.

Republicans' Missed Opportunity

I personally admire and respect George and Laura Bush and greatly appreciate their service to our nation. They restored moral dignity and honor to the White House. I also appreciate the service of the Republican leaders who presided during my time in Congress. But I can no longer stay silent about what I believe our leadership did to the Republican Party and our country while we had the presidency and the majority in Congress.

The Siren Song of Socialism

It wasn't just one mistake; it was many. The Iraq War, which I supported and believed was necessary, was poorly managed and proved to be an albatross around the necks of Bush and the Republicans. This mismanagement of the war and the response to Hurricane Katrina, profligate spending, jail sentences for Republicans who traded earmarks for bribes, and sexual immorality among our members finally sent the Republican majority packing in 2006. Democrats had mismanaged government for years, and Republicans were elected to change Washington. It turned out that Washington changed us.

Republicans, who are supposed to carry the banner of freedom, betrayed the trust of the American people. We were supposed to provide a clear contrast with big government, big union, and antibusiness Democrats and convince Americans that freedom can work for everyone. Instead, we allowed big-spending Republicans to rule and ruin our party.

Throughout my time in Congress, I saw one "conservative" after another fall victim to the siren song of socialism (I fell for it a few times myself). There was always a good excuse to vote for another increase in spending, even for the most ineffective and wasteful programs. The earmark game created a bidding war for more spending: "You can have $50 million for your local projects if you support my $200 million bridge to nowhere." By 2008 it was hard to tell the Republicans from the Democrats.

This book is critical of both parties. At times it will seem more critical of the Democrats because their policies are consistently collectivist and socialistic. Republicans will get their share of criticism because many in leadership at the national level have betrayed the principles of freedom and conservativism that once defined our party. But to engage Americans in the fight to save freedom, it is essential that I point out the real ideological and policy differences between the two parties.

> To the frustrated, freedom from responsibility is more attractive than freedom from restraint. They are eager to barter their independence for relief from the burdens of willing, deciding, and being responsible for inevitable failure. They willingly abdicate the directing of their lives to those who want to plan, command, and shoulder all responsibility.[3] —Eric Hoffer

A Brief History of Socialism

Even after fighting for more than ten years against the policies I believe are moving America toward socialism, the word *socialism* still sounds— even to me—like a conspiracy theory exaggeration. Unfortunately the threat of a social democracy in America is not only real; we may be nearing the point of no return.

Why is socialism a threat to America? Because it doesn't work and it never has! Despite its utopian promises, socialism undermines every foundational principle of a free society. *Socialism is a socioeconomic system in which property and the distribution of wealth are subject to control by government.* Socialists are critical of capitalism, consumer choice, private property, and values based on religious faith (all of which are basic elements of freedom).

European socialism was always closely associated with labor unions. In 1864 the International Workingmen's Association was founded in London, and Karl Marx was invited to come as a representative of German workers. The First International became the first major international forum for the promulgation of socialist ideas. Unions in Europe and America continue to advocate collectivist views and promote more government control of cultural and economic functions.

In 1945 the post-World War II insecurity of the European people, along with an increased dependence on government from the war, led to a Labor Party/Socialist takeover of much of Europe. England, France, Italy, Sweden, Czechoslovakia, Belgium, Norway, and other European countries were controlled by Labor parties or Social Democrat parties that implemented social reforms and socialist economic policies. In 1949, however, the Social Democrats were defeated in Germany's first democratic elections. Not surprisingly, Germany became Europe's most powerful and productive economy, while most of Europe declined into economic stagnation.

Social democracies in Europe initially focused on social reforms to improve the lives of the working class. More radical economic socialists soon began to demand that main streams of economic activity be brought under government direction. The nationalization of industries and government economic planning spread throughout Europe. Capitalism became the whipping boy for social reformers.

The attacks on capitalism are likely to sound familiar to contemporary Americans. Increasingly the wrath of political candidates has been directed at property owners (the rich) and free enterprise, so-called corporate greed, has become the root of all evil. Demands for more equality and justice through government control of the culture and the economy are front and center in every political debate.

The McCain-Obama debates in 2008 were symptomatic of how politicians are abandoning the cause of freedom and promoting socialist solutions. Both candidates blamed the massive Wall Street and financial market collapse on corporate greed. Obama went further, citing markets running wild after deregulation. Neither candidate defended free enterprise or explained how bad government policies had been the root cause of the problem. Both candidates proposed more government solutions. Obama confidently made his case with socialist principles.

The socialist principles of "equality" and "justice" sound like ideas we should all support, but the socialists' definition of equality is not equality of opportunities but an equality of outcomes. They are not speaking of equal justice under law. Socialists promote a more arbitrary "affirmative justice" government action to combat perceived discrimination or suspected prejudice. To save freedom, Americans must understand these advocates of government-imposed social and economic justice want to transform America into a social democracy that, whether they know it or not, advances the cause of socialism.

> Loss of freedom seldom happens overnight. Oppression
> doesn't stand on the doorstep with toothbrush,
> moustache, and swastika armband—it creeps up
> insidiously . . . step by step, and all of a
> sudden the unfortunate citizen realizes that
> it is gone.[4] —Baron Geoffrey Lane

America's Slide toward Socialism

America's slide toward socialism began long before I was sworn in as South Carolina's 4th District U.S. representative in January 1999. A few seeds of the concentration of power and government dependency were planted soon after the thirteen states ceded "limited" power to the new federal government in 1787. Despite the wise checks and balances set up by our founders and their warnings that freedom declines as government grows, political ambitions and the corrupting influence of power were at work before the ink was dry on the Constitution.

Before the American Revolution, freedom was second nature to Americans. It was bred into our DNA long before the Declaration of Independence and the signing of our Constitution. Established as trading colonies, America was built on capitalism and free trade. Americans were people of good character and strong faith who came to the New World seeking freedom of religion. We benefited greatly from the English rule of law and their standard currency.

Personal responsibility and intact families were essential for survival because there were no government programs to assist those in need. Churches and voluntary organizations provided charity and emergency support for families in need. Government was limited, informal, and a relatively insignificant part of colonial life. The key components of free-dom had already converged in the New World before 1776.

When England attempted to raise taxes and expand its control, Americans reacted with indignation because freedom had become so ingrained in their hearts and minds. Taxes were considered abominable, but "taxation without representation" was intolerable. Many thought it better to die than relinquish their freedom. They decided to fight the greatest army in the history of the world with their hatchets and hunting rifles. Despite all odds, Americans won their independence and expanded freedom even more.

After the Revolutionary War and the signing of the Constitution, the United States of America quickly grew into one of the world's strongest political, economic, and military powers. We were the envy of the world. But the great irony of democracy is that it tends to destroy the very things that make it work. The new government soon began to undermine the foundations of freedom.

One of the first symptoms of the shift toward more government power was the patronage system. President Andrew Jackson (1829–1837) "consolidated and celebrated partisan party control over the 'spoils of office,' which meant in effect that the party organizations colonized nineteenth-century U.S. public administration."[5] The winners of elections created an expanding number of government functions in order to give jobs to their supporters. Jackson became the father of the modern Democratic Party, and his patronage system concentrated more power in Washington by establishing the permanent government bureaucracy that continues to expand to this day.

Our founders avoided the construction of a centralized bureaucracy, but the patronage system became "the meat and potatoes of nineteenth-century politics. . . . The major political parties in nineteenth-century America's patronage democracy flourished not as business conspiracies, nor as programmatic representatives of collective interests, but because they were so adept at using governmental resources for widely and eclectically distributing divisible benefits."[6] Government began its slow march of replacing the charitable work and community service of private citizens, families, churches, private charities, and mutual aid societies.

After the Civil War, which was the result of America's failure to apply our principles of freedom to slave labor, expanding bureaucracies at the local and state level took increasing responsibility for the needy. "Coping with unfortunates who were impaired or who had to ask for poor relief, and teaching children basic skills and values—these were the 'social functions' explicitly performed by nineteenth-century American governments."[7]

At first these functions were decentralized, with local governments in villages, towns, counties, and cities providing autonomous services with little federal involvement. "Decentralized federalism allowed local, state-level, and private initiatives to compete with one another—and often to imitate one another as well, in waves of analogous institution-building."[8] Local and state public/private partnerships for mutual aid proved to be a reasonably effective model that did not lead to centralized autocratic control.

The federal role in patronage politics and social provisions began to grow rapidly after the Civil War. The patronage system spurred the growth of benefits for Civil War veterans and survivor benefits for widows and children. The political parties began to compete for who could promise the richest benefits. Veterans' benefits soon expanded to old-age and survivor benefits for manual laborers. "Pension patronage flourished both through Congress and through party controls over the leadership. . . . The statutes quickly became so bewilderingly complex that there was much room for interpretation."[9]

Patronage democracies have historically evolved into paternalistic states with even more government control. In the early twentieth century, there were many calls for the U.S. to imitate the welfare programs adopted in Europe, particularly in Germany. "By 1910 . . . actual pensions or prospective eligibility for them [Germans] reached 52 percent of the economically active German population and 22 percent of the total population."[10] Increasingly, academicians and politicians in America began to believe government had the responsibility of protecting citizens against the ordinary risks of life.

Dr. I. M. Rubinow, a Socialist Party member and author of *Social Insurance* (1913) and *The Quest for Security* (1934), had a significant impact on the development of twentieth-century U.S. social policies. He wrote that government-sponsored social insurance "may and has been decried as rank paternalism, and this indictment must be readily admitted. For social insurance, when properly developed, is nothing if not a well-defined effort of the organized state to come to the assistance of the wage-earner and furnish him something he individually is quite unable to attain for himself."[11]

Professor Henry Rogers Seager, another influential proponent of government paternalism, was concerned in 1910 that traditional American individualist attitudes would stand in the way of desirable social reforms. He wanted our country to move toward a view of government as a moral agency with a humanitarian mission. "To become 'a truly civilized society,' the United States must develop a 'deepening sense of social solidarity and quickening of appreciation of our common interests.' And that Americans must 'begin to think of government as . . . organized machinery for advancing our common interests.'"[12]

President Franklin Roosevelt (1933–1945) used America's vulnerability during the Depression to implement his New Deal. This new social agenda created the Social Security program, provided extensive protections of unions, and began the farmer assistance program. The seeds of socialism took root.

Until 1929 Americans generally resisted the autocratic, paternalistic style of government that was seen in Europe. It took the Great Depression to drive Americans into the arms of the federal government. The decade between 1929 and 1940 convinced Americans they could not trust capitalism and free markets. Ironically, there is considerable evidence that the Depression was caused not by the failure of capitalism but by the mismanagement of our currency by the newly formed Federal Reserve.[13]

The American worldview changed dramatically after the Great Depression and World War II. This was the pivotal point in American history when we took a sharp left turn from a free republic and headed down the road toward a social democracy.

FDR's predecessors had presided over a republic. Central to the functioning of that republic was a set of checks and balances designed to limit the concentration of political power. Truman's successors presided over a system defined by the concentration of power, both in Washington and, within Washington, in the executive branch.[14]

> Remember, democracy never lasts long. It soon wastes, exhausts, and murders itself. There never was a democracy yet that did not commit suicide. —President John Adams

America's Fall from Wealth and Independence

After World War II, America was on top of the world. Our powerful economic and military machines saved the world from tyranny and ushered in a generation of peace and prosperity.

> By the end of World War II, the country possessed nearly two-thirds of the world's gold reserves and more than half its entire manufacturing capacity. In 1947, the United States by itself accounted for one-third of world exports. Its foreign trade balance was comfortably in the black. As measured by value, its exports more than doubled its imports. The dollar had displaced the British pound sterling as the global reserve currency. . . . Among the world's producers of oil, steel, airplanes, automobiles, and electronics, it ranked first in each category. In 1948, American per capita income exceeded by a factor of four the combined per capita income of Great Britain, France, West Germany, and Italy.[15]

The United States achieved the self-sufficiency and freedom of action George Washington hoped for: "to give it, humanly speaking, the command of its own fortunes."[16] But freedom and abundance have historically undermined the principles that lead to success. Americans used their new wealth and prosperity to consume and indulge. The federal government used its new wealth and power to grow and expand its reach around the world and into more areas of America's culture and economy. The American people became more dependent on the government (more than 50 percent of Americans now receive a significant portion of their income from government programs),[17] and the federal government became more dependent on other countries.

As power began to concentrate in Washington, D.C., and the federal government began to take an ever-expanding role in planning and controlling more of our culture and economy, America began to transition from a wealthy and independent nation to one now characterized by debt and dependency. Instead of developing our own energy resources, America went from an exporter of oil to chronic dependency on foreign oil. Our first warning came with the "oil shock" of 1973, but despite commitments by politicians to reduce our dependence on foreign oil, America's dependency has doubled since 1973.

In the 1960s, the Supreme Court began to purge religious faith and traditional values from public life. The expansion of the welfare state resulted in an exponential increase in unwed births and broken homes. The decade of the 1960s resulted in a cultural revolution that undermined many of the foundational principles that had created America's success, including faith, family, and freedom.

In the mid-1970s, America transitioned from an exporting nation to a nation heavily dependent on foreign goods. We've had a negative trade balance every year since 1975.[18] Federal government intervention in local schools resulted in a continuous and systematic decline in America's education system relative to other advanced nations. Federal health-care programs such as Medicare began America's journey toward a socialized health-care system.

> In the 1960's . . . the empire of production began to come
> undone. Within another twenty years—thanks to permanently
> negative trade balances, a crushing defeat in Vietnam, oil shocks,
> "stagflation," and the shredding of a moral consensus that could

not withstand the successive assaults of Elvis Presley, "the pill," and the counterculture, along with news reports that God had died—it had become defunct.[19]

A Crisis of Values

Centralized government and collectivists principles were both catalysts and facilitators of America's decline, but at its root the cause of America's problems was a crisis of values. Our federal government and opportunistic politicians became the "enablers" by telling Americans they could have it all without responsibility, risk, and sacrifice. Many Americans became the addicts of government promises.

The traditional values of personal responsibility, hard work, frugality and saving, independence, family, and faith gave way to government promises of more security, more income, more health care, more education, more . . . more . . . more. Too many Americans began to look to the federal government to solve almost every problem, and they became gullible clients of politicians promising to satisfy every need.

As the debt and dependency of people and the government increased, America found itself in difficult times in the last years of the 1970s. President Jimmy Carter attempted to blame both the people and the government: "In a nation that was proud of hard work, strong families, close-knit communities, and our faith in God, too many of us now tend to worship self-indulgence and consumption."[20] Carter continued by explaining that we have "a system of government that seems incapable of action . . . a Congress twisted and pulled in every direction by hundreds of well financed and powerful special interests."[21]

Carter missed the real cause of America's problems. Government was trying to do too much. Government becomes "incapable of acting" when it attempts to serve a large number of particular needs rather than promoting the general welfare. When the federal government began to involve itself in planning and directing specific aspects of America's culture and economy, it was inevitable there would be destructive and costly consequences.

The Siren Song of Socialism

The more the government tried to do, the bigger the problems became, and the less the people did for themselves. Government responded to its failures by growing in size and scope as it tried to fix the problems it caused. Americans responded by throwing up their hands and demanding that government fix the mess. Politicians were more than willing to promise that government would solve all our problems.

Ultimately, it has been America's political leadership that has undermined the values of our people. When the government took responsibility for schools, some parents lost control of their children's education. When government took responsibility for the poor, voluntary charity from churches and community groups declined. When government took responsibility for retirement security, many Americans quit saving. When government and employers took responsibility for health insurance, individuals became dependent on others for their health care.

President Reagan believed the values of the American people should guide the actions of government. But he understood that the traditional values held by Americans should not be underminded by government. He also understood that, if government was allowed to continue to grow, the values of the American people would be replaced by a valueless secular bureaucracy. In his 1981 inaugural address Reagan promised to "check and reverse the growth of government."[22]

> For decades we have piled deficit upon deficit, mortgaging our future and our children's future for the temporary convenience of the present. To continue this long trend is to guarantee tremendous social, cultural, political, and economic upheavals. . . . You and I, as individuals, can, by borrowing, live beyond our means, but for only a limited period of time. Why, then, should we think that collectively, as a nation, we're not bound by that same limitation?[23]

Unfortunately Reagan had to deal with a Democrat Congress intent on expanding domestic spending for social programs. In order to get the spending he wanted to rebuild our military and back down the Soviets, Reagan was forced to give the Democrats the money they wanted for social programs. America's debt and dependency increased dramatically. Overall federal spending nearly doubled during the Reagan years, and federal deficits skyrocketed.[24] America's dependency on foreign oil also increased significantly during the Reagan years.

The values of the people and the actions of government are inextricably entwined. As the spending and debt of the federal government increased, so did consumers debt. As the U.S. government increased its dependence on foreign governments for oil, products, and loans, Americans increased their dependence on government. As federal politicians stopped thinking about America's future and started thinking about the next election, Americans ceased to save for the future.

Like the sailors in Homer's *Odyssey* who could not resist the siren song, American voters have been led astray by politicians who offer quick-fix government promises. Too many Americans have stopped looking within themselves for hope and opportunity; we have sailed too close to the island of socialism.

The crucial point of which people are still so little
aware is, however, not merely the magnitude of the
changes which have taken place during the last generation
but the fact that they mean a complete change in
the direction of the evolution of our ideas and social
order. For at least twenty-five years before the specter of
totalitarianism became a real threat, we had
progressively been moving away from the basic ideas on
which European civilization has been built.[1]
—Friedrich Hayek

CHAPTER THREE

The Allure and Dangers of Socialism

Big Government Robin Hoods and Their Merry Men

Long ago in the kingdom of Nottingham, when the good King Richard was away at war, an evil sheriff unjustly took the lands and possessions of a young noble named Robin of Loxley. Left without a home, Robin lived outdoors in the dense and beautiful Sherwood Forest. He made his living by stealing from rich travelers and distributing the loot among the poor in the kingdom.

Despite the evil sheriff's best efforts, he could not catch Robin or his band of followers. They became masters of disappearing deep into the woods and reappearing only to surprise poor townsmen with the gold and silver from their latest heist. The people loved their benevolent bandits and called them Robin Hood and his Merry Men.

Socialism begins with envy of the rich and the temptation to use government force to take from the rich and give to the poor. But social and economic equality are more often an excuse used by power-hungry politicians to provoke the discontent of the masses. Their real goal is to centralize power on behalf of a few elites who consider themselves uniquely qualified to manage society.

Envy of the rich and the desire to help the poor are sentiments held by many Americans. One study exploring the egalitarian impulses in human nature found that 70 percent of participants "reduced or added to another person's money, most often by taking from the richest players or by donating to the poorest players."[2] This "Robin Hood Impulse" becomes easy fodder for wily politicians who capitalize on the charitable inclinations of voters by convincing them that the government will help the poor with other people's money at no cost to them. This appeal becomes even stronger if politicians can convince voters that the government is justified to take money from the rich and give it to the poor *and* the middle class (essentially everyone is a beneficiary).

The Allure of Socialism

America's progression from freedom toward socialism parallels the journey of other modern democracies. Friedrich Hayek, born in Germany and writing in England in 1944, saw the dangers of growing socialism in Europe and attempted to warn the world in his book *The Road to Serfdom*. Although clear and substantive warnings that socialism means slavery had already been issued by the greatest political thinkers of the nineteenth century, De Tocqueville and Lord Acton, Hayek said, "We have progressively abandoned that freedom in economic affairs without which personal and political freedom has never existed in the past."[3]

Socialists redefine the word *freedom* to mean a freedom from necessity and responsibility or as Hayek wrote "to be truly free [from] the 'despotism of physical want.'"[4] Peter Drucker, one of the twentieth century's greatest authorities on economics and management, observed:

The Allure and Dangers of Socialism

The less freedom there is, the more there is talk of the "new freedom." Yet this new freedom is a mere word which covers the exact contradiction of all that Europe ever understood by freedom. . . . The new freedom which is preached in Europe is, however, the right of the majority against the individual.[5]

Socialists package this new freedom with the promise of equality and security. Most would agree that civilized societies should strive to assure that all citizens have "some minimum of food, shelter, and clothing, sufficient to preserve health and the capacity to work."[6] The socialist, however, seeks to go much further by guaranteeing a determined standard of living and the protection of certain levels of income by taxing wealthy individuals and profitable businesses.

History has proven that it is impossible for governments to manage the economic and social structure of society without diminishing economic progress and severely restricting the freedoms of individuals. Nevertheless, the political promise of equal outcomes and security by the political class has lured many Americans into the trap of government dependency. We seem to have forgotten that freedom has a price, and that price is hard work and risk.

When government attempts to insulate the people from the normal risks of life, it diminishes the energy and productivity that come from work, struggle, and persistence. Hayek decried calls for government-sponsored security and deemed a phrase used by Benjamin Franklin to be the rule of liberty for free countries: "Those who would give up essential liberty to purchase a little temporary safety deserve neither liberty nor safety."[7]

The goals of socialism are focused on eliminating risk that, according to socialist-leaning politicians, can only be achieved by centralized power, planning, and organization. Few understood as Hayek did that it was precisely this philosophy of centralized power advancing under the banner of National Socialism in Germany that led to World War II:

Germany wants to organize Europe which up to now still lacks organization. I will explain to you now Germany's great secret: we, or perhaps the German race, have discovered the significance of organization. While other nations still live under the regime of individualism, we have already achieved that of organization.[8] —German chemist Wilhelm Ostwald

The desire to organize society leads to the centralization of power, and power always corrupts the best intentions of man.

The Dangers of Socialism

The corruption of leadership in a socialized society is only exceeded by the degradation of the people. Americans have seen the destruction our welfare system has wreaked upon the poor. Our attempts to help the poor have discouraged the behaviors and attitudes that help to move people up the economic ladder—deferral of gratification, sobriety, thrift, and dogged industry.[9] As social philosopher Irving Kristol writes, "It's hard to rise above poverty if society keeps deriding the human qualities that allow you to escape from it."[10]

Myron Magnet, writing in *The Dream and the Nightmare* in 1993, described the damage inflicted by America's socialistic welfare policies.

The new culture held the poor back from advancement by robbing them of responsibility for their fate and thus further squelching their initiative and energy. Instead of telling them to take wholehearted advantage of opportunities that were rapidly opening, the new culture told the Have-Nots that they were victims of an unjust society and, if they were black, that they were entitled to restitution, including advancement on the basis of racial preference rather than mere personal striving and merit. It told them that the traditional standards of the larger community, already under attack by the counterculture, often didn't apply to them, that their wrongdoing might well be justified rebellion or the expression of yet another legitimate "alternative life-style."[11]

The greatest danger of socialism is it diminishes the importance and responsibility of the individual. All initiative, creativity, entrepreneurship, productivity, faith, love, and charity begin at the individual level. Socialism is based on the concept of the ineffectual individual who has no meaning except by losing his blemished and unwanted self into a larger movement. As Eric Hoffer explains in *The True Believer:*

> When we renounce the self and become part of a compact whole, we not only renounce personal advantage but are also rid of personal responsibility. There is no telling to what extremes of cruelty and ruthlessness a man will go when he is freed from the fears, hesitations, doubts and the vague stirrings of decency that go with individual judgment. When we lose our individual independence in the corporateness of a mass movement, we find a new freedom—freedom to hate, bully, lie, torture, murder and betray without shame and remorse.[12]

America is clearly sliding toward socialism. Government is now the nation's largest property owner (nearly one-third of the land mass); it "owns" over one-third of the profits of all businesses and more than one-third of the incomes of most working Americans. It controls and restricts the development of America's energy resources. Government controls the majority of education and health-care services in America. It owns the primary retirement income plan for most Americans (Social Security). Government, through a burdensome regulatory system and direct interventions into the financial markets, effectively controls a significant portion of the nation's economic development and business activity.

America's style of socialism is more subtle and, on the surface, appears more benign than early twentieth-century European socialism. America's federal government has not yet taken over or nationalized any industry (although they are getting close as I am writing this book); but it has increasingly expanded its control through regulation and intervention, its ownership through confiscatory taxes, and in the case of health care, more control through fixed prices and mandatory service requirements.

On the cultural front, the socialization of values has turned right and wrong upside down. Courts and legislatures have decreed that many behaviors once considered "wrong" by society—abortion, unwed sex and births, divorce, homosexuality, pornography, gambling, laziness, etc.—are now "rights." The costs and impact to America's culture of these decisions have been devastating. Behaviors once considered wholesome, constructive, and "right"—prayer, belief in right and wrong, sexual abstinence, traditional marriage, personal responsibility, delayed gratification—are discouraged and even held in disdain by the governing elites.

The siren song of socialism already has many Americans under its control; and unless we change our course, it will devour our prosperity and our hope for a better future. All we have to do is look at our own economic and cultural decline or the slow economic growth and high unemployment in some of the more socialized countries in Europe. Freedom and socialism cannot exist together; they are incompatible. The fight to save freedom must begin today!

The Addictive Power of Socialism

Why don't Americans just stand up and demand a return to the principles of freedom? I'm afraid that's like asking a drug addict just to quit using drugs. Americans are heavily dependent on government, and many do not believe freedom can be trusted to take care of them. Political candidates sound much more enticing when they promise more security and government benefits than when they speak of personal responsibility and cutting government spending.

Why don't congressmen and senators stop supporting policies that expand debt and dependency? I'm afraid that's like asking a drug dealer to stop selling drugs. After more than ten years in Congress, I still can't explain the behavior of my colleagues, but I'll offer some personal opinions. It has a lot to do with the groups that support the two political parties.

> The argument for collectivism, for government doing something, is simple. Anybody can understand it. "If there's something wrong, pass a law. If somebody is in trouble, get Mr. X to help them out." The argument for voluntary cooperation, for a free market, is not nearly so simple. It says, "You know, if you allow people to cooperate voluntarily and don't interfere with them, indirectly, through the operation of the market, they will improve matters more than you can improve it directly by appointing somebody." That's a subtle argument, and it's hard for people to understand. Moreover, people think that when you argue that way you're arguing for selfishness, for greed. That's utter nonsense.[13] —Milton Friedman

Robin Hood's Merry Men

Very loyal, well-organized groups and constituencies that want more centralized government and collectivist policies heavily support Democrats. Republicans are supported by smaller groups and individuals who are less loyal to the party, less organized, and more focused on particular issues. Republican supporters generally want less government, less regulation, less taxation, more traditional values, and more individual freedom. The key difference is that all of the major groups supporting the Democratic Party demand more centralized control and government power to benefit their cause.

Labor unions are one of the most powerful forces in Washington, and they support Democrats almost exclusively. Union membership in the private sector has been declining for many years and is now only about 7.5 percent of the workforce.[14] However, about 20 percent of employed Americans work for the government at some level or for a firm that depends on taxpayer financing[15] and more than 35 percent of government workers are members of a union.[16]

With unionization on the decline in the private sector and global competition making union shops increasingly obsolete, union bosses are dependent on the federal government to give them an advantage when trying to unionize more businesses. Federal laws have made unions the most powerful political force by allowing union bosses to use members' dues for political purposes without the permission of members. Unions are the only organizations in America that can compel dues as a condition of employment and use members' dues for direct contributions to candidates and for grassroots political activity. And union bosses take every opportunity to use their political advantage. Some union contracts with employers even include a holiday on election day so union members can work the polls for Democrats.

The Democrat Party reciprocates by shamelessly promoting the union agenda in Congress. Democrats currently have as one of their top national priorities to eliminate the traditional secret ballot workers have always been accorded when union bosses are attempting to organize their workplace. Democrats hope to replace the secret ballot with a "card check" that will allow union thugs openly to intimidate workers who hesitate to sign up. Under the new Democrat majority, the U.S. House of Representatives has already passed the bill that eliminates the secret ballot.

Almost every spending bill that goes through Congress has some provision that promotes the use of union shops by local and state governments. Unions also control our education policy. All attempts to give parents more choices of schools are viciously attacked by the teachers unions (nearly 40 percent of teachers are members of unions). Federal education policy is much more about protecting unions and teachers than parents and students.

For union bosses, gaining members and political power is paramount. Union influence is pervasive in Washington and around the country. Did you ever wonder why so many Democrats supported amnesty and citizenship for illegal immigrants? Just think of millions of new dues-paying farm and service worker union members . . . and millions more Democrat voters.

Democrats are fiercely loyal to union bosses and vice versa. Both know the more the federal government supports the expansion of unions, the more money and votes will be available for union bosses and Democrat candidates. States with the highest number of union members, such as California and New York, are solid Democrat states. Southern and mid-western states with low union memberships have traditionally voted Republican.

Another powerful group that supports the Democratic Party almost exclusively is composed of trial lawyers, also referred to as plaintiff's attorneys. This group is one of the largest financial contributors to Democrat candidates and the national Democratic Party. Writing about trial lawyers and the large 1998 tobacco settlement, the *National Review* writes:

> Those legal fees are estimated at between $3 and $5 billion per year for the next twenty-five years. While the fees the tobacco companies will have to pay are still in arbitration in over forty states, three years ago lawyers representing just three states— Texas, Mississippi, and Florida—were awarded $8.2 billion. These lawyers can be counted on to invest their newfound wealth in the industry that made them rich: the out-of-control system of tort litigation that underwrites, and is protected by, the Democrat party.[17]

Over the decade of the 1990s, the legal profession contributed a total of $357 million to federal candidates. The fifty-six-thousand-member Association of Trial Lawyers of America, now called the American Association for Justice, gives nearly 90 percent of its millions to Democrats.[18] They get a good return on their investment. Democrats consistently block any attempt at legal reform that would reduce frivolous and abusive lawsuits. Trial lawyers make millions by suing the businesses that create jobs and the doctors who provide health care. Democrats get millions in campaign contributions by making sure the gravy train keeps rolling.

There are many good trial lawyers that serve a vital function in our economy and culture. I support the contingency fee system that encourages lawyers to take the cases of plantiffs who cannot afford representation. My complaint with the national trial lawyer groups is they constantly work to expand the risks and liabilities of doing business in America, and fight all attempts to develop reasonable reforms.

A third major support group for Democrats includes America's minorities. After decades of discrimination, Republican talk of "less government" is actually threatening to minorities who believe government is their protector and guarantor of a better life. More than 90 percent of African-Americans vote Democrat even though on the issues they often prefer Republican policies. African-Americans are more religious, pro-life, and are inclined to support school choice even though these policies are contrary to the Democrat platform.

That platform has one purpose: to increase the number of people dependent on government and, therefore, on the party of government. Seniors who depend on the federal government for their income (Social Security or federal pension)[19] and health care (Medicare) now comprise 20 percent of our population. Democrats use every election as an opportunity to attempt to frighten those seniors by telling them that Republicans will reduce or eliminate these programs.

The poor and other American's who can be classified as "government beneficiaries" also consistently support the Democratic Party. This group includes nine million on food stamps, two million receiving housing subsidies, five million with federal loans or scholarships, and millions more receiving government disability benefits. Economist Gary Shilling says the "portion of Americans receiving government benefits stands at 52.6 percent," which is up from 28.3 percent in 1950.[20] Is there any wonder those fighting the slide to socialism are losing ground?

Democrats have united all of these groups in a common struggle against the injustices of a free society, free enterprise, and religious-based moral judgments. In his presidential campaign Barack Obama spoke often of common struggles and called on Americans to unite "by binding our grievances." Socialists understand that uniting people behind centralized power requires a belief that without the help of government they will stand alone against oppression and injustice. The struggle of one group must be linked to the struggle of others and people must be "agitated" to unite and fight. According to the International Socialist Organization:

> We need socialists in every workplace to agitate . . . on the shop floor. We need socialists in every neighborhood to take up the questions of housing, police violence, health care, and everything else that comes up. We need students to agitate on college campuses. We need socialists in every corner of society inhabited by working people, and we need these socialists working nonstop—organizing struggle and carrying on political discussions. . . . But a socialist organization has to be centralized. Why the need for centralized organization? Because the other side is organized. The basis of their power is the profit they make at workplaces—highly organized systems built around exploiting workers. . . . This, then, is the case for why you should be a socialist. As individuals on our own, we can't accomplish much—not even with the best grasp of what's wrong with the world and how it could be different. But as part of an organization, we can make a difference.[21]

The Democratic Party has become synonymous with government security. Democrats agitate and unite by reminding voters that America has been unfair, and without the protection of government, they will be alone and powerless. In so many words "freedom" is their enemy. Ironically the more dependent Americans become on government, the more insecure and fearful they become. Democrats use this fear to manipulate their votes at election time.

Republicans have become America's minority party because they have been poor salesmen of the benefits of true freedom. As Americans have become more dependent on government, Republicans have tried to use a "Democrat lite" approach, trying to appeal to voters' desire for more security. George W. Bush tried to appeal to America's need for security with his big-spending, "compassionate conservative" agenda. But few Republicans have been willing to tell Americans the truth: people are most secure when they are most free.

The political support for Republicans is much more fragmented and less party-loyal than Democrat supporters. Republicans are accused of being "in the pocket of big business." The fact is most big businesses play both sides by supporting Republicans and Democrats. While Republicans are associated by the media with Wall Street, the big firms like Goldman Sachs give much more in political contributions to Democrats.

There are no large political groups supporting only Republicans. The U.S. Chamber, the premier representative of American business, balances their political risks by supporting incumbents whether they are Republican or Democrat (incumbents usually win). Even though the Chamber's top priority in 2008 was to stop Democrat attempts to eliminate the secret ballot when unions try to organize a workplace, they endorsed incumbent Democrat Senator Mary Landrieu from Louisiana who opposed their position. This seat was considered the only possible "pick up" opportunity for Senate Republicans in the 2008 elections, but the Chamber aggressively supported Landrieu's reelection.

Other groups such as the NRA and pro-life groups support candidates who are in line with their positions. They are not loyal to the Republican Party. Physicians, who have traditionally supported Republicans because of the need for lawsuit reform, gave more political contributions to Democrats in 2008 (to "cover their bases," as one physician told me, since the Democrats are going to be in power for a long time).

The sad fact is almost all of the organized political power in America today is on the side of a larger, more centralized, more socialistic government. They support the Democratic Party because Democrats support more centralized government and more government control. Republicans have traditionally been supported by independent voters who want more freedom, less government, and less taxation. Republican supporters are decreasing in number as more Americans become dependent on the government and as the number of people who pay taxes declines.

Robin Hoods are running our government. Freedom is in trouble in America. Time is short. We must act now!

> Freedom has cost too much blood and
> agony to be relinquished at the cheap price
> of rhetoric.[22] —Thomas Sowell

Rightful liberty is unobstructed action, according
to our will, within limits drawn around it by
the equal rights of others.
—President Thomas Jefferson

CHAPTER FOUR

The Fight for Freedom
Why Freedom Is Worth Fighting For

*Over seven hundred years ago, on September 11, 1297, King Edward I
of England sent seven thousand troops to squash a rebellion by the Scots.
Sir William Wallace, who was called the Guardian of Scotland by his fellow
countrymen, convinced the Scots they should be independent from England.
The king had no patience with these Scottish peasants and sent his best fighting
men to reassert his control.*

*When the king's troops arrived at the Scottish border, their commander
sent a message to Wallace offering him the opportunity to surrender and live.
His response: "Take back this reply, that we are not here to make peace but to do
battle, to defend ourselves, and liberate our kingdom. Let them come on and we
shall prove this in their very beards!" So the English planned their attack.*

*But there was one small obstacle. The troops had to cross the River Forth
to get to Wallace. The only passage across the river was Stirling Bridge, a bridge
so narrow only two horsemen could walk abreast as they crossed. Moving troops
into position was a long and tedious process. The English commander was so
confident, however, that he only sent two thousand troops across to quell the
Scottish rebels.*

*The king's two thousand troops quickly found themselves trapped on
the wrong side of the bridge. They were ambushed by six thousand angry*

Scotsmen. The narrow bridge made retreat impossible and restricted the passage of reinforcements. The English troops were massacred, and the Scottish fight for freedom became legend.

Why Fight?

Thirteenth-century Scotsmen could see and feel the oppression of British rule. Freedom was only a distant hope and dream, but it inspired them to fight and to give their lives in battle. In America today few seem willing to fight for something they think they already have. Until recently the threat of losing our freedom was not real enough to create a sense of urgency, much like the threat of a thunderstorm does not keep people from going to the beach on a beautiful day.

Prior to recent terrorist attacks, economic tribulation, and the unprecedented government intrusion into the financial industry, most Americans of this generation were bathing in the sunshine of security and—relative to the rest of the world—enough prosperity to sedate any desire to fight. But the dark cloud on the horizon now seems to have covered the entire American sky. More Americans are asking, "What can we do?"

It is difficult for people who are worried about their next paycheck or mortgage payment to make the connection between the expansion of government and the increasing burden of taxes; or to understand how decisions by government have increased the cost of gas, food, and electricity; or how government schools have led to the decline of the quality of education and career advancement opportunities; or how laws and regulations have increased the difficulty in finding affordable health insurance; or how high taxes, lawsuits, and overregulation have led to the loss of American competitiveness and jobs.

> None but the people can forge their own chains; and to flatter the people and delude them by promises never meant to be performed is the stale but successful practice of the demagogue.[1] —John Randolph

Ironically, as Americans have begun to feel more pain caused by the mismanagement and expansion of government, we still call on the government for relief. We don't seem to know where else to turn.

People will not fight for freedom unless they understand it, value it, and believe it is at risk. Americans and freedom-loving people around the world must develop a deeper understanding and appreciation of freedom. To the oppressed, freedom may simply mean escape from their oppressors. To the poor, freedom may be the deliverance from want. To the anxious, freedom is synonymous with security.

These desires to be free from difficulty and danger are understandable, but they have led to a willingness to make government our master. Politicians with mostly good intentions have promised to help with more government solutions, but unless these leaders and policymakers develop a better understanding of freedom, their good intentions will continue to destroy not only our freedom but the very people they are trying to help.

The pursuit of physical, emotional, and spiritual freedom is arguably the highest purpose of mankind. Amartya Sen, a Nobel Prize winner in economics, writes, "The success of a society is to be evaluated . . . primarily by the substantive freedoms that the members of that society enjoy."[2] The pursuit of freedom is in many ways a moral cause that attempts to elevate individuals to a place where they can make their own decisions based on their personal value system. Yet despite endless calls for liberty, the conflict of the ages continues to wage between those who would use force to control others and those who are willing to fight for the freedom to control their own lives.

The dilemma for democratic governments is how to balance the use of force with the requirements of freedom. Civilization by its definition must restrain the destructive tendencies of mankind in order for people to live together in peace and constructive interaction. Governments must have laws and the ability to enforce them. Without some control there will be chaos, and there is no freedom in chaos.

The ironic political question has always been: how much societal control is necessary for freedom to thrive, and at what point does control by government destroy freedom? If this were the primary point of contention in political debates, all governments would be moving to find the optimum balance between freedom and control. Unfortunately, from ancient civilizations to the present, many leaders and governments have denied the societal benefits and moral calling of freedom. Freedom is a threat to power and control. Those who seek power (even to do "good") must solidify their control by restricting freedom.

> God grants liberty only to those who love it, and are
> always ready to guard and defend it.[3] —Daniel Webster

Freedom the American Way

The American founders attempted to deal with the conflict between government control and individual freedom through a system of representative democracy and a separation of powers. The federal government was given limited authority over the people, but the people were given the power to choose their government and their representatives. The individual states maintained considerable independence, and power at the federal level was divided between three branches of government. This division of power was based on the belief that "man is corrupt; and therefore his best chance to attain justice and freedom lies in keeping the hands of ambitious men from that power which invites corruption."[4]

The plan devised by our founders and ensconced in the Constitution worked. The United States became the greatest nation in the history of the world, and its people became the freest. The American success story demonstrated the indivisible nature of freedom, prosperity, and security. But now it seems many Americans have forgotten what made us successful.

Voting trends over the past decade, especially in the 2008 elections, confirm that Americans increasingly prefer candidates who promise an expansion of the role and scope of the federal government. This trend indicates Americans have forgotten the value of freedom and may no longer understand that it was freedom, not government, that created the greatest nation in history.

It is not an overstatement to say *freedom* describes the highest state of human existence. For more than two centuries, this elusive treasure has thrived in the United States of America. Freedom is hard to define. We can't see it or touch it. Yet freedom has been written about and spoken of throughout history as the height of individual achievement and the ultimate goal of civilization.

> Freedom is a means to human excellence, to human happiness, to the fulfillment of human destiny. Freedom is the capacity to choose wisely and to act well as a matter of habit—or, to use the old-fashioned term, as an outgrowth of virtue. Freedom is the means by which, exercising both our reason and our will, we act on the natural longing for truth, for goodness, and for happiness that is built into us as human beings. Freedom is something that grows in us, and the habit of living freedom wisely must be developed through education, which among many other things involves the experience of emulating others who live wisely and well.[5]

By all objective measures (which we'll discuss in later chapters), *freedom* is on the decline in America. It is imperative Americans pause to understand how and why this is happening. The philosophy of socialism has crept into almost every aspect of American life, and this philosophy has slowly and indiscernibly stripped many Americans of their prosperity, security, dignity, and hope for the future.

As part of America's baby-boom generation, I have seen the subtle changes over many decades. There have been thousands of media accounts during my lifetime of people dying in pursuit of freedom. Hundreds of Germans died trying to get to freedom by tunneling under, crashing through, or flying over the Berlin Wall. Many Cubans and Haitians drowned when their makeshift rafts sank en route to America. Russian defectors were smothered while hiding in shipping crates trying to get to our shores. A Chinese escapee almost froze to death hiding in the wheel well of a jet plane on its way to the U.S. Yet today America is adopting many of the policies of the countries so many have fled.

> A wise and frugal government, which shall restrain men from injuring one another, which shall leave them otherwise free to regulate their own pursuits of industry and improvement, and shall not take from the mouth of labor the bread it has earned. This is the sum of good government. —President Thomas Jefferson

The Importance of Freedom

Freedom of speech, freedom of religion, freedom of association, free enterprise, financial freedom, freedom to vote for government leaders—freedom in all its contexts has proven to have incredible power for good. Freedom can change hopelessness into opportunity. It can turn a meaningless life into a life full of purpose. Freedom can transform an idea into a multimillion-dollar enterprise. Freedom can turn poverty into riches. It can change enemies into friends. Freedom can convert evil to virtue. Unquestionably freedom has the power to make possible many of the hopes and dreams of all mankind. Government's goal should be to allow freedom to work for everyone.

We all need to take the time to understand what freedom is and what makes it work. This is a tall order in today's microwave culture. People are so used to sound bites and simple solutions that they have little patience for detailed explanations of our problems or in-depth discussions about alternative solutions. This impatience with understanding explains how Americans can vote for candidates who block the development of America's own energy supplies and then complain about high gas prices. It explains how voters can support an elected official who votes against policies that would help individuals buy their own health insurance and then act surprised when there are so many uninsured Americans. It explains how people can vote for politicians who support higher taxes, regulations, and lawsuits against businesses and then have no clue why jobs are going overseas.

Soon the same politicians who voted to spend the money in the Social Security Trust Fund on bridges to nowhere will be on the news asking who stole all the money. And after voting to cut what Medicare pays doctors, they will call doctors greedy for not taking senior citizens as patients and demand the government do something to fix it. The same members of Congress who voted for wasteful pork barrel earmarks and to spend America deep into debt will ask for an investigation into why interest rates and inflation are on the rise. If Americans aren't willing or able to connect the dots between cause and effect, they will continue to vote for the people who cause most of their problems . . . and infringe on their liberty.

Yet today, more than at any time in our history, America is placing its hopes and dreams on the belief that freedom is our most valuable national asset and our strongest defense against our enemies. We are told the spread of freedom will make our country and the world safe, peaceful, and more prosperous. The war against terror has taught us the strength of our military alone cannot achieve these goals. We are using freedom as our weapon against terror, as our instrument of peace, as our reason to intervene in the affairs of other nations, as our explanation for trading with communist countries, and as the glue that will ultimately hold this fragile world together.

Throughout our history, America has done much to protect and defend the cause of freedom. But in recent decades, attempts to spread freedom have been awkward and inept at best. The number of "democracies" is increasing, but liberty is not.[6] Democratic elections in places without democratic institutions or the rule of law have produced Islamic theocracies and terrorist-run governments in the Middle East. Russians can vote, but freedom is in decline. Democracies flourished in Africa in the 1990s, but chaos and instability have actually made corruption and lawlessness worse in many countries.[7] Venezuela is a democracy with a dictator as president. India has been a democracy since 1947, but it has become less tolerant, less secular, less law-abiding, and less free.[8] Too many democratic elections merely legitimize power grabs. Nearly half of "democratizing" countries in the world can now be classified as democracies without liberty.[9]

And then there's Afghanistan. The world celebrated as millions of Afghanis risked their lives to participate in democratic elections. But Americans are now worried that Afghanistan may be another premature democracy not ready for political freedom. America's brave military has once again demonstrated a willingness to fight for freedom, but the question remains as to whether the Afghanis have that same love for freedom and the resolve to build the institutions to help them keep it.

Democracies don't create liberty. Liberty creates democracies. The fact that the United States, the consensus home of freedom, does not understand freedom or how it works is a problem of global concern. If America does not understand freedom, how can we possibly spread it to other countries? More troubling is the question: how can we presume to preserve freedom for ourselves and our posterity if we no longer understand the factors that create it and make it work?

As America attempts to sell our brand of freedom to the world, it is critical we evaluate the quality of the product we are selling. We are betting everything that freedom is the answer. We have spent trillions of dollars and hundreds of thousands of American lives to establish freedom here and abroad. New democracies all over the world are looking to America as their example. It has never been more important that we understand what freedom is and what must be done to allow it to work.

Before continuing our attempts to spread freedom abroad, America must assess what has gone wrong with freedom at home. The country that triumphed over communism and socialism has become increasingly government dominated and socialistic. We must first be the model for freedom before we attempt to spread freedom to the rest of the world.

Americans once known for personal responsibility and independence have become increasingly dependent on their government for their income, health care, education of their children, housing, food, and other subsidies. Our culture and people, once known for their character and virtue, are statistically among the world leaders in murder, rape, violent crime, gambling, pornography, abortion, divorce, and unwed births. Once boasting the world's best and brightest children, America is better known today for being near the bottom of achievement scores.

Liberal politicians in Washington are clamoring for more government solutions to the problems caused by more government. Conservatives are at a loss when trying to explain to voters (who have not been educated in how freedom actually works) that by saying no to counterfeit government compassion, we are simultaneously saying yes to real liberty. Liberals in politics, as well as the media and academia, are increasingly anticapitalist and anti-private property—attitudes consistent with socialistic ideology. Freedom is in peril in America, which means the future of freedom around the globe is at risk.

There are real solutions. Freedom can be saved and secured for future generations around the world if Americans will take the time to understand its origins and essential components. Our goal must be to stop America's slide toward a socialized democracy that destroys the principles of liberty. Our freedoms are being threatened, and Americans must once again stand up and fight to protect this sacred trust that so many have fought and died for.

Every generation of Americans has had to fight for freedom, and our generation is no exception. The difference today: our greatest enemy is not a foreign government or even a terrorist group. The dual threat to America's freedom is the lack of understanding of the meaning of freedom in the hearts and minds of Americans and the public policies deployed by elected officials who have lost sight of why America is great.

The smallest minority on earth is the individual.
Those who deny individual rights cannot claim
to be defenders of minorities.[10] —Ayn Rand

The Two Sides of Freedom: Society and the Individual

If freedom were a coin, one side would be *society,* and the other the *individual.* Society determines what you're allowed to do and provides the external support systems for you to live in freedom. Your capabilities as an individual ultimately determine your ability to live independently and your qualifications to live in freedom. There can be no freedom unless individuals have the capabilities to succeed in a free society.

Society plays an instrumental role in developing the external factors (like laws and enforcement) that allow people to act with autonomy, to make choices in all areas of their lives, and to be protected from those who would threaten their lives and property. Amartya Sen refers to external environmental factors as society's "instrumental" role in developing freedom:

> The instrumental role of freedom concerns the way different kinds of rights, opportunities, and entitlements contribute to the expansion of human freedom in general, and thus promoting development. . . . The effectiveness of freedom as an instrument lies in the fact that different kinds of freedom interrelate with one another, and freedom of one type may greatly help in advancing freedom of other types.[11]

An environment of freedom requires a government of laws that protects the rights of individuals, discourages destructive behavior, and promotes individual and societal actions benefiting the common good. Freedom also requires a diversity of institutions such as marriage and family, schools, churches, a free-enterprise economy (capitalism), a participatory political system, and voluntary associations to play an instrumental role in the development of individual capabilities and to create opportunities and choices. Milton and Rose Friedman write that private sector institutions such as capitalism reduce the need for central control by government:

> Economic freedom is an essential requisite for political freedom. By enabling people to cooperate with one another

without coercion or central direction, it reduces the area over which political power is exercised. In addition, by dispersing power, the free market provides an offset to whatever concentration of political power may arise. The combination of economic and political power in the same hands is a sure recipe for tyranny.[12]

Free institutions, along with a government that operates according to a predictable framework of law, will work together to develop individual capabilities and to create the choices and protections that are necessary for independent people to thrive. Freedom exists in a country where capable, independent citizens live in a free environment supported by strong institutions.

Amartya Sen refers to the internal characteristics and abilities of people as the "intrinsic" capabilities[13] that allow them to live with a degree of autonomy, self-sufficiency, and independence. No one is completely independent. People are entirely dependent on their ecosystem, culture, and society for food, water, shelter, and other basic needs.[14] Citizens who band together for their common defense are safer. Everyone is psychologically healthier when they have others to meet their belonging needs.

Seeking independence does not mean eradicating dependency and becoming ultimately independent and self-sufficient. Rather, optimum independence requires an understanding of the difference between healthy, normal dependency that must be accepted as a condition of being a part of civilization and unhealthy forms of dependency that result in a loss of dignity and purpose when others control your life.[15] A better word for healthy dependence is interdependence. People who contribute, who give and take from those around them, have a constructive interdependent relationship with society.

An unhealthy dependence exists when people lose the ability to provide for themselves and their families. This can be caused by the inadequate development of skills by the individual or the diminishing of skills that occurs when others consistently provide for necessities that should be provided by the person. The lack of continuous development of individual skills often results in an unhealthy cycle of dependency. Incapable individuals become increasingly disabled, dependent, and needy. Positive impulses to dream, work, improve, save, and advance disappear as expectations of provisions by others increase. Ultimately, for the dependent citizen, the meaning of freedom becomes the freedom from risk and want.

Individual capabilities allow a person to succeed in a free society. Freedom, or liberty as our founders called it, relies on an independent citizenry with the character and capabilities to seize the opportunities freedom provides.

> Liberty exists when individuals—endowed with unalienable
> rights, empowered with virtue and individual capabilities,
> committed to personal responsibility, and protected by the rule
> of law—are allowed to make their own choices in pursuit of a life
> that they value.[16]

Everything that is really great and inspiring is created by the individual who can labor in freedom. —Albert Einstein

---

The Individual Is the Foundation of Freedom

The pursuit of freedom is focused on the individual. There can be no freedom unless individuals have the capabilities, including skills and values, to live independently and succeed in a free society. There can also be no freedom unless a society recognizes the rights of individuals to make choices and take actions based on their own values. A third requirement for a free society is that individuals must be constrained from taking actions that violate the freedoms of others.

The recognition of the individual as the focus of freedom has proved difficult in practice throughout history, including in America. Rights and privileges in societies around the world have historically been based on class, caste, religion, race, gender, economic status, ethnicity, or other group identification. Even in America, basic rights were once denied to African-Americans, women, Native Americans, and others who were discriminated against because of their group affiliation.

Today an opposite but equal threat to freedom has developed: special rights for individuals *because* of their membership in a particular group. The concept of "equal justice under law" (carved in stone above the doors of the Supreme Court) for individuals dissipates as government withholds or extends specific benefits based on classification by group.

The goal of equality can be a positive force but not equality as it is sometimes defined today. Everyone must have an equal opportunity to pursue success, but everyone does not have an equal right to success. All people are born with equal value as human beings because we are all created in the image of God, but everyone has different gifts, abilities, and drive. What we do with our abilities and how we perform during our lives determines our level of success.

While all people are of equal value before God, all behavior is not. Able-bodied people who won't work must not be compensated equally with those who work hard. If they are, the value of work will be diminished. Those who disobey laws must not be treated equally with those who obey laws. If they are, laws will mean nothing.

Society must recognize and elevate the value of the traditional family as providing the best chance for children to succeed. If it does not, marriage will be meaningless, and more children will be born without two parents. Same-sex couples must not be honored with the institution of marriage. If they are, the moral standing of marriage will be reduced to that of homosexuality.

Freedom requires that individuals be treated equally based on their equal standing before God and society, but freedom will not work unless society has the right to discriminate between constructive and destructive behavior—against what we as individuals consider good or bad. Without the freedom to discriminate between good and bad, our culture will decline and our society will deteriorate. Socialism replaces individual values and judgments with a government-mandated tolerance for destructive behaviors.

In a free society the individual must be free to make value judgments and to act on those values. Freedom requires the individual to be the central actor on a stage with many freedom-enhancing institutions. The illustration below reflects the traditional American perspective that assumes not only that individuals can control their own lives; they can also change the world around them. Institutions help develop our capabilities as well as provide the outlets to exercise our freedom to choose jobs, products, services, political candidates, churches, and schools.

Freedom Requires the Individual to Be the Central Focus

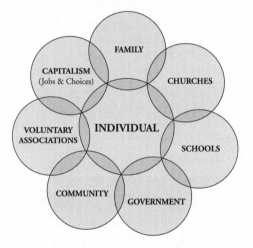

Socialists Devalue the Individual

The socialist or collectivist perspective is that the individual has value, security, and opportunity primarily as part of a group. The group perspective is essentially "you and me against the world." People find their identity not in themselves but with their group: union, minority, ethnicity, club, religion, or nationality. This group mentality has proved destructive to nations and to individuals.

The Fight for Freedom

The worldview of those without an individual identity leads them to believe life is something that happens to them, and they have little control over their lives or the world around them. Ironically, these people often see themselves as exploited victims and, at the same time, superior to others who are not a part of their group. They believe they are oppressed because of their individual characteristics or group association, but they also believe their victimization and association with others who have experienced similar oppression makes them better than nonmembers.

Those who find their identity in a group association tend to look to government to manage the world around them. They have little faith in private sector institutions because they don't trust free markets and free people to protect and provide preference to their group. In fact, they tend to believe those outside their group will discriminate against them without the intervention of government. Their worldview precludes a belief that their own initiatives can change their circumstances or that free people and free markets will voluntarily solve problems and improve the quality of life for everyone.

Government leaders in America have expanded centralized control under the guise of protecting and providing for people who have been victimized by our free society. It is easy to prove there has been injustice or that some citizens do not make good decisions for themselves. There are always people who cannot provide for themselves. According to their socialist thinking, compassion demands more government control and fewer independent choices.

If people believe they are helpless, they will want government to be their master. That's why many political candidates try to convince voters they are hapless victims who need a strong government to save them.

> If you think of yourselves as helpless and ineffectual, it is certain that you will create a despotic government to be your master. The wise despot, therefore, maintains among his subjects a popular sense that they are helpless and ineffectual.[17] —Frank Herbert

SAVING FREEDOM

Barack Obama became a master of "victimology" during his 2008 campaign for president. He painted a picture of America as a collection of groups who have been victimized by injustice. In his speech on May 18, 2008, responding to the controversial anti-American sermons of his pastor, Reverend Jeremiah Wright, Obama asked voters to "build a coalition of white and black, Latino and Asian, rich and poor, young and old [who are] irrevocably bound to a tragic past." His speech called for unity and change, but he attempted to unite Americans around their dissatisfaction with their country: "Continue on the path to a more perfect union . . . means binding our particular grievances—for better health care, and better schools, and better jobs—to the larger aspirations of all Americans—the white woman struggling to break the glass ceiling, the white man who's been laid off, the immigrant trying to feed his family."

Obama offered hope not in an American identity but a hope that America could change from its repressive past. The enchantment of Barack Obama to the disenchanted was derived from the fact that much of what he said was true. There has been much injustice. But instead of inspiring Americans with hope and pride in the greatness of our country and the strides we've made toward justice, he inspired people to unite around the wrongs and injustices that they have suffered because of their affiliation with a victimized group. Obama's platform was the antithesis of liberty because it diminished the importance of individual responsibility and destroyed confidence in freedom-enhancing institutions in the private sector. He offered hope in more government.

Socialists will cite slavery, racism, and other historical injustices in America as examples of how freedom doesn't work. This myth must be laid to rest once and for all! Slavery was government sponsored and an obvious violation of our founding principles. State and local governments created segregated schools and colleges (mandated by the federal government in the 1896 "separate but equal" U.S. Supreme Court ruling of *Plessy v. Ferguson, 163 U.S. 537*). Slavery and segregation in America were not the fault of freedom, but the fault of government policies antithetical to freedom.

The Fight for Freedom

Socialists use the perceived victim status of groups to promote a collectivist or group-oriented approach to government, even when government is responsible for the injustice. The contrast between America's social and political philosophies is the most distinct on this point. Those with socialist leanings generally push for group-oriented, universal, government-directed solutions to societal problems. Those who believe in freedom believe government should facilitate free choices and equal treatment for all individuals. I'll mention a few examples.

Those with a group focus prefer a universal, one-size-fits-all, government-directed, health-care system. Conversely, a focus on the individual will demand that people have their choice of affordable health-care plans that they can own and keep from job to job and into retirement.

Those who see individuals as incapable of making good decisions want a universal, government-owned, national pension plan (Social Security) with all retired Americans dependent (at least in part) on the government for their income. Those who understand how freedom works will fight for the right of every American to have a personal Social Security account they own and the government can't spend.

True socialists will jealously guard the universal, government-run education system and fight all attempts to create more choices with competitive, independent schools. This gives the government (and those who run the government) control over the values and beliefs of every generation. Freedom lovers believe parents should have many choices of schools, and the money spent on public education should follow students to the school of their choice.

Democrat politicians who are heavily influenced by labor unions want to force workers to join unions. They have demonstrated this intention by voting to take away the secret ballot that protects workers from intimidation when unions are trying to organize their place of employment. Freedom fighters believe a worker's right to a secret ballot election should be protected and no workers should be forced to join a union.

People often ask me, "Why can't members of Congress just get along and work together?" The reason is some members are pushing a collectivist, socialist-leaning agenda, and others believe it is our job to allow freedom to work for everyone. There is no functional compromise between freedom and socialism. When you hear a bill passed with "bipartisan support," you can bet your bottom dollar it expanded the role of government in some area of your life.

In the last scenes of the movie *Braveheart*, William Wallace (played by Mel Gibson) was being tortured and killed by the evil king. Screaming in agony with his dying breath he shouted, "Freedom!" Wallace's fight for freedom continues to inspire people today, and America now needs that kind of inspirational leadership to save freedom.

He is free who knows how to keep in his own hand
the power to decide, at each step, the course of his life,
and who lives in a society which does not
block the exercise of that power.[1]
—Salvador de Madariaga y Rojo

CHAPTER FIVE

Free to Choose
The Risks and Rewards of Making
Your Own Decisions

*There was once an old sow with three little pigs. All three left home to seek
their fortunes. The first little pig built a house of straw. Presently a wolf came
along, knocked on the door, and said, "Little pig, little pig, let me come in."*

*The pig answered, "No, no, no . . . not by the hair of my chinny, chin
chin." The wolf replied, "Then I'll huff, and I'll puff, and I'll blow your house
down." So he huffed, and he puffed, and he blew down the house and ate up
the little pig.*

*The second little pig built his house with sticks. Then along came the wolf
and said, "Little pig, little pig, let me come in."*

*The little pig answered, "No, no, no . . . not by the hair of my chinny, chin
chin." The wolf replied, "Then I'll huff, and I'll puff, and I'll blow your house
down." So he huffed, and he puffed, and he blew down the house and ate up
the little pig.*

*The third little pig built his house with bricks. Then along came the wolf
and said, "Little pig, little pig, let me come in."*

*The little pig answered, "No, no, no . . . not by the hair of my chinny, chin
chin." The wolf replied, "Then I'll huff, and I'll puff, and I'll blow your house*

down." So he huffed, and he puffed, and he huffed and puffed, but he couldn't blow down the brick house.

When the wolf saw he couldn't blow down the little pig's house, he invited the pig to meet him to gather turnips the next morning at 6:00 a.m., but the little pig got up at five, gathered the turnips, and was safely at home before the wolf got to the field.

The wolf tried several more times to lure the little pig out of his house, but each time the little pig outsmarted him. Then the wolf decided to break into the little pig's home by sliding down the chimney. But the little pig saw him climbing up his roof, so he hung a large pot of water over a blazing fire in his fireplace. The wolf slid down the chimney right into the boiling water. The little pig quickly put the cover on the pot, boiled up the wolf, and had him for supper. Then the little pig lived happily ever after.

Life is hard. None of us likes to see people suffer, even if their suffering is caused by their own bad decisions. Those of us who are parents know the pain of watching our children suffer for their own choices (and we know the pain of suffering for our own bad decisions, too). We also know the importance of letting our children make more of their own decisions as they get older to prepare them for the cold, cruel world.

Elected officials don't want people to be eaten up by wolves. That's why we should insist on laws that protect private property and enough police to enforce the law. But the slide toward socialism quickens when politicians seek to protect people by limiting their choices and their freedom to make them.

In the story above, two of the little pigs paid a high price for making bad decisions. Of course in the real world, society should do everything it can to keep people from carelessly putting themselves in life-threatening situations. But the lesson of this story should focus on the third little pig that did make good and thoughtful decisions.

In the longer version of the *Three Little Pigs*, the wolf tried many times to lure the third little pig from his home. Each time, through thoughtful decisions, the pig outsmarted the wolf. And every time the pig made a decision, he became better at making good decisions. The process of making his own choices helped him make better decisions and secure his own future.

More Choices Mean More Freedom

Making choices is making freedom. Freedom of choice is a major criterion for creating a free society.[2] Peter Bauer, author of *Dissent on Development*, argued that making choices is central to developing the capabilities to be free:

> I regard the extension of the range of choice, that is, an increase in the range of effective alternatives open to the people, as the principal objective and criterion of economic development; and I judge a measure principally by its probable effects on the range of alternatives open to individuals.[3]

When a child is allowed to make some choices for herself and accept the consequences of her decisions, she enhances her ability to make better choices in the future. This may be as simple as allowing the child to decide what her family will have for dinner. When she sees her decision sitting on the table and everyone enjoying her decision, she begins to understand she can change the world around her and make it better. Developing this worldview is essential to creating the capacity for people to live in freedom.

Thomas Aquinas, the thirteenth century Dominican friar, wrote passionately about freedom, virtue, and the importance of individuals gradually acquiring the capacity to make better choices. He believed individuals having the freedom to choose and the ability to make good choices was the key to a successful society. Paraphrasing Aquinas, George Weigel writes:

> Freedom is in fact the great organizing principle of the moral life—and since the very possibility of a moral life (the capacity to think and choose) is what distinguishes the human person from the rest of the natural world, freedom is the great organizing

principle of a life lived in a truly human way. That is, freedom is the human capacity that unifies all our other capacities into an orderly whole, and directs our actions toward the pursuit of happiness and goodness understood in the noblest sense: the union of the human person with the absolute good, who is God.[4]

Allowing people to make their own choices is foundational to the meaning of freedom. The process of decision-making and the opportunity for individuals to make decisions in pursuit of a valued outcome are both the "means" to developing the capability to live free as well as the desired "end" of the process of development.[5] When an individual goes through the process of making a decision, he is developing his capability to live free. This is the "means" to freedom. The opportunity to pursue a personal objective through one's own initiative and decision-making is freedom, the "end" goal of the development process.

> The system under which people make their own choices—and bear most of the consequences of their decisions—is the system that has prevailed for most of our history.[6] —Milton and Rose Friedman

Real freedom of choice means individuals accept the risks, consequences, and rewards of making their own decisions. Freedom is a risk and reward system at every level. This is true when people choose personal relationships such as marriage or economic relationships such as employment. Risks and rewards are factors every time an individual chooses to buy a product or service. When government tries to remove the risks, rewards, and consequences of decision-making, it destroys freedom.

Socialists attempt to reduce risks and promote fairness by centralizing decision-making and creating more standard or universal services for everyone. Under socialism a small number of people make many of life's choices for millions of people. *Freedom is the complete opposite of socialism because it is based on millions of people making their own decisions from a wide array of choices offered by thousands of competing suppliers.*

Freedom: The Success Model

A few years after the fall of the Soviet Union and the toppling of the Berlin Wall, I saw a television documentary that included an interview with a former Soviet official who visited the U.S. as part of a government delegation during the Cold War. He was asked what impressed him most about the U.S. during his visit.

The interviewer was surprised by the Soviet official's answer. He did not mention the New York skyline, the grand monuments in Washington, D.C., or America's beautiful mountains, lakes, and rivers. The Soviet was astounded by America's grocery stores. He could not believe the incredible variety of goods in such abundance. He was amazed at the diversity of shoppers and that the "common" people appeared to find what they needed at prices they could afford, while the more affluent shoppers also found what they wanted in the same store.

The Soviet's answer did not surprise me because I had long considered America's grocery stores to be showcases of free enterprise. I know a little about the grocery store business. I worked as a stock boy and bag boy in a grocery store. After college I worked for a consumer product manufacturing company that marketed their products in grocery stores. Later I worked for advertising agencies that developed advertising and promotion plans for products sold in grocery stores.

The grocery store business is built around the concept of millions of customers making their own decisions about what they buy. The retail grocer does everything he can to have all the products that a wide variety of customers want at a better price than his competitors. Since the demand for products, sizes, and prices changes constantly, grocery store managers must work diligently to make sure the merchandise on their shelves is what the customer wants.

Manufacturers selling to grocery retailers must be equally creative and diligent. They must constantly study their customers to find out what they want, including what sizes and prices are most preferred. Their research and development departments systematically try to improve their products while trying to lower costs. Marketing departments regularly hold focus groups with their own customers and the customers of competitors to find out how to improve their product and its perceived value. Advertising is used to tell customers of the superior qualities of their products. Competition ensures that only the best manufacturers and retailers will survive. This results in the best quality products at the lowest possible prices and millions of individuals are able to make their own decisions about what to buy based on their means and values.

Socialists will argue that this showcase of free enterprise is not fair. Some people can buy steaks while others can afford only hamburgers. Some customers are poorly educated and will make bad dietary decisions for their families. Much of the expense of advertising, promotion, and packaging could be eliminated so prices could be reduced.

But what socialists don't understand is that hamburger is more available at lower prices because some people buy steaks. Most people can afford better diets for their families because so many businesses are competing to provide better products at lower prices. And the increased volume that comes from effective advertising actually lowers the per unit prices of consumer goods.

The reason the Soviet official was so impressed with America's grocery stores was that he saw the Soviet grocery stores that were a product of socialism. In the Soviet Union, the "state" controlled what products were produced and sold. Selection was limited and prices were high. The contrast between free enterprise and socialism is sharp and clear to the people who have lived under socialism.

There are many other success stories for freedom in America. When I was in college, IBM was America's premier computer company. Only governments and large organizations could afford computers and only PhDs could operate them. Computers were large enough to fill a room. There were only a few competitors selling computers and only a small number of people making the purchase decisions. Innovation and improvements in computer technology were slow and imperceptible.

Free to Choose

Little changed in the computer industry until a young man named Steven Jobs developed a personal computer in his garage. He called it Apple. Suddenly the computer market changed from a business controlled by a few to an industry with millions of people making their own decisions based on their own values. The number of competitors exploded, as did innovations and improvements. Average people, once considered not smart enough to operate computers, quickly became the primary target market for new, consumer-friendly technologies. Even I could use one. I started my business with an Apple IIe.

Personal computers have improved the lives of millions, but they would never have been invented under a centrally controlled system. The same is true for today's telecommunication industry. When telephone communication was controlled by the government-regulated AT&T monopoly, it took decades to move from a rotary dial to a push button phone. When the courts broke up AT&T and created a free-enterprise telecommunication industry, innovation and consumer choices expanded dramatically almost overnight.

Cell phones, digital transmission, the Internet, iPods, Blackberries . . . you name it. Choices increased exponentially when millions of people began making their own decisions from a large array of products offered by hundreds of competitors. This is the model for success in America. This is decentralized power and control. This is freedom. It works in the economic sphere for grocery stores, computers, and telecommunications, just as it works in the social and political spheres, and as it could work with education and health care—millions of people making their own decisions from a wide variety of competing choices.

> When freedom prevails, the ingenuity and inventiveness of people creates incredible wealth. This is the source of the natural improvement of the human condition.[7] —Brian S. Wesbury

Socialism: The Model for Failure

As noted earlier, making the case for freedom does not mean making the case for no laws or regulations. The infrastructure for freedom requires a strong and predictable framework of law and order. Consumers must be protected from fraudulent claims and dangerous products. Marketers must provide adequate product information to allow consumers to make good decisions. But every effort should be made in a free society to avoid centralizing decision-making and reducing individual choices.

Unfortunately America has centralized decision-making for some of our most important services, including education. Education is paramount in a free society because it is a pivotal factor in developing the individual capabilities necessary for individuals to succeed and for society to prosper. A poor education hinders the ability of people to live successfully on their own and ultimately leads to an expansion of government.

I have worked closely with public schools as clients when I was in business. Decision-making in government schools is centralized and heavily bureaucratic. Instead of working to meet the needs of a wide variety of students, government schools focus on delivering a standard service to all students. While some attempts are made to provide choices such as honors classes or career classes, there is no urgency to "win the business" of a variety of students with different learning styles, aptitudes, and interests. In fact, there is a great fear among public school administrators that offering too much variety could lead to accusations of discrimination if every student is not offered the same thing.

There is no constant effort to change and improve services in government schools and no danger that bad schools will be put out of business by competitors if their services are sub-par. Parents and students have little say about which services are offered. Unless they can afford a private school, they are stuck with whatever is provided by the school to which they are assigned by the central planners. Most parents are essentially trapped, and despite the best intentions of many school board members and administrators, most government schools reflect a "you'll take what we give you" mentality.

Free to Choose

President Bush thought the requirements to measure progress in No Child Left Behind would improve schools. They didn't. In fact, many teachers tell me the effort to "teach the test" in order to meet the requirements of NCLB is actually resulting in a poorer education. I don't have to recount the terrible statistics of America's education system. We are losing ground to practically every other industrialized country in the world. At a time when our workforce has to compete with the best and brightest workers in a dynamic and competitive global economy, we are failing our children by keeping them in a government-run, socialist system.

America is now applying the same socialistic model to health care. Decision-making has been centralized into large government and insurance company bureaucracies. Laws and regulations make it difficult for individuals to own their health insurance and to make their own health-care decisions with their doctors. Federal tax laws allow businesses, but not individuals, to deduct the cost of health insurance. Workers are dependent on employers or the government for their insurance and most lose their insurance every time they change jobs.

Medicare takes 2.5 percent of every worker's paycheck to provide health insurance during retirement. Most seniors think the Medicare system is an example of how government can work. Unfortunately the federal government has not saved any of the money taken from workers since it was created in the 1960s. Today Medicare is bankrupt and will require tens of trillions of dollars to keep its promises to future seniors. Medicare already pays physicians and hospitals less than their cost to treat a patient. That's why more and more health-care providers are refusing to treat Medicare patients.

Medicare demonstrates why socialized medicine does not work. The expertise of doctors and the needs of patients are secondary to a dehumanizing, bureaucratic, inefficient government system. Medicare is built on debt and dependency. It forces patients and physicians to become dependent on the government. And it lumps huge debts on future generations of Americans.

Social Security is another promise to seniors America must keep, but it is another government program built on debt and dependency. Today's generation of seniors is happy with Social Security because they will, on average, get more from the program than they put in. But like Medicare, the federal government has not saved one penny of the 12.5 percent it takes out of every American's paycheck for Social Security. In 2017 Social Security taxes will no longer pay promised retirement benefits to seniors, and there is no money in the so-called Social Security Trust Fund.

There are freedom solutions to education, health care, and Social Security, as well as for American energy supplies, our tax code, and transportation system. These will all be discussed in detail in chapter 13, "The Plan to Save Freedom." It is difficult to understand why any American would continue to insist on centrally planned programs for America's most essential services. The evidence is clear despite all the best intentions in the world: there is no example of any effective and efficient federal government program. Freedom does not create perfect solutions, but there is abundant evidence that choices and competition improve the quality of life for almost everyone.

It is the "almost" that gets the attention of socialists. Instead of attempting to improve the capabilities of a few who are not succeeding, socialists want to organize society around the assumption that no one has the capabilities to succeed on his own. Instead of helping the few who can't afford to purchase affordable, competitively priced health insurance, they want the government to pay for health care for everyone. Instead of helping a few manage their personal Social Security accounts, the socialists want everyone to be dependent on the government for their retirement income. *Socialists want to organize society around the lowest common denominator for the benefit of those who are least capable of living free.*

Freedom is not something that anybody can be given;
freedom is something people take and people are
as free as they want to be.[8] —James Baldwin

Free to Choose

Americans today love freedom, but mistake the blessings of freedom with the substance of freedom itself. Self-government is a blessing of freedom. Self-control is a requirement for this blessing to exist. The pursuit of happiness is a blessing of freedom. Taking responsibility for yourself and sharing in the responsibilities of being a part of a community are prerequisites to the pursuit of happiness.

Security, opportunity, and prosperity are all blessings of a free America, like flowers in a garden. Tilling the soil, fertilizing, weeding, and watering are the hard work required to make the flowers grow. Working the "soil" of liberty by continuously developing individual capabilities and freedom-enhancing institutions is the hard work required to produce the blessings of freedom.

Freedom requires hard work and patience, two disciplines in short supply today. People are sometimes weak, flawed, and even evil. Developing the capacity for people to live free is a long and arduous process. It is always tempting to shortcut the process of developing individual capabilities and the societal infrastructure for freedom with a (supposedly) quick and easy government solution. But turning to government is giving up on freedom. We cannot allow the difficult process of developing freedom to cower us into accepting dehumanizing socialistic solutions.

Evil is not the last word about the human condition, and an awareness of the pervasiveness of evil is not the place to start thinking about freedom, or indeed about political life in general. We are made for excellence. Developed through the four cardinal virtues—prudence (practical wisdom), justice, courage, and temperance (perhaps better styled today, "self-command")—freedom is the method by which we become the kind of people our noblest instincts incline us to be: the kind of people who can, among other possibilities, build free and virtuous societies in which the rights of all are acknowledged, respected, and protected in law.[9]

SAVING FREEDOM

The essence of freedom is much broader, more complex, multi-dimensional, and dynamic than is commonly understood in the world today. Freedom's meaning has been cheapened by political rhetoric that suggests moral license, entitlement, equality of outcomes, and a lack of responsibility and discipline. Freedom so defined is not worthy of the high cost in blood and sacrifice, which has always been required to win and keep it.

Freedom is in fact a "discipline" that must be continuously pursued to be achieved and preserved. Freedom requires constant development directed toward the skills, values, and overall capabilities of the individual and the freedom-enhancing institutions in society providing the opportunities, choices, and accountability for freedom's expression. No wolf can blow down that house.

Every American must make a choice: will we aspire to make freedom work to the greatest degree possible for everyone, or will we use human frailties and the failures of society as excuses to replace freedom with more government control and socialism? I'll take my stand with those who fight for freedom!

Part II
PRINCIPLES AND INSTITUTIONS OF FREEDOM

Unless the Lord builds a house, its builders labor
over it in vain; unless the Lord watches over a city,
the watchman stays alert in vain.

PSALM 127:1

The natural progress of things is for liberty to yield
and government to gain ground.
—President Thomas Jefferson

CHAPTER SIX

Freedom versus Big Government

Unlimited Government Leads to Unlimited Debt and Socialism

Long ago in a distant land, a very old man called his son to his dying bed. There he revealed an amazing secret: the old man's father had bequeathed him a genie he kept locked in a small cage and hidden in a closet. The genie provided two services to the kingdom where the man's family lived for generations. First, he protected the people from any person or country that attempted to harm them. Second, he guaranteed all the citizens of the kingdom were treated equally and fairly. Because of these two protections, their kingdom was the happiest and most prosperous in the land.

The man told his son to bring the genie's cage to his bedside. "The genie is now your responsibility," he said, "but you must never ask him to do any more than the two services he has provided for years. If you do, he will grow in size and strength with every new request. Then he will break out of his cage and become a threat to the kingdom instead of a blessing."

The son promised to heed his father's warning, and for several years he kept his promise. Then a neighbor's home burned along with all of the possessions in the house. Instead of waiting for the community to help the man rebuild his home as was the kingdom's custom, the son decided to ask the genie to help. The whole community was amazed at the beautiful new home with all the man's possessions restored. They held a great celebration for the son and gave him a beautiful award. But soon another man's home was destroyed by a flood, and instead of rushing to help, the community came to the son's house and demanded that the genie restore the man's home.

The son relented and asked the genie to help. This time the genie grew large enough to break out of the cage. He escaped, and everywhere he went someone asked him to do something new. He grew and grew and began to demand more and more food and possessions from the kingdom. The genie built a huge castle on a hill and demanded that all citizens bring him half of everything they produced. But citizens continued to ask for more and more, and the genie continued to grow and demand more and more from the citizens. The people became weaker and poorer, and their kingdom eventually disappeared from the land.

America's founders knew they were putting a powerful genie in a cage when they formed the federal government. They knew that historically all democratic governments grew until they consumed the freedom of the people and ultimately collapsed under their own weight. They knew the American people would have to remain constantly vigilant to restrain the growth of government. And they knew, like the genie in the story above, the federal government would grow every time we asked it to do something new. But our founders left us a "cage" to protect ourselves against the genie of government growth: the Constitution.

After my first election to Congress in 1998, I spent November, December, and the first few weeks in January 1999 setting up my office, hiring staff, and fighting to get on the committees that aligned with my priorities: tax reform, Social Security reform, health-care reform, and education choice. Most of these issues were handled by the powerful Ways and Means Committee that was reserved for senior members or "vulnerable" Republicans who needed to raise a lot of money. Apparently, outside groups gave a lot of money to committee members who could tinker with the tax code. They were less interested in people like me who really wanted to reform the tax code. I never got on the Ways and Means Committee during my six years in the House.

Swearing-in ceremonies for the new Congress were in late January. My wife and four children traveled to D.C. to watch from the House gallery as I took the oath of office. Every member of the House has to stand in the House chamber, raise his right hand, and recite the oath of office at the beginning of each new Congress. I had never given a lot of thought to the oath until I took it, and frankly was a little surprised by what it actually said. I guess I expected to swear allegiance to my country and agree to do whatever I thought was best for my state and the American people. But the oath was a simple pledge to defend the Constitution:

> I, Jim DeMint, do solemnly swear that I will support and
> defend the Constitution of the United States against all enemies,
> foreign or domestic; that I will bear true faith and allegiance to
> the same; that I take this obligation freely, without any mental
> reservation or purpose of evasion; and that I will faithfully
> discharge the duties of the office on which I am about to enter.
> So help me God.

There is nothing in this oath about representing my district and state or helping the poor and downtrodden. There was nothing about responding to the woes of the American people. There was no list of duties because everything we were supposed to do in Congress was written in the Constitution. All federal officers, the president and his cabinet, justices on the Supreme Court, and members of the armed services all take an oath to protect and defend the Constitution. It must have been really important at one time.

After taking the oath as a group in the House chamber, I met my wife and children to have our pictures taken with the new speaker, Dennis Hastert. We were encouraged to bring our own Bibles for a simulated swearing-in ceremony. I put my left hand on my personal Bible, raised my right hand, and the camera flashed. I was a United States congressman.

I rarely heard the Constitution spoken of again—not when considering legislation, not when considering any new government program. It was never used as justification for legislation because there was little we did that fit within the limited powers of the federal government specified by the Constitution. Congressman Ron Paul from Texas, a physician and former presidential candidate, was known as "Dr. No" because he voted no on almost every piece of legislation. He argued that just about everything Congress did was unconstitutional. He was usually right.

The Constitution Limits the Role of the Federal Government

The Constitution is a relatively short document that outlines how the federal government is to be organized, how laws are made, and the specific "powers" granted Congress (legislative branch), the president (executive branch), and the Supreme Court (judicial branch). The first ten amendments to the Constitution, packaged as the Bill of Rights, specify the rights of individuals and the states. We have included a copy of the U.S. Constitution in the back of this book for your convenience.

The best and most comprehensive analysis of the Constitution, in my opinion, is *The Heritage Guide to the Constitution*. This book, which represents the work of many legal scholars, was compiled by the Heritage Foundation under the leadership of former Attorney General Edwin Meese III.[1] No one should receive a college diploma in America without a course on this book.

I'm not a legal expert and won't try to extract the brilliant legal commentaries from Heritage's excellent work. The intent of the Constitution is clear, even to a nonlawyer like me. It doesn't take a legal scholar to see that the main purpose of the Constitution is to limit the role, scope, and power of the federal government. It does this by dividing and specifying the duties and powers of the federal government and by reserving all other powers to individuals or the states. The Tenth Amendment confirms the limitations of the federal government dictated by the Constitution:

Freedom versus Big Government

The powers not delegated to the United States by the
Constitution, nor prohibited by it to the states, are reserved to
the states respectively, or to the people.

The Constitution gives Congress the power to make laws for specific federal purposes, raise revenues (taxes), and spend money; it charges
the president with the responsibility to execute the laws and command
the military, and it gives the Supreme Court and other federal courts
the responsibility of ensuring equal justice under the law. The areas in
which Congress is allowed to make laws and spend money are confined
primarily to protecting Americans against "enemies foreign and domestic"
by establishing and funding the military and by punishing counterfeiters
and pirates on the high seas (Article I, Sec. 8). Congress is also given the
power to regulate commerce *between* (not within) the states and foreign
nations and to establish post offices and post roads.

Section 9 of Article I then tells Congress several things it can't do,
including showing preference to states and spending money unless it is
properly appropriated by law. This is where most of Congress's mischief
originates. Politicians and even some judges have said this section gives
Congress "the power of the purse" to spend money on anything it pleases.
This is categorically absurd! It is clear in context that Congress only has
authority to fund actions consistent with those powers given to Congress
in Section 8.

The modern-day interpretation of Section 9 of Article I completely
undermines all the restraints in size and scope of the federal government that were the primary purpose of the Constitution. Today Congress
makes laws, spends money, and raises taxes for small local projects (traf-
fic lights and water projects), for preferential requests from specific states
(museums), and to satisfy demands from special interest groups (farmers,
unions, minorities, senior citizens, veterans, etc). It won't be easy to turn
this around because most American voters are now dependent in some way
on federal beneficence.

The federal government now provides funding and heavily regulates public education, health care, retirement income (Social Security), farming, transportation, research, water and sewer services, banking and financial services, electric utilities, environmental standards, business and labor relations, and a myriad of other activities not found in the Constitution. It is perhaps naive and unrealistic to believe that Americans who are heavily dependent on these federal services would ever support a return to a pure Constitutional framework. I do believe, however, that if Americans could grasp the disastrous long-term impact of allowing our federal "genie" continued growth, they would force elected officials and judges to focus more on the protective "cage" provided by the Constitution. Then we could begin to restrain the growth of the federal government.

Why Restrain the Growth of the Federal Government?

Most members of Congress act like the Constitution is no longer relevant and seem to believe we should continue to expand federal programs whenever and wherever we see fit. But no reasonably informed, thinking American could believe unrestrained government spending would be good for our country. I will discuss in later chapters the corruption, incompetence, mismanagement, and devastating societal impact of congressional meddling in all areas of American cultural and economic life. The focus of this chapter, however, is the financial condition of our country. The most compelling arguments to stop the growth of the federal government are our government's unsustainable levels of spending and debt, which could result in the financial collapse of our government and our private sector economic structure.

The following chart illustrates the current course of government spending as a percent of the total U.S. economy (Gross Domestic Product or GDP). Government spending represented only a small fraction of the private economy until the twentieth century. Since World War II government spending has hovered around 20 percent of GDP.[2]

> If anyone thought U.S. Treasury bonds are a riskless investment, think again. Am I suggesting the U.S. government will default on its obligations? In my opinion, no other outcome is imaginable. If you doubt this conclusion, try to imagine federal, state, and local government paying off $10 trillion. It's not going to happen, as the readiest method of default open to government is the debasement of the national currency. This means an end to American international power—financial and military. It means an end to the old international order, which has existed since 1945. It means global revolution. Wave hello to socialism.[3]—J. R. Nyquist

Economic cycles over the past several decades have confirmed that good economic growth can occur when government spending stays below 20 percent. The U.S. economy has usually slowed and declined as government spending exceeded 20 percent.[4] As the chart below confirms, government spending now exceeds 20 percent and will surpass 40 percent in about thirty years. This chart and the one that follows are not the work of some radical anti-government group. They are the product of the Congressional Budget Office and the federal Office of Management and Budget. And they were created before the massive $850 billion Wall Street bailout of 2008 and the trillion-dollar economic stimulus package passed by President Obama in 2009.

Government Spending as a Percent of GDP

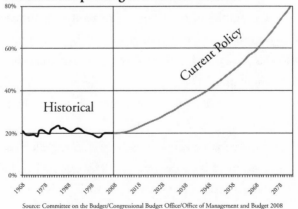

Source: Committee on the Budget/Congressional Budget Office/Office of Management and Budget 2008

Equally troubling is the growing national debt owed by the American people. Over recent decades America's debt has grown but has stayed below 50 percent of GDP because our economy has continued to grow. Based on current projections, however, our debt will soon explode and dramatically eclipse our total economy. Unless major reforms are enacted quickly, Americans will face devastating economic consequences (this chart was also created before the multitrillion-dollar bailouts).

Debt Held by the Public as Percent GDP

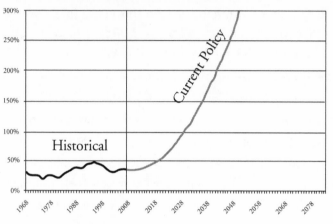

Source: Committee on the Budget/Congressional Budget Office/Office of Management and Budget 2008

Americans have been told so many times about an impending "crisis" they no longer take these alarms seriously: the energy crisis, the Social Security crisis, the housing crisis, the mortgage crisis, the Wall Street crisis, the auto industry crisis, the recession crisis, and of course, the global warming crisis are all examples of recent problems used for political manipulation. Global warming, which is now being used as an excuse to expand dramatically the power and control of government, may not even be a man-made phenomenon. The science on this issue is far from conclusive. Yet Congress is in a virtual panic to implement massive taxes on our economy to punish the users of coal and gas.

Unlike politically manufactured crises, the catastrophic financial course of the federal government is an absolute fact. Without major reforms there is no plausible survivable scenario for our economy. This is not a problem that might occur in the distant future. The nation's debt, out-of-control spending, and loose monetary policy are creating worldwide economic insecurity. It seems inexplicable that Congress is completely ignoring this problem.

Ignoring the Warnings

During the hurried debate and political panic of the Wall Street debacle in late 2008, I remember many of my Senate and House colleagues expressing disbelief that there had been no warning of the crisis. The fact is there were ample warnings for more than ten years. Congressional leaders chose not to act because the government-sponsored entities (Fannie Mae and Freddie Mac) and Wall Street were doing their bidding, in addition to making consistently large financial contributions to their campaign accounts.

Easy and cheap credit were allowing more people to buy homes and cars, accomplishing the dual goals of artificially raising the standard of living for lower-income Americans and keeping our economy running on steroids. The problem with steroids is they eventually destroy the people who use them. Loose monetary policy created a financial house of cards destined to crash. But unqualified borrowers and unscrupulous lenders were not the only ones who suffered. Much of the savings of responsible, hardworking Americans evaporated almost overnight.

Once the panic ensued, many politicians were quick to blame others and claim "they had sent a letter" warning of the coming crisis. Baloney. Congress, well-known for its doublespeak and dishonesty, outdid itself during the "economic rescue" debate. The people who blocked reforms and received the most campaign contributions from the guilty parties were the ones in charge of negotiating the irresponsible bailouts. The result was several trillion dollars borrowed against America's future and an unprecedented intrusion by the federal government into the private economy.

I'm afraid neither Congress nor the majority of the American people learned their lesson. We are now ignoring a much more serious warning. America's massive and growing debt is today's greatest threat to America's prosperity. Early in 2008 the comptroller general of the United States,

David M. Walker, began to travel the country trying to warn Americans about our unsustainable level of spending and debt. Almost no one paid attention. His warnings did not appear on the nightly news of the major television networks.

Mr. Walker's presentation, titled "Saving Our Future Requires Tough Choices Today,"[5] revealed that mandatory spending (required by law) for Social Security, Medicare, and Medicaid (entitlements) had grown from 16 percent of federal spending in 1966 to 40 percent of the entire federal budget in 2006. The large wave of baby boomers now reaching retirement age promises to make this problem much worse.

Most of this spending has been taken from funds that should have been used for the primary constitutional responsibility of the federal government—defense. Military spending dropped from 43 percent in 1966 to 20 percent in 2006. While "smart bombs" and other new high-tech weapons systems have lulled Americans into a false sense of security, our military is fighting with one hand tied behind its back. In the age of terrorism, our intelligence capabilities are woefully lacking. Our Air Force is flying many antiquated planes (often more than forty years old), and the scheduled replacement rates guarantee a worsening situation. So much of our military spending is directed by political earmarks from congressmen and senators with parochial interests that we make it harder for our military leaders to develop coherent plans to defend our nation.

My point is this: there is a terrible cost to unrestrained government spending and debt. Part of that cost is the neglect of real national priorities such as defense. The other costs are the devaluation of our currency, the destruction of our private-sector economy, and the loss of wealth and quality of life for all Americans.

Despite any claims by politicians, the warnings about unrestrained spending and debt have been loud and clear and summarily ignored. Mr. Walker's presentation goes on to point out that mandatory spending (including interest on the debt) in 1966 was 33 percent of the federal budget, which left 67 percent for all other spending including defense. In 2006 mandatory spending was 53 percent of federal spending. This means the money left over for defense, roads, and other priorities is quickly shrinking—even at America's current high tax rates.

Mr. Walker calculates America's national debt in 2007 to be $10.8 trillion (this increased to about $12 trillion after the 2008 borrowing for the "economic rescue"). When future obligations for current mandatory spending are added, our total national debt is $52.7 trillion. The current total net worth of all American households is only $58.6 trillion. This means when assets and liabilities are combined, Americans owe almost as much as they are worth. The average American family now owes $455,000. With an average household income of $48,201 a year, there is no plausible scenario where America can manage its current debt level.[6] Yet Congress continues to spend like there is no tomorrow.

The implications of our national debt are further complicated by the fact that a large and growing portion of our debt is held by foreign countries. Approximately $3 trillion of America's national debt is held by other countries, with China and Japan holding more than 40 percent of this debt. The biblical admonition from Proverbs certainly applies: "The borrower is a slave to the lender" (Prov. 22:7). America's foreign policy and trade enforcement decisions are heavily influenced by our dependence on other countries to lend us more and more money. Because of our large and growing debt, America can no longer control its own destiny.

Why Presidents and Congress Continue to Borrow and Spend

In July 2008 I put the two previous charts on posters and took them to the Senate floor to sound the alarm. With exasperation (and I'm afraid anger) I chided my colleagues for continuing to create and expand new government programs in the face of catastrophic spending levels and debt. In the previous week we passed an expansion of the Medicare prescription drug plan (Medicare already has trillions of dollars of unfunded liabilities), and a $300 billion bailout for the mortgage industry (with the federal government taking possession of the nation's riskiest nonperforming loans). We were then getting ready to pass a $50 billion foreign aid bill that was a massive expansion of President Bush's $15 billion program (which I supported) to help AIDS victims in Africa.

While we were debating the $50 billion foreign aid bill, Treasury Secretary Paulson announced he would be asking Congress to give him a "blank check" to save Fannie Mae and Freddie Mac, the government-sponsored enterprises that had grown out of control carrying trillions of dollars in debt. Given the projected expansion of our national debt and all the emergency-spending projects we were considering, I thought it reasonable to propose an amendment to reduce the foreign aid bill to $35 billion, still more than twice the amount of the original program. My amendment received only thirty-one votes, and the $50 billion foreign aid passed overwhelmingly. A month later we passed the nearly $1 trillion Wall Street bailout.

As a businessman I had to go back to my office and scratch my head. By any business standard, the federal government is already bankrupt. Cash flow is negative and expenses are projected to outpace revenues for the foreseeable future. Debt is nearly half of total sales (tax revenues) and will surpass total sales within twenty years. In spite of all this, I am convinced the foreign aid bill would have still passed had we doubled it to $100 billion.

A "normal" person might scream, "What are you guys thinking?" It's taken me a while to figure it out, but I now realize why presidents and Congress continue to spend in the face of financial disaster. First, presidents, congressmen, and senators are rewarded for increasing spending and punished for opposing new spending bills. I'll share a few examples of how this happens.

Veterans are often used as political pawns in Congress's political spending game. If Republicans offer a bill to increase funding for veterans programs by 10 percent, Democrats will offer an amendment to increase it by 15 percent (even though everyone knows this exceeds the budget and violates common sense). If Republicans vote against the 15 percent increase, veterans groups will immediately send out e-mails and newsletters telling all their members Republicans voted against veterans. Republicans could then expect thirty-second television commercials to run against them in their next election that say something like, "DeMint voted to cut funding for our nation's brave fighting men and women."

I've actually been in the Republican cloakroom (cloakrooms are like baseball dugouts, connected to the Senate floor for both teams, only with chandeliers and couches) when our leaders said we should vote for the higher amount for veterans because the Democrats already agreed to reduce it later secretly in conference with the House. In other words, we could do a "show" vote for veterans and then reduce the amount in secret.

Any attempt to mess with veterans' spending is punishable by phone calls, letters, e-mails, and thirty-second commercials. In 2007 a veterans' bill was being debated in the Senate. One issue was the Veterans Administration's plan to downsize an underutilized veterans' hospital in Los Angeles near Hollywood. By selling off several acres of unused prime real estate, the VA estimated they could add $5 billion to the veterans' budget. But Hollywood friends of the two California senators wanted to keep the area as a park, so the bill included an earmark to prohibit the VA from selling the property. I thought this was preposterous in light of the need to get more money to veterans' health care.

My amendment to remove the $4 billion park earmark and use the funds for veterans' medical care failed miserably, so I voted against the veterans' bill. I was the only senator to vote against it, and I've been doing damage control with veterans in South Carolina ever since. Even though serving veterans has been a top priority of my office since I came to Congress, some liberal interest groups have tried to convince them I'm trying to cut their programs and their funding. Those senators who voted for the veterans bill will receive accolades from veterans for years to come and no criticism for contributing to the national debt.

The same phenomenon occurs with almost every piece of legislation. In 2008 a giant $600 billion farm bill came through the Senate. The bill provided large subsidies to many millionaire farmers—including some members of Congress—who were already enjoying historic profits because of high food prices. While the bill had some good and necessary provisions, I thought it was irresponsible to increase farm spending dramatically during a time of war, economic downturn, and massive federal debts. I voted against the farm bill and became public enemy number one with some farmers in South Carolina.

Soon after the farm bill, an aviation bill was moving through the Senate. Some Senators tried to attach $8 billion for the Highway Trust Fund, that had nothing to do with aviation, without even a vote. I objected to rushing the provision through Congress, and within one hour I was getting phone calls from paving contractors in South Carolina complaining about my insensitivity to the need for better roads. The next week the Senate was trying to rush through a housing bill that included a $300 billion bailout for mortgage companies. I objected to passing it without debate or amendments. The next day I was on a conference call with home builders trying to explain I wasn't trying to destroy the housing business in South Carolina.

Immediately following the housing bailout bill, the Senate moved to the $50 billion foreign aid bill I mentioned above. There was a lot of pressure to allow it to pass without a vote, but I objected and forced a floor debate. I was called insensitive, and celebrities from Bono to Bishop Tutu were on my case about delaying this wonderful humanitarian effort. Helping the sick around the world is a wonderful cause, but it is irresponsible to borrow more money and diminish the future for our children and grandchildren to gain the praise of the world.

The net result of my efforts to restrain the growth of spending is that I will be accused of voting against veterans, farmers, good roads, affordable housing, and sick children in Africa. I will have to raise millions of dollars to defend myself against these baseless charges in my next campaign. That will be more difficult because the organizations that are a major source of campaign funds are the organizations representing groups wanting something from the federal government. Thousands of organizations have PACS (political action committees) that can each contribute up to $10,000 to candidates for every election.

Freedom versus Big Government

Through communications to their members and fund-raising for candidates, special interest groups are the most important allies or enemies for members of Congress. These groups have little interest in the size of the national debt or long-term problems resulting from reckless government spending. Their view is short-term, much like most members of Congress who don't look past the next election. Members of Congress who vote for more government spending will be rewarded by most of these groups, while members who vote against special interest spending will find strong and active opponents in the next election.

Another reason government spending continues to increase is the earmark system. This is the practice that allows members of Congress to request spending for specific projects in their states or districts. I will expose earmarks in great detail in the next chapter, but for this discussion earmarks can be viewed as a way to encourage congressmen and senators to vote for large increases in spending. If a congressman receives $1 million for a local road project, he will think twice before voting against the giant spending bill that includes his project, even if the bill is grossly over budget. If committee chairmen can give a majority of members a few earmarks, they are almost guaranteed the votes they need to pass their bill regardless of the level of spending.

A more subtle but equally potent reason for irresponsible spending by the president and Congress is that increasingly politicians see the federal government as America's charity and themselves as generous instruments of compassion. Most members of Congress view their job as doing good deeds with other people's money. The boundaries of the Constitution are irrelevant.

Myron Magnet exposed the disastrous results of government-centered compassion in his 1993 book, *The Dream and the Nightmare, the Sixties' Legacy to the Underclass*. He exposed the guilt-motivated actions of the "haves" as they attempted to use government to remedy the problems of the "have-nots."

Instead of ending poverty for the Have-Nots—despite the
civil rights movement, despite the War on Poverty—the new

99

cultural order fostered, in the underclass and the homeless, a
new, intractable poverty that shocked and dismayed, that seemed
to belong more to the era of ragged chimney sweeps than to
modern America, that went beyond the economic realm into
the realm of pathology. Poverty turned pathological . . . because
the new culture that the Haves invented—their remade system
of beliefs, norms and institutions—permitted, even celebrated,
behavior that, when poor people practiced it, will imprison
them inextricably in poverty. . . . Worse, during the sixties and
seventies, the new culture of the Haves, in its quest for personal
liberation, withdrew respect from the behavior and attitudes
that have traditionally boosted people up the economic ladder—
deferral of gratification, sobriety, thrift, dogged industry, and so
on through the whole catalogue of antique-sounding bourgeois
virtues.[7]

Today this same elitist perspective by elected federal officials have
them attempting to help and centrally manage almost every area of
America's (and increasingly the world's) economy and culture—with
equally devastating results. Whether education, health care, financial
markets, farming, law, taxes, or retirement programs, it is difficult to find
any federal program that has not led to waste and corruption while destroying the quality and efficiencies of private, competitive markets.

Presidents, congressmen, and senators are counting on the inability
of Americans to connect the dots between reckless spending and future
economic problems for our nation. Historians will not blame a future
economic meltdown on the congressmen and senators who voted for the
$50 billion foreign aid bill. An addiction to spending by hundreds of
congressmen and senators over many years protects them all from individual accountability.

We saw this lack of individual accountability clearly during the
"high gas prices" crisis in 2008. The Democrats were mostly responsible for restricting the development of American energy for decades.

President Carter shut down nuclear generation, President Clinton vetoed the opening of the oil reserves in Alaska (ANWAR), and Democrats voted almost unanimously for years—at the behest of left-wing environmental groups—to restrict the development of America's oil and natural gas reserves. Yet when Americans cried out in anger over high gas prices, the Democrats successfully blamed "big oil," greedy speculators, and President Bush. Politicians have learned they never have to take the blame, so they continue to respond to the demands of special interests to grow government and spend more money.

The Politics of Socialism

Despite the increasingly obvious dangers of spending and debt, politicians have manipulated many interest groups into joining their destructive slide toward socialism. Veterans and senior citizen groups are now among the most powerful lobbying groups in Washington. They constantly demand more spending and more government programs, and their demands are often justified. Our government promised our veterans health care for life, and every year the veterans' health-care system and overall veterans' benefits become increasingly expensive.

Our government also promised all seniors retirement income and health care, and now the cost of Social Security and Medicare is threatening to bankrupt our nation. Seniors groups like the AARP are at the forefront promoting socialist solutions to fulfilling our promises to seniors.

When President George W. Bush attempted to reform Social Security with personally owned accounts (a freedom concept), the AARP ran national television ads to frighten seniors that these accounts were "risky." Remarkably they convinced seniors and the majority of Americans that it was safer to spend Social Security taxes than to save them (the federal government now spends every dime of Social Security taxes). The AARP's motives are questionable; they sell millions of dollars worth of those "risky" investments to seniors.

When Republicans in 2008 attempted to continue giving seniors the choice of private health insurance policies in addition to traditional

Medicare, the AARP ran ads against the congressmen and senators who supported the private policies. The AARP sells supplemental insurance to seniors with traditional Medicare. Seniors with private insurance are much less likely to need supplemental insurance. The AARP appears to be acting in its own interest instead of the interest of seniors and our nation.

The goals of Social Security and Medicare are laudable, but politicians have not been able to resist pandering to voters by expanding benefits and beneficiaries. Social Security began as a 2 percent payroll tax on the first $3,000 of income (1 percent from employee and 1 percent from employer) with benefits to a relatively small number of poor American seniors. Today it is the world's largest government program, consuming more than 20 percent of the total U.S. budget and costing American workers 12.4 percent of every paycheck.

Almost all American seniors now receive Social Security benefits, and for over half of our senior citizens, it is their primary source of income. Now heavily laden with trillions of dollars in unfunded liabilities, the program is financially unsustainable and in desperate need of reform. But it has proved to be political suicide to suggest any changes to save Social Security because so many voters are dependent on the program for their retirement income. The politics of Social Security are essentially the politics of socialism; dependent voters reward those candidates who promise more spending and more government-sponsored security.

The Social Security Act of 1935 also created the welfare program called Aid to Families with Dependent Children, which was later expanded dramatically by President Lyndon Johnson's War on Poverty in the 1960s. Millions of Americans became directly dependent on the government for their income, food, and housing. Most of these government-dependent Americans now vote for candidates who promise even more from government.

The AFDC welfare program unwittingly encouraged unwed births, leading to an exponential increase in broken homes, poverty, crime, child abuse, and school dropouts. Numerous costly federal programs have since been created to address these problems caused by the unintended consequences of poverty and welfare programs. While welfare reform in 1995 significantly reduced the welfare rolls, government incentives for unwed births continue, and the long-term damage to American families and culture is significant.

President Johnson's Great Society program created Medicare and promised virtually free health care for America's senior citizens. Medicare takes another 2.5 percent of every American's paycheck. Like Social Security, Medicare now consumes more than 20 percent of the federal budget and is hopelessly underfunded. With virtually all Americans over sixty-five years old now dependent on the government for their health care and at least part of their income, seniors have become pawns of politicians who try to win elections by promising more benefits and by creating fear that their opponents will cut benefits to seniors.

Younger Americans will pay a high price for America's slide toward socialism. *USA Today* reported in May 2008 that every American family was liable for nearly $500,000 to pay for Social Security, Medicare, and other federal benefits. (Keep in mind, this was before Congress added trillions more in federal spending for bailouts and stimulus.)[8] The federal government has saved none of the taxes it took from Americans to fund these programs, so higher taxes from younger workers will be needed to fund retirement benefits for seniors.

Presidents Roosevelt and Johnson are considered by many to be compassionate American heroes, but those of us in Congress today must now figure out how to clean up their messes. The seeds of socialism are now sprouting all around us: growing dependency on government, unprecedented debt and unfunded liabilities, and increasing government control in all areas of our lives. If left unchecked, the continued expansion of government will eventually lead to socialistic political, economic, and cultural systems.

Principles and Institutions

Government is an essential *institution* for the development and protection of freedom. We must have a framework of law, order, and justice for freedom to grow and thrive. Government makes the rules and enforces them much like the officials at a football game. Players and coaches have the freedom to do whatever they want as long as they follow the rules. When they don't, the officials throw a flag and impose a penalty. But the officials don't call the plays or decide who gets to play. Officials don't manage the game, and the federal government shouldn't try to manage America.

> When all government, in little as in great things, shall be drawn to Washington as the Center of all power, it will render powerless the checks provided of one government on another and will become as venal and oppressive as the government from which we separated. —President Thomas Jefferson

America's government has grown well beyond the constitutional framework provided by our founders. Our federal government is no longer the referee for our economy and culture; it is now the biggest player on the field. Our federal government is trying to manage many aspects of America's economy and social services. It is not an exaggeration to say the results have been catastrophic. Not only has the government inhibited the growth of our economy and undermined our culture, it has put our country on an unsustainable financial course that must be reversed immediately.

Instead of continuing to try to manipulate the economy, further exacerbating uncertainty among banks and investors, the federal government needs to stabilize the dollar by reducing spending and debt. "Markets and economies don't need government help; they simply need their governments to make stable the currencies they issue."[9] If the value of the dollar collapses, America collapses. There is nothing backing up the value of the American dollar except faith that our governments, businesses, and people can pay their bills. That faith is under serious scrutiny today.

Freedom versus Big Government

Americans can solve any problem if we recognize the causes and unify around the solutions. There are solutions to our exploding spending and debt, and they will be discussed in detail in the Action Plan section of this book. One of the best plans, The Road Map for America's Future, developed and introduced by Congressman Paul Ryan, puts America back on a sustainable financial course by fixing Social Security, Medicare, Medicaid, and our tax code in one piece of legislation. This plan will also make America more competitive in global markets by eliminating taxes on exports. In his introduction to this legislation, Congressman Ryan gives America two choices:

> The status quo leads to a level of government spending,
> financed by taxes or debt, that will cripple the U.S. economy,
> depriving future working families of their potential prosperity,
> and future retirees of the very benefits government promises.
> The other path transforms health care, federal entitlements,
> and federal taxes; restrains the growth of government spending
> to sustainable levels; and fulfills America's promises from one
> generation to another.[10]

The principle that has been lost by today's politicians is *limited government*. When our legislators ignore the limits established by the Constitution, there is no limit to government at all. When we laugh at champions of a balanced budget (which all states have to adhere to), we throw off all restraints on spending. The government then becomes the instrument of compassion and the means for every good deed dreamed up by our politicians. The only solution is for the American people to stop asking more from their "genie"—the federal government—and force it back into its "cage"—the Constitution.

Once government has embarked upon planning for the sake of justice, it cannot refuse responsibility for anybody's fate or position.[1]
—Friedrich Hayek

CHAPTER SEVEN

Big Government's Impossible Dream
Making Everything Right for Everyone

There was once a middle-age rural gentleman who, after a lifetime of responsible hard work, became obsessed with books about chivalry. He began to fancy himself as a brave knight who traveled the world with horse and armor in search of adventure and to right all the wrongs he saw in the world.

He finally abandoned his common life, found some rusty armor, mounted his old hack horse, and set out to save the world, calling himself Don Quixote de La Mancha and his noble steed Rosinante. He also persuaded his neighbor, Sancho Panza, a plump laborer, to mount his donkey and join him. And he dubbed a peasant girl he hardly knew to be his princess and named her Dulcinea.

Don Quixote's quest quickly becomes a comedy of errors and disasters. He attacked traveling silk merchants for not agreeing that Dulcinea was the most beautiful maiden in the world. Dulcinea was not with him, so the merchants had no way of knowing what she looked like. Quixote was severely beaten after he attempted to defend her honor.

Quixote charged windmills, mistaking them for giants. His virtue was compromised when a maid at an inn mistakenly went to his bed in the night.

107

He attacked a puppet show after getting carried away by the spectacle of Moorish knights doing battle with Christians. And Sancho was thrown out of an inn after Quixote refused to pay his bill. In the end Sancho paid the highest price for Quixote's misadventures; he was beaten, robbed, and humiliated as a result of his knight's attempts to do good.

After beginning his quest with noble motives, Quixote eventually became a thief rather than a savior. He became involved with a bandit named Roque Guinart, believing they could help the poor by stealing from the rich. He finally returned home in failing health and utter defeat, leaving multiple disasters in his wake. As he lay on his deathbed, Quixote denounced chivalry and knighthood. He died disillusioned and defeated.

Why do smart people do stupid things? That's a good question for Don Quixote and for Congress. How could so many otherwise intelligent people in Congress continue to spend, waste, and borrow at ever increasing rates—literally mortgaging the future of America—and still believe they are nobly serving their country? The question is important because as government grows, along with debt and dependency, socialism replaces freedom. The story of Don Quixote actually helps explain why well-intended congressmen and senators would blindly destroy the freedoms that created the American success story.

I was once a normal husband, father, businessman, and community volunteer. As I got older, I wanted to do more to leave the world a better place for my children and grandchildren (really). I began to read books and articles about American history and our quest for freedom. Finally, at age forty-seven I decided to mount my trusty steed (an old Ford Taurus), enlist the help of Sancho (family and friends), and ride off to attack windmills (the federal government).

When I arrived in Congress in 1999, I found 435 Don Quixotes in the U.S. House and another 100 in the Senate. We were all there to do good, correct wrongs, and make America and the world a better place. The problem was we all had very different ideas about what we were supposed to do and how we were going to do it.

My "impossible dream" was to reduce the size and cost of the federal government, return power to states and communities, and promote individual freedom. Most of my fellow Quixotes, however, seemed to be there to use the federal government as their swords and lances. They intended to use the federal government to do good and to correct all the wrongs in America.

Ignoring Constitutional Limits Created a Dysfunctional Government

Once congressmen and senators take their focus away from constitutional limits, the federal government becomes the means and ends to all our good intentions. This is when we begin to look stupid. Instead of building consensus and taking actions that promote the "general welfare," Congressional debates deteriorate into disagreements over a myriad of targeted actions—picking winners and losers—based on the particular interests of 535 Don Quixote knights and the king in the White House.

The problem has been compounded by the fact Congress and many presidents have not only ignored the Constitution; they have rejected any institutional accountability that could restrain the exponential growth in spending and debt. One commonsense way to slow the growth of government would be a law requiring an annual balanced budget, but Congress has consistently rejected all attempts to pass a balanced budget requirement.

States are required to balance their budgets. This forces governors and state legislatures to make tough choices every year about spending and taxes. Every American family has to make the same commonsense decisions to balance their personal priorities with their income and expenses. But the federal government just keeps spending and borrowing and charging it to Sancho (the American people). There are good reasons the approval ratings for Congress have reached an all-time low.

The federal government is increasingly dysfunctional because congressmen and senators are focusing on their own priorities and the special interests of major political groups rather than the good of the nation. With so many competing interests, there is no agreement on what should be done. The only way to pass legislation is to ball up hundreds or even thousands of special interests favors into almost every bill. As long as a majority of congressmen have something they want in the bill, it passes.

Democracies become corrupt, incompetent, and dysfunctional when their focus turns from working for the good of the whole to serving the many interests of a wide range of subgroups. The reason for this dysfunction should be obvious; it is impossible for politicians and bureaucrats in Washington to manage a complex array of public and private functions at the national and international levels, while also trying to manage public and private functions within our fifty states and thousands of local communities.

That's why America was designed with a republican form of government, not a national government. We are a republic composed of fifty semi-independent states with separate legislatures and budgets. Each state has its own system of local governments to further disperse political power. The collective power of state and local governments was intended to counterbalance the power of the federal government. In addition, private enterprise with limited government interference was intended to disperse economic power to millions of independent decision-makers.

Alexis de Tocqueville noted in 1835 how the constitutional limits of the federal government, along with the checks and balances held in place by state and local governments, protected the people from what he called "the tyranny of the majority":

> But in the United States, the majority, which so frequently
> displays the tastes and the propensities of a despot, is still
> destitute of the more perfect instruments of tyranny. In the
> American republics, the activity of central government has
> never as yet been extended beyond a limited number of objects,
> sufficiently prominent to call forth its attention. The secondary
> affairs of society have never been regulated by its authority; and

nothing hitherto has betrayed its desire of interfering in
them. . . . The townships, municipal bodies, and counties may
therefore be looked upon as concealed breakwaters, which check
or part the tide of popular excitement. If an oppressive law were
passed, the liberties of the people would still be protected by the
means by which that law would be put into execution.[2]

Another constitutional protection from "the tyranny of the majority" is our representative form of democracy designed by our founders.
Americans don't vote on every decision; they elect representatives to
make laws and oversee enforcement. The Constitution created inter-
mediaries between the people and their government to protect individuals
and minorities from the threat of "mob rule" and to avoid a permanent
ruling class of career politicians.

The obvious intent of our founders was for common people to serve
short terms in Congress as representatives *from* their communities and
states. They were not to represent particular interests *for* their constituents. They were to swear an oath to defend and protect the Constitution
of the United States of America. Unfortunately the distinction between
"representatives from" and "representatives for" has been lost. Today, most
members of Congress proudly serve the special interests of their constituents and political allies.

The Tyranny of Special Interests

America's constitutionally limited, republican form of government
is now alien to most members of Congress, federal judges, and federal
agencies. These politicians, judges, and bureaucrats see themselves as rulers of all political, legal, economic, humanitarian, and cultural activities
in America. They may delegate some responsibilities to other public and
private entities; but make no mistake, the final say for all matters rests at
the federal level.

As power has concentrated in Washington, every special interest in
America has focused its attention on gleaning favor and money from the

federal government. My office in Washington stays full with a parade of groups and lobbyists who want something from the federal government. Because the government now makes so many important decisions for so many interests and has control over so much money, lobbyists have grown like weeds in Washington. As Newt Gingrich has said:

> Lobbyists are a consequence of big government, not a cause of it. The more money centered in government the more value there will be in hiring a lobbyist. The more lobbyists are hired, the more politics will be dominated by the political contributions of the lobbyists and their employers. The more power the lobbyist and their employers amass over the politicians, the more politics will define the economy. It will become more profitable to influence a politician than to invent a product. If the market rejects you, or your ideas fail to compete, with your lobbyist's help you may be able to get government to protect you from your own failure.[3]

The proliferation of special interests in Washington has created a threat to freedom quite different from the "tyranny of the majority." Majority interests in America are now secondary to the politics of special interests. The election of 2008 demonstrated how a political party could bundle the interests of numerous groups and create a new ruling majority—a new tyranny of special interests.

This new political dynamic is the antithesis of the intent of our Constitution and a serious blow to the cause of freedom. The rights of individuals, protected by equal justice and the rule of law, are now subjugated to the special rights of groups that are guaranteed by a strong, centralized government. The "common good" is now viewed as a conglomeration of disparate interests of multiple groups demanding special treatment.

There are a lot of good reasons for Americans to fight back against this centralization of special interest power in Washington, but the most important reason is it creates a dysfunctional government. It may be a cliché, but it's true; Washington is broken. Almost everything our federal government attempts to do becomes a disaster. We mandate that cars burn corn ethanol and cause a world food crisis. We combine social engineering with monetary policy and create a worldwide financial crisis. This is truly a "Don Quixote" government; we have left one catastrophe after another in our wake as we have attempted to save the world, dry every tear, and solve every problem.

Americans don't trust their government because our government cannot be trusted to do what it says. It is an impossible dream to think America can continue to be the leader of the free world unless we reverse the growth of the federal government, reduce our debt, and start recultivating the seeds of freedom.

Earmarks: The Gateway Drug to Socialism

Solving serious problems requires our discovery of what caused them. The bottom line, root cause of much of America's current overspending, debt, and governmental dysfunction is the practice of earmarking. There is nothing in Washington that symbolizes special interests and the deterioration of constitutional government more than earmarking. My friend Senator Tom Coburn from Oklahoma has described earmarks as the "gateway drug for wasteful government spending." He's right. And that means earmarks are one of the primary reasons for the growth and dysfunction of government, and America's slide toward socialism.

I didn't know what an earmark was when I got to Congress. I think the name comes from bending back the corner of a page to mark something special in a book. Earmarks are how individual congressman and senators direct federal spending to their particular interests or causes. That means there are a lot of "bent corners" on the pages of just about every bill we pass in Congress.

As a new congressman from South Carolina, I stood in the shadows of legendary senators Strom Thurmond and Fritz Hollings, as well as the shadows of several senior congressmen who were known for "bringing home the bacon." When I came to Washington, I thought it was my responsibility to direct as much federal spending back to my congressional district as I possibly could.

So I began my political career believing earmarking was a harmless and important way to represent my district. After a few years in Congress, my mind began to change as I saw the damage the practice of earmarking was doing to our government and country. It became clear that asking for earmarks for my state stood in direct contradiction to my solemn oath to defend the Constitution.

My first experience with earmarks came a few months after I was sworn in as a congressman. I was a junior member of the Transportation Committee in the House. We were working on a giant transportation spending bill, and I was told I needed to get all my earmark requests in to the committee to let them know what projects I wanted for my district.

Before I submitted any requests, I received a call from a senior staff member on the committee. He told me, since I was a member of the committee, I would be given $30 million for my district. I just needed to let them know how I wanted to spend it so they could list the earmarks in the committee report. For a new congressman trying to make his mark, this was like receiving a large gift certificate to my favorite store.

Working with local officials back home, I came up with a list of worthy local road projects and allocated the money to each project as I deemed best. My staff then developed press releases to announce all my great work to the folks back home. I was a hero, at least to those people interested in the projects I deemed worthy of taxpayer money.

There were more than seventy members of the Transportation Committee, so after everyone got their allocation of money, the final bill was a foot thick. The more senior members of the committee got a lot more money and leaders of both parties who were not on the committee got a large allocation of earmarks to help "grease the skids" to get the bill to the House floor for a vote. No one paid much attention to the ridiculous earmarks in the bill (for example, hundreds of thousands of dollars for the Cowgirl Hall of Fame), to the bad policies, or to the fact the final bill was well over budget. It passed easily because most members of Congress had earmarks in the bill.

I was hooked, and like all bad habits it took me a while to break it. Now I'm a recovering earmarker on a crusade to stop this practice because I believe it is the main driver to wasteful government spending and our growing debt. My experience with the Transportation Committee was just the tip of the iceberg. Every year twelve appropriation subcommittees in the House and the Senate work to develop spending bills for different areas of the federal government. In the spring the twelve committees invite all 535 members of the House and Senate to submit their earmark requests. Christmas comes early every year in Congress.

Appropriation bills must be passed before Congress adjourns in late fall or the government shuts down. The threat of a government shutdown is enough to frighten most members into voting for any conglomeration of bloated spending bills with thousands of earmarks. Congressional leadership in both parties know how to use earmarks to manipulate their members into voting for almost anything.

Thirty years ago Congress added only a few hundred earmarks each year. Now earmarks exceed ten thousand a year and account for more than $20 billion in total spending.

Proponents of earmarks will say earmarks represent a small amount of money compared to the total federal budget, but I've learned that bloated, overbudget spending bills can be easily passed because earmarks are put in the Christmas stockings of members who are expected to vote for the final bills regardless of overspending or bad policies.

Instead of working on national priorities—fixing our antiquated tax code, saving Social Security and Medicare, reducing our debt, downsizing federal agencies, and devolving some federal functions to the states— earmarks encourage Congress to spend most of its time and effort on parochial interests at the state and local level. Earmarks shift the focus of

Congress from the "general welfare" of the country to thousands of special interest projects, many of which are detrimental to the good of our country as a whole.

Earmarking encourages wasteful, irresponsible spending. A 2007 report by the Department of Transportation Office of Inspector General requested by Senator Tom Coburn (R-Oklahoma) contains the following findings on the problems created by transportation earmarks:

- Department of Transportation (DOT) earmarks have increased in number by 1,150 percent in ten years (1996–2005), with the value of earmarks in the same time frame jumping 314 percent.[4]

- Ninety-nine percent of earmarks (7,724 out of 7,760) "were not subject to the agencies' review and selection processes or bypassed the states' normal planning and programming processes."[5]

- Earmarks may not be the most effective or efficient use of funds. The IG report identifies five ways in which earmarks impact programs in the Federal Highway Administration, the Federal Transit Administration, and the Federal Aviation Administration, as follows:

   o "Earmarks can reduce funding for the states' core transportation programs."[6]

   o "Earmarks do not always coincide with DOT strategic research goals."[7]

   o "Many low priority, earmarked projects are being funded over higher priority, nonearmarked projects."[8]

   o "Earmarks provide funds for projects that would otherwise be ineligible."[9]

   o "Earmarks can disrupt the agency's ability to fund programs as designated when authorized funding amounts are exceeded by 'overearmarking.'"[10]

Big Government's Impossible Dream

The federal farm program is another example of how parochial interests and earmarks can trump true national priorities. The farm program is a big government giveaway disguised as assistance to small farmers. It lavishes welfare-style subsidies on large corporate farmers, "hobby" farmers, and many agriculture-related businesses overflowing in profits. The most recent farm bill passed in May 2008 spent more than $600 billion. It was opposed by nearly every major editorial board and others from all political spectrums: the *New York Times*,[11] *The Washington Post*,[12] *USA Today*,[13] *Los Angeles Times*,[14] *National Review*,[15] and more.

The bill contained outdated subsidy formulas giving welfare to millionaire farmers and continues to direct billions to food industries experiencing record profits. You are probably asking why, if just about all observers on the left and right condemned the bill, did it pass the House (318–106) and Senate (81–15). The answer is simple: special interest political power and earmarks.

- The Citizens against Government Waste found more than $2 billion in earmarks in the bill.[16]
- *USA Today* found that more than $9 million in farm subsidies have gone directly to eight senators and four House members or their relatives.[17]
- *The Washington Post* found at least $15 billion in wasteful farm subsidies.[18]
- The Cato Institute uncovered an earmark to Plum Creek Timber for $500 million and noted that the company spent $2 million in lobbying and campaign contributions to secure the taxpayer handout.[19]

Another problem with earmarks is they restrict the ability of our federal agencies to operate efficiently. For example, as congressmen and senators bemoan the nation's deteriorating roads and bridges, former Transportation Secretary Mary Peters explained that congressional earmarking was the major cause of our infrastructure problems:

Wasteful spending over the last few decades has further
degraded our ability to direct our limited transportation
resources to the most productive investments. The clearest
evidence of our failure to prioritize investments has been
the disturbing growth of Congressional earmarks in surface
transportation reauthorization bills, from a handful in the 1982
bill to more than 6,000 in the 2005 bill, SAFETEA-LU. The
amount of the SAFETEA-LU earmarks was more than $23
billion.[20]

Leaders of all our federal agencies will offer a similar analysis.
Testifying before Congress, Admiral Conrad Lautenbacher, the head of
NOAA (the agency that manages national weather forecasts and hurricane
warning systems) reported:

It's a very hard budget to execute because of the twenty-six
hundred line items, and when there are a number of issues of
which we are trying to work on this year that are locked in to
these line items, it makes it very hard to keep the current services
going at the levels I know you all expect.

> The maintenance of a free society is a very difficult and
> complicated thing. And it requires a self-denying ordinance
> of the most extreme kind. It requires a willingness to put up
> with temporary evils on the basis of the subtle and
> sophisticated understanding that if you step in to try
> to do something about them, you not only may make
> them worse, but you will spread your tentacles and
> get bad results elsewhere.[21] —Milton Friedman

In 2008, I tried to pass a one-year moratorium on earmarks, but it
failed after the leadership of both parties maneuvered appropriators to

pressure members to oppose the bill. But we're making progress. Americans are beginning to catch on and more are beginning to oppose earmarks. Several high-profile congressmen and senators who ran their campaigns on "bringing home the bacon" have lost their bids for reelection. I believe we're close to stopping this destructive practice.

One Giant Step toward Socialism: The Wall Street Bailout

The more our federal government tries to solve every problem, the more problems it causes. The more problems it causes, the more it spends and the bigger it grows as it tries to fix the problems it has caused. As Ronald Reagan said, "The more the plans fail, the more the planners plan."[22] And inevitably the bigger our federal government grows, the more freedom evaporates as America slides precariously closer to socialism.

Just before the pivotal election in 2008, President Bush and Secretary Henry Paulson convinced Congress to pass a Wall Street bailout bill giving the Treasury Department nearly a trillion dollars (all borrowed) to buy up bad loans clogging up the credit markets. The explanation for this massive intrusion into the private markets was too complicated for almost anyone to understand, but Americans instinctively knew something was desperately wrong with this plan. They blamed Bush, McCain, and the Republicans in Congress.

The result was a bloodbath for Republicans in the 2008 election and the installation of a powerful majority of Democrats who believed they were elected with a mandate to expand government regulation and control of the financial markets. Democrats believed the financial and economic crisis was caused by deregulation and a failure of capitalism. They are now working within our own government and with other governments around the world to further centralize government power over the financial markets in the U.S. and internationally.

> With their economies in recession and a credit crunch
> steepening the slide, policy makers around the world race

119

to contain the damage. Calls for expansion of government spending, taxes and regulation, even for radical revision of our economic system, an end to capitalism, are rampant.[23]

During the crisis largely manufactured by Wall Street and the White House, few Republicans or industry leaders proffered a defense of capitalism and America's free enterprise economic system. Many Republicans parroted the accounts of "corporate greed" and joined the Democrats in calling for more regulations. Congressional Republican leaders were mostly mute. But many Americans seemed to intuitively know the truth; the crisis had been caused by our Don Quixote government.

As Congress plumbs the causes of our current mess, the main one is hiding in plain sight: Reckless monetary policy that did so much to create the credit mania and then compounded the felony with a commodity bubble and run on the dollar whose damage is now becoming apparent. The American people intuitively understand what's been done to them, which is why they are so angry. If the next president ignores the monetary roots of our troubles, he is courting the same fate as George W. Bush.[24]

The financial crisis that led to the massive intervention of the federal government into the private market was the result of bad policies and negligent oversight for several decades by Congress, the White House, and the Federal Reserve. In an attempt to help poor Americans, Congress passed a law in the late 1970s requiring banks to give a portion of their loans to low-income borrowers who did not otherwise qualify to receive a loan.

Congress also created two government-sponsored enterprises (Fannie Mae and Freddie Mac) to make it easier for low-income Americans to buy homes. These "companies" were given special interest rates, preferred tax treatment, and an implied government guarantee, allowing them to become a monopoly in the mortgage industry. That's how they got "too big to fail."

Fannie Mae and Freddie Mac bought home mortgages from local banks regardless of the qualifications of the borrower. This encouraged banks and local mortgage companies to make "no down payment" loans at low-interest rates to people who could not afford to make the payments. Easy mortgage money for just about every American encouraged an over-supply of homes with inflated prices.

During this same period the Federal Reserve (whose main mission is to protect the value of the dollar) provided easy, cheap credit to banks across America. This created an economy on steroids that grew at an artificially fast pace using debt rather than equity. As the federal government increased its addiction to spending and debt, so did the private sector.

Fannie Mae and Freddie Mac were the "big fish" drug dealers in this economic crack house of cards. They bought up trillions of dollars of mortgages, bundled them into mortgage backed securities (MBS), and then sold them to investors with the implied (wink, wink) guarantee of the federal government. These securities were marketed as being as safe as Treasury notes but with a better return.

Governments and national economies, like people, can only run on steroids for so long. When a few homeowners began to default on their mortgages, it was no longer just a problem between borrowers and their local banks. The nonperforming loans were not held by local banks. They were bundled with hundreds of other mortgages into MBSs and sold as packages all over the world. The investors who bought the bundled mortgages could not simply pluck the bad loans from their packaged securities. This was like having one bad apple locked in a bushel of good apples. The value of the whole bundle became questionable, so the market value of these mortgage-backed securities dropped precipitously.

Multiply this phenomenon thousands of times, and you have a credit crisis. Banks, domestic investors, and foreign creditors demanded action. Since our government gave a "money-back guarantee" on these mortgages, everyone wanted their money back. That's why Secretary Paulson was not interested in fixing the causes of the problem.

I believed Congress needed to respond immediately to the crisis, but I didn't want any more Don Quixote-style government solutions. We needed to start by admitting the government caused this problem. It was ridiculous to blame the crisis on the failure of private markets or deregulation. No amount of regulation could have prevented the inevitable collapse of the house of cards created by inept government action.

We needed to change bad laws and regulations, break up Fannie Mae and Freddie Mac and make them private companies, and force the Federal Reserve to focus on its mission of protecting the dollar rather than manipulating our economy. We also needed to promote private sector solutions by lowering the corporate tax rate, eliminating the capital gains tax, opening America's energy resources to stop the export of $700 billion worth of American liquidity each year, and giving Americans more confidence that their bank deposits are safe. The administration would have none of this. They created a false choice between their demand for a blank check or "doing nothing," even though many counter-proposals were on the table.

I was adamantly opposed to the bailout and led the opposition to the bill in the Senate. Before the vote, I went to the Senate floor to challenge my colleagues to think about the gravity of what they were getting ready to do:

> This is a sad and tragic time in America. We are the nation
> that has been called the bastion of freedom and we are the nation
> that has sacrificed blood and treasure to share that freedom with
> the world. We have fought against communism and socialism.
> We have helped to establish democracies and free enterprise
> economies around the world. Millions of people now participate
> in electing their leaders and millions have been taken out of
> poverty as capitalism created prosperity wherever it was planted.

Big Government's Impossible Dream

Yet, as the blood of our young men and women falls on foreign soil in the defense of freedom, our own government appears to be leading our country into the pit of socialism. We have seen this government socialize our education system and make our schools among the worst in the world. We have seen this government take over the majority of our health-care system, making private insurance less and less affordable every year. We have seen this government socialize our energy resources and bring our nation to its knees by cutting off the development of our own oil and gas supplies. And now we see this Congress yielding its Constitutional obligation to a federal bureaucracy, giving it the power to control the financial system in America.

My efforts to stop the bailout failed, in part because Republican and Democrat leaders packed the bill with earmarks and targeted provisions for special interests. House and Senate leaders promised to pass a clean bill without unrelated measures and both Obama and McCain urged swift action without add-ons. But after the House failed to pass the bailout on its first attempt, Senate leaders decided to go back to business as usual. They added the unrelated Wellstone Mental Health Parity bill to attract Democrats and an unrelated tax extenders package to attract Republicans, as well as some new tax breaks as "sweeteners" to help the medicine go down. These sweeteners included special tax breaks for makers of children's wooden arrows, wool clothing, and Puerto Rican rum, to name just a few.[25]

A few in the media told Americans the truth:

As the national economy teetered on the edge of the abyss, with risky, unprecedented legislation hanging in the balance, Congress opened the spigot on all the fat and gravy it could pump. We can only hope the Chinese are willing to cover the bill.[26] —*The Seattle Times*

And then, even worse, the Senate, in effect, bribed reluctant House members into switching their votes by unconscionably loading the measure with more than $100 billion in tax breaks sought by lobbyists of every stripe and hue. Favors were done for interests ranging from solar energy producers to rural counties hurt by federal logging cutbacks to Hollywood producers to stock-car racetrack owners to manufacturers of toy wooden arrows for children. We kid you not. With nothing less than the American standard of living at stake, lawmakers took care of their pals. That's how nakedly corrupt Congress now is.[27]

—*The N.Y. Daily News*

> In an amazing display of historic ignorance, economic destructiveness, and ideologically driven dishonesty, Washington politicians are in the process of combining the worst of the 1970s bad economic policies with the worst of Detroit's economic and (America's) educational decay. We are in grave danger of turning all of America into the kind of declining economy and bureaucratic mess which Detroit became over the last forty years.[28] —Newt Gingrich

The High Cost of Socialism

Like Sancho in the Don Quixote story, Americans will bear the brunt of the good intentions of our knights in Congress. Despite political promises to reduce pain and to make things right for everyone, the top-down decision-making and bureaucratic management of government always deliver an inferior service at a higher price than competitive, free-market providers.

Once government begins to intervene into the free-enterprise system, the natural accountability of private sector risks and rewards is thrown out of balance. We have seen it in the financial crisis, in the auto and agriculture industries, in the deterioration and high cost of health-care services, and in America's government-run education system. The federal government's management of America's energy resources has also obscured the reliable economic balancing of supply and demand and left Americans heavily dependent on unreliable and high-cost energy suppliers.

Americans will not only pay for our slide toward socialism with inferior services; we will pay with high taxes and the devaluation of our dollar. Socialism creates a vicious cycle of political promises, government spending, and mounting debt. America's current debt, now at about $12 trillion, cannot be paid back under any plausible scenario. At our current rate of spending, we will not even be able to pay the interest on our debt without borrowing more money. In fact, we are already there. Our government has to borrow more money almost every day just to pay back the loans already coming due.

Absent major reforms and the downsizing of government, there are only two ways the government can deal with our current national debt: raise taxes dramatically and/or devalue our currency. The devaluation of our dollar will likely begin soon because other countries are already losing confidence in our ability to pay back our debt.

When the value of our dollar falls, everyone's quality of life declines because we can buy less with our current incomes. The value of our savings and investments also declines as the cost of everything we buy increases. If the government continues to spend and borrow more money—even to "bail" us out—we dig a deeper hole, and the value of the dollar will drop even more.

If politicians raise taxes to pay for more spending or to repay debt, everyone pays—even if the taxes are targeted at the "rich." Taxes take money out of the private economy and permanently increase the cost of government. Money left in the private economy is either spent or saved, both of which improve the overall economy.

When money stays in the private economy, there is an economic multiplier to every dollar spent. If you spend a dollar at the grocery store, the grocer uses it to pay an employee. That employee uses it to buy clothes at a local retailer who uses if to pay his employees . . . and on and on.

Consumer spending strengthens our economy and creates jobs. Likewise, when money is saved or invested, it also creates jobs because savings and investments are used to finance the growth of companies with stocks or as loans to businesses or consumers.

Conversely, when money goes to the government in the form of taxes, it increases the size of government and creates a permanent cost to taxpayers. Every dollar the government spends this year becomes part of the baseline budget for next year. All new spending is added onto last year's spending. So when the government takes a dollar in taxes, it eliminates the economic multiplier in the private sector and creates a permanent cost compounded over time by bigger government.

Higher taxes don't solve problems; they weaken the private sector economy and grow the size of government. The question is not whether it is fair for someone to make millions while others struggle at minimum wage. The question is how do we help the guy making minimum wage make millions—or a least a decent income?

Principles and Institutions

Considering America's debt and current economic situation, the principle of limited government is not only a preferred conservative political philosophy; it is an urgent necessity for the survival of our republic.

> Conservatism is more than a quaint belief-system to be embraced and debated over donuts at Starbucks. It is more than a list of talking points. It is the foundation of the civil society. The liberal uses crises, real or manufactured, to expand the power of government at the expense of the individual and private property. He has spent, in earnest, seventy years evading the Constitution's limits on governmental power. If conservatives don't stand up to this, who will? If they don't offer serious alternatives that address the current circumstances AND defend the founding principles, who will?[29]

Big Government's Impossible Dream

In addition to limited government, there are many principles at stake in the battle against socialism. We have discussed the constitutional principle that directs representatives of the people to work on behalf of the "general welfare"—the good of the nation as a whole—not special interests. There is also the republican constitutional principle that reminds Americans that power and control in America must be dispersed between federal, state, and local governments.

Another principle is that political power must be counterbalanced by private sector economic power. America's free enterprise capitalistic economic system with its millions of decision-makers is the foundational democratic institution in American. We cannot allow our government to become a major force in our private economy.

Freedom is protected by a wide range of public and private institutions guarding against the concentration of power. The concentration of power at the federal level destroys this balance, weakens other institutions of freedom, and destroys freedom itself. Americans must not continue to allow one institution of freedom, the federal government, to dominate and diminish the role of other institutions or to demean the individual values that made our country great and free.

America needs champions of freedom at the state and local levels who will challenge the growing concentration of power in Washington. Governors and state legislatures could take much more control of education, health care, transportation, energy, and other services that would give their citizens more independence from the federal government. This could help begin the process of downsizing the federal government. Business leaders could unite around common goals to reduce corporate taxes, duplicative regulations, and frivolous lawsuits at the state and federal levels. Every dollar and decision we keep from Washington today means more freedom for all Americans tomorrow.

The modern world arose only in Christian societies.
Not in Islam. Not in Asia. Not in a "secular"
society—there having been none.[1]
—Rodney Stark

CHAPTER EIGHT

The History of Faith and Freedom

Remembering the Source of America's Strength

There once was a child named Samson whose mother dedicated him to God at birth. As was the custom of men who were wholly dedicated to God, Samson made a vow never to cut his hair. God honored Samson with great physical strength and told him the outward sign of his strength would be his long hair.

Samson's strength became legendary. He defended his country from all its enemies. He once killed more than one thousand invading Philistines using only the jawbone of a donkey. All the people rested safe and secure because they trusted in Samson's great strength.

Samson fell deeply in love with a woman named Delilah, but he didn't know the Philistines paid her to find the source of his strength. Delilah pleaded persistently with Samson to tell her the secret of his strength, but he resisted. Finally Delilah wore Samson down and convinced him to tell her. He confessed that his great strength came from his long hair.

When Samson fell asleep, Delilah cut off Samson's hair and called in the Philistines. With his strength gone, the Philistines bound Samson with chains and blinded him. They threw a big party to celebrate their victory and to mock

Samson. They tied Samson's arms to two large columns holding up the roof of the great hall where all the Philistines gathered to drink and laugh.

Humiliated, weak, and blinded, Samson pleaded for God's forgiveness and prayed for one last measure of strength to bring judgment onto his enemies. Samson felt God's power return to his arms, with one last surge of strength, he jerked the large columns together and brought down the roof, crushing himself and all the Philistines.[2]

Samson believed his great strength came from his hair. The people he protected believed their strength came from Samson. They all forgot it was God who gave Samson his strength and protected all the people from their enemies. Samson's long hair was an outward symbol of his dedication to God. He lost his strength, his freedom, and his life when that physical symbol of God's power was cut off.

When we forget the real inner source of our power, our outward physical strength begins to disappear. Before long we become confused and fearful as we scramble to find the reasons for our weakness and failures. America is scrambling and it is time to rediscover the source of our strength and success.

In America today secular socialists insist that religion be securely locked in a separate compartment and held at a safe distance from any public policy debate. They promote a perverted interpretation of "separation of church and state" upheld (or extremely confused) by our federal courts. They maintain that religion lacks the logic and reason necessary to guide the progress of the American republic.

> Most textbook accounts of the birth of our nation now carefully ignore the religious aspect, as if a bunch of skeptics had written these famous lines from the Declaration of Independence: "We hold these truths to be self-evident, that all men are created equal, that they are endowed by their Creator with certain unalienable Rights, that among these are Life, Liberty, and the pursuit of Happiness."[3]

An objective review of world and American history provides undeniable evidence that religion—far from being just a derivative of freedom—has been the primary catalyst and preserver of America's unique freedoms and success.

> Statesmen my dear sir, may plan and speculate for liberty, but it is religion and morality alone which can establish the principles upon which freedom can securely stand. . . . The only foundation of a free Constitution is pure virtue. —President John Adams

The Dawn of Freedom and Law

A millennium before democracy rose in Greece, one of its basic tenets was introduced to the world by a nation without a homeland. Rescued from slavery in Egypt and exiled in the desert, the Israelites became the first people to subject themselves to a rule of law. The Ten Commandments applied not only to the Jewish people, but equally to their leaders. From that moment forward, throughout the Old Testament, kings and peasants alike were held subject to The Law. This rudimentary "rule of law" planted the early seeds of individual liberty, as Mosaic Law laid out the contours of future notions of rights, freedom, and equality.

In the sixth century BC, Greek democracy began to flower, and further political steps were made toward the fruition of these principles we now take for granted. Eventually, all Athenian citizens were free to speak and vote in the Assembly, the first serious attempt at self-government. Those principles took another step forward during the rise of the Roman Republic, which codified a series of rights and privileges in the Twelve Tables, which were prominently placed in the Forum for all Romans to see.

Yet despite these advances, the public and private values of Greco-Roman societies ultimately proved as arbitrary as the stories of gods that entertained and frightened their people. There were no consensus values. Justice was more dependent on the mood of the rulers than the laws.

In the end the "rule of law" became the "rule of men." Freedom spurred prosperity, which in turn tempted leaders toward more centralized power. As the concentration of power corrupted the leaders, dependency and immorality corrupted the people.

The warnings against the centralization of power were almost as prevalent in Greece and Rome as they are in America today. As historian Will Durant summarized, "Without checks and balances a monarchy becomes despotism, aristocracy become oligarchy, democracy becomes mob rule, chaos, and dictatorship." The Roman leader Cicero warned that the man who will be chosen as leader of an ungoverned populace would be "bold and unscrupulous . . . who curries favor with the people by giving them other men's property."[4]

These warnings were apparently prescient. Both Rome and Greece eventually collapsed from within. In Durant's words, "Class war, not Caesar, killed the Roman Republic."[5] Rome's class war has been blamed on its transition from a republic to a democracy. The people began to demand more from their government, and the leaders began to "curry favor with the people by giving them other men's property."

Despite their eventual failure, Greece and Rome helped further the notion that, as Will Durant wrote, "Man became free when he recognized that he was subject to law."[6] This was a key principle in the founding of the American republic. In 1775, John Adams, referencing Livy, the Roman philosopher, and Aristotle, the Greek philosopher, defined a republic to be "a government of laws and not of men."

The Birth of Christ and the Dawn of Freedom

Jesus Christ was born into an Israel in decline and occupied by the Romans. The birth of Christ and the Christian faith built on the Jewish foundation of law created a new foundation for freedom itself.

> While the other world religions emphasized mystery and intuition, Christianity alone embraced reason and logic as the

primary guide to religious truth. . . . The church fathers taught that reason was the supreme gift from God and the means to progressively increase their understanding of scripture and revelation. Consequently, Christianity was oriented to the future, while the other major religions asserted the superiority of the past. . . . Encouraged by the scholastics and embodied in the great medieval universities founded by the church, faith in the power of reason infused Western culture, stimulating the pursuit of science and the evolution of democratic theory and practice. The rise of capitalism was also a victory for church-inspired reason, since capitalism is in essence the systematic and sustained application of reason to commerce—something that first took place within the great monastic estates.[7]

Early church scholars viewed the Christian religion as the systematic and persistent pursuit of truth, not a sentimental and unfounded belief in God. Their rational approach to theology led to the development of the scientific method.

Christianity fostered a very strong conception of individualism consistent with its doctrines concerning free will and salvation. In addition, medieval monasticism cultivated regard for the virtues of work and plain living . . . [and] new ideas about human rights. For capitalism to develop, it was essential that Europe ceased to be a collection of slave societies. . . . Christianity was unique in evolving moral opposition to slavery. . . . By the tenth century slavery had disappeared in most of the West.[8]

While some early Christian clerics expressed antagonism toward commerce and finance, these sentiments were "resoundingly rejected in the twelfth and thirteenth centuries by Catholic theologians who stoutly defended private property and the pursuits of profits."[9]

Leading Christian theologians such as Augustine and Aquinas celebrated reason as the means to gain greater insight into divine intentions. Another church leader, Quintus Tertullian, wrote in the second century: "Reason is a thing of God, inasmuch as there is nothing which God the Maker of all has not provided, disposed, ordained by reason."[10]

In that same spirit Clement of Alexandria warned in the third century: "Do not think that we say that these things are only to be received by faith, but also that they are to be asserted by reason. For indeed it is not safe to commit these things to bare faith without reason, since assuredly truth cannot be without reason."[8] Christianity's emphasis on using reason to confirm truth and strengthen personal faith became the catalyst for using reason to develop scientific methods, capitalist economic theories, innovation and entrepreneurship, standard currencies, and "rule of law" political systems.

> The so-called Scientific Revolution of the sixteenth century has been misinterpreted by those wishing to assert an inherent conflict between religion and science. Some wonderful things were achieved in this era, but they were not produced by an eruption of secular thinking. Rather, these achievements were the culmination of many centuries of systematic progress by medieval scholastics, sustained by that uniquely Christian twelfth-century invention, the university. Not only were science and religion compatible, they were inseparable—the rise of science was achieved by deeply religious Christian scholars.[11]

The economic and cultural contrasts between Christian Europe and non-Christian nations in Asia, Africa, and the Middle East have been noted by many researchers and social scientists. Distinguished Oxford historian Joseph Needham, after spending several decades attempting to discover a materialist explanation for the lack of progress in China, finally concluded:

> The failure of the Chinese to develop science was due to their religion, to the inability of Chinese intellectuals to believe

in the existence of laws of nature because "the conception of a divine celestial lawgiver imposing ordinances on non-human nature never developed. It was not that there was no order in nature for the Chinese, but rather that it was not an order ordained by a rational personal being, and hence there was no conviction that rational personal beings would be able to spell out in their lesser earthly languages the divine code of laws which he had decreed aforetime."[12]

This same principle of a "celestial lawgiver" creating predictable natural laws for the study of science has similar implications for the development of governmental laws. When people believe temporal human laws reflect eternal spiritual values, they are more likely to follow them voluntarily without the threat of government force. Adherence to laws becomes a service to God and mankind, not an involuntary imposition of force by an impersonal government. A large part of America's early success can be attributed to the fact our laws had moral authority because they were derived from biblical principles the people revered.

Like Asian cultures, Islamic nations have faced religious barriers to progress in the areas of science and law. "Allah is not presented as a lawful creator but is conceived as an extremely active God who intrudes on the world as he deems it appropriate. This prompted the formation of a major theological bloc within Islam that condemns all efforts to formulate natural laws as blasphemy in that they deny Allah's freedom to act."[13] Without a belief in fixed laws, there can be no systematic discovery of scientific truth or development of political and economic freedom.

Freedom and the Reformation of Christianity

In my last term in the House, I was in a small breakfast meeting with the legendary Dr. Henry Kissinger, the secretary of state and foreign diplomat for several administrations. We were talking about tensions in the Middle East and assessing the hope for reforms and peace. As we spoke about democracy and freedom, Dr. Kissinger said, almost in passing, "There would be no America as we know it without the Reformation."

This seemed a stunning statement coming from a Jewish academic with a comprehensive knowledge of history and personal experience with governments and religions all over the world. His comment stirred me to think more about the connection between the reformation of Christian thought and the founding of America.

No one should pretend the Christian Church has ever completely represented the perfection or holiness of Jesus Christ. All human institutions have their imperfections and the organized Christian Church—regardless of denomination—has been no exception.

Despite the contributions of the early church to the foundations of freedom—individualism, virtue and morality, science, capitalism, and fixed laws—many leaders of the organized Christian Church eventually succumbed to the corruption that inevitably results from the concentration of power. To be clear, I was raised a Catholic, went to Catholic school, and deeply appreciate the contribution that the Catholic Church today makes in the causes of life and freedom. However, the medieval church—highly centralized and allied with government power—was not immune to the temptations that occur when even the best of intentions are combined with absolute power.

It was against this backdrop that a simple monk named Martin Luther, the father of the Reformation, burst upon the scene. Other than Jesus Christ and His apostles, Luther may have done more to unleash the power of freedom than any other man in history. He was born in Germany in 1483 and, while studying Paul's epistles as a professor of theology at Wittenberg, discovered the truth of Romans 1:17, "For therein is the righteousness of God revealed: . . . The just shall live by faith" (KJV). Luther's newfound understanding of Scripture led him to teach that salvation was through faith in Christ alone and "not by works of righteousness which we have done" (Titus 3:5 KJV).

Luther's life was transformed, and soon so was the rest of the world. He was excommunicated from the Catholic Church for opposing church dogma. On trial for his life for heresy in front of Emperor Charles V, Luther refused to recant, and his reply continues to shake the world:

> Since then Your Majesty and your lordships desire a simple
> reply, I will answer without horns and without teeth. Unless
> I am convicted by Scripture and plain reason—I do not accept
> the authority of popes or councils, for they have contradicted
> each other—my conscience is captive to the Word of God.
> I cannot and I will not recant anything, for to go against
> conscience is neither right nor safe. Here I stand, I cannot do
> otherwise. God help me. Amen.[14]

Over many centuries the early Christian Church had become a top-down organization, with authority centralized at the top and often welded to the power of the state.

The simplicity of personal faith, which characterized first-century Christianity, had evolved over the centuries into a complex array of religious requirements that encouraged uniformity rather than individualism. The Bible was not translated into the common language, so a largely uneducated population had neither the capability nor the opportunity to read the Scriptures for themselves. Priests alone held the keys to heaven.

Martin Luther turned the Christian Church upside down. He said, "Each and all of us are priests," and taught that individuals could, through the saving grace of Jesus Christ, approach the throne of God on their own. This radically new focus on the individual laid the foundation for revolt, reform, and war in Europe, and planted the seeds of freedom that would soon sprout in America.

Luther took his message directly to the people, placing an unprecedented emphasis on education for the laity. He translated the Bible and printed his own works into the common German language. His prolific writings coincided with the development of Gutenberg's printing press, and by 1523—only two years after he stood before Charles V—a million copies of Luther's religious and political treatises were circulating throughout Germany.[15]

As religious wars and persecution persisted in Europe, the New World offered a refuge for many war-weary believers. "Thousands of Martin Luther's spiritual descendants preferred the wilderness hardships of the New World to the religious tyranny of the Old."[16] Christians flocked to the American colonies, bringing with them a strong faith in God, a deep sense of individual responsibility, and an unwavering demand for freedom to worship according to the dictates of their conscience.

A New Worldview and a New World

Secular historians often overlook the profound impact of the Protestant Reformation on the cause of freedom. The Reformation stressed that even individuals without power and position had intrinsic value in society and should read the Bible for themselves. They had worth and purpose as individuals because they believed they were created in God's image. They began to think, reason, and pursue truth and knowledge on their own. Their faith gave them hope, their hope gave them courage, and their courage led them to action. Millions of autonomous individual actions worked together to create an explosion of freedom.

Christianity's new focus on the individual emphasized more personal accountability to God—focusing on an inner faith that created a strong sense of individual responsibility and morality. George Will, who has spoken of Martin Luther as one of America's founding fathers, describes how Luther's work encouraged the self-control that makes self-government and individual freedom possible.

> Luther's words announced the ascendance of private
> judgment—of conscience—this driven man demonstrated that
> the modern notion of freedom—freedom from external restraints
> imposed by others—can mean submission to a hard master,
> one's conscience. . . . An Italian contemporary, Machiavelli, was
> secularizing politics, orienting it toward man's passions rather

than God's laws. Luther was peeling politics off religion, in a quest for religion's essence.

Christianity's assessment of man, at once high and severe, is about right for political philosophy: Man can be magnificant, but is magnificant rarely, and never spontaneously—without help from nurturing institutions. Luther had a haunting sense of the utter fallenness of mankind, and of mankind's total dependence on God's grace. . . . This insulated him from the political temptation to believe in the perfectibility of man through the improvement of social arrangements . . . with seven words—"each and all of us are priests"—he asserted an idea of equality that evolved into an underpinning of popular sovereignty.[17]

It would be a mistake to believe the American colonies were only settled by holy and righteous men and women. America had its share of "get rich quick" opportunists, thieves, and unscrupulous businessmen. The difference in America was a cultural and political consensus of biblical values reflected by strong institutions: the traditional and extended family, churches, mutual aid community groups, businesses, and government.

Biblical tenets were not practiced by all, but they were translated into values, principles, and policies by pervasive institutions that established societal standards. Biblical standards established visible boundaries in the American colonies that judged the actions of all—believers and nonbelievers. The connection between God, the Bible, Christianity, virtue, law, individual responsibility, and freedom were unquestioned by those who shaped America's founding.

Because freedom is God-given, it requires responsibility as well as gratitude. Freedom does not mean the right to do whatever a person pleases. That would not be freedom but would be chaos and anarchy—the worst kind of bondage. The Biblical concept of freedom involves the ability to make choices and to assume responsibility for those choices.[18]

In my fight to save freedom, I have found people of faith to be indispensible allies. Though theological differences continue between Jews, Catholics, and Protestants of all denominations, there is a growing unity regarding the importance of Judeo-Christian values in our culture and politics. People of faith are increasingly standing up for the rights of the unborn, the dignity of the individual, the rights of parents and personal responsibility . . . all essential elements in the foundation of freedom.

While there are certainly other religions prevalent in our country, this does not mean that the Judeo-Christian values and principles that built America should be dismantled to accommodate cultures with different values. In fact, the Judeo-Christian belief that each individual is ultimately personally responsible to their Maker was crucial to our founder's understanding that we must embrace the freedom of religion for everyone, regardless of creed or value system.

America's Freedom Awakening

The seeds of the Reformation, planted years earlier by Luther, grew to their full maturity in the American colonies. Settlers in Connecticut established the first constitution written on American soil. While this constitution did not require church membership for government participation, its preamble affirmed the biblical purposes of civil government, "to mayntayn and presearve the liberty and purity of the gospel of our Lord Jesus which we now professe, as also the discipline of the Churches, which according to the truth of the said gospel is practiced amongst us."[17] (Those guys spelled like I do!)

Americans also placed a preeminent value on education. One of the first things the Pilgrims did when they arrived in 1620 was to establish schools to ensure that all children could read the Bible for themselves. Higher education during America's colonial period was also shaped by Christianity. Many of today's Ivy League schools were established in the colonies to fill the pulpits of America with trained, fervent ministers and to prepare missionaries to take the gospel into the wilderness. Harvard, the first American college, was founded in 1636. Its stated purpose, summed up in their 1646 Rules and Precepts, would surprise most Harvard students today:

> Every one shall consider the main end of his life and studies
> to know God and Jesus Christ which is eternal. Seeing the Lord
> giveth wisdom, every one shall seriously by prayer in secret seek
> wisdom of Him.[19]

The spiritual fires of America's colleges, churches, and people began to cool early in the 1700s. Prosperity and security reduced the need for a God who protected and provided for His people. Materialism and European rationalism began to replace spiritual fervor. But out of this state of spiritual decline and lethargy erupted one of the most powerful movements since the Reformation: the Great Awakening.

Historians differ on the actual beginnings of this time of spiritual renewal, but many mark the date and place at 1734 in Northampton, Massachusetts, when Jonathan Edwards's sermons began to affect the whole community. Large numbers of citizens began to experience conviction, conversion, and renewed spiritual life. Edwards wrote at the time, "This town never was so full of love, nor so full of joy, nor so full of distress as it has been lately. . . . I never saw the Christian spirit in love to enemies so exemplified, in all my life as I have seen it within this half-year."[20]

This spirit of revival spread throughout Massachusetts and Connecticut and soon spread to all the colonies.

The Great Awakening is credited by many historians with providing the spiritual fervor and courage that led to America's demand for independence. It transformed lives, influenced society, and shaped the generation whose ideas and arms gave birth to our republic.[21] John Adams considered America's spiritual awakening to be the American Revolution:

> What do we mean by the American Revolution? Do we
> mean the American war? The Revolution was effected before the

war commenced. The Revolution was in the minds and hearts of the people; a change in their religious sentiments of their duties and obligations.[22]

> It was religion that gave birth to the English colonies in America. One must never forget that. . . . I think I can see the whole destiny of America contained in the first Puritan who landed on those shores, as that of the whole human race in the first man. . . . Despotism may be able to do without faith, but freedom cannot. . . . When a people's religion is destroyed . . . then not only will they let their freedom be taken from them, but often they actually hand it over themselves.[23] —Alexis de Tocqueville

Unlike any other revolution in history, the American war for independence was fought for freedom, a freedom inspired by the faith of millions of Americans in Jesus Christ. Secularists have consistently tried to revise history and ascribe other reasons for the unique motivation and outcome of the American Revolution, but there is no other credible explanation for the events and actions that resulted in the founding of the American republic.

Other revolutions, such as the French Revolution of 1789 or the Russian Revolution of 1917, were about power. As Alexander Hamilton observed during the bloodletting in Paris during the 1790s, "There is no real resemblance between what was the cause of America and what was the cause of France. The difference is no less great than that between liberty and licentiousness."[24]

In both the French and Russian revolutions, small and ruthless groups seized the reins of power in the name of the people. These fierce little factions overthrew the existing institutions of God and government and replaced them with atheistic dictatorships.[25]

To maintain their iron-fisted grip on power, revolutionary leaders in France and Russia resorted to executions rather than elections. Forty thousand Frenchmen were beheaded during their revolution, most of them peasants. And the millions of Russians killed by Lenin and Stalin in their consolidation of power exceeded the combined death tolls of both world wars.[26]

My Personal Awakening

My own life's journey has helped me see the connection between spiritual awakening and freedom. Growing up in the late sixties and early seventies, I was part of America's counterculture. I set my moral standards low and fell short. I had a fast car and a slow brain. Religion was an imposition on my freedom and I had no time for it. God was someone I planned to do business with when I was too old to have fun. Until then I was not interested in any religious rules or guilt trips.

When I finished college, I married my high school sweetheart. We were on our own and free. I had a good job and a company car (a used Ford Torino) and making more money than I could spend ($12,000 a year). Did I mention a slow brain?

This was the kind of freedom I had dreamed about—no one to answer to but me (except maybe my wife, my boss, my landlord, the IRS). I could set my own rules and schedule. But in the midst of all this freedom, I had never felt so empty and unsatisfied.

I'm not sure why, but at one point, I dug out an old Bible I was given as a child. Several times in my life I pulled it out and started reading the first chapter of Genesis. In those attempts I never finished that first chapter, and the pages smelled musty from years in a box. History repeated itself, and I closed the Good Book again without finding anything of value. But somehow I knew the answers I was looking for were spiritual.

One day while rummaging through a bookstore, I came across a book that I vaguely remembered a friend of mine in college receiving from two guys from Campus Crusade. The more I read and thought about events the Bible had already accurately predicted, the more I found myself convinced that it just might be true.

And once you allow yourself to believe the Bible might be true, you are in big trouble. There are still a lot of prophecies yet to be fulfilled. One of them promises that Jesus will return to Earth one day and separate the sheep from the goats. Some people may need Billy Graham to convince them they are goats, but my "deep spiritual insights" up to that point in my life enlightened me enough to know I was not one of the sheep. I knew, even if God graded on the curve, I was at the bottom of the class. This meant if Jesus returned, I would be left behind or worse.

I knelt down on the shag carpet in my apartment and asked Jesus to come into my life, to forgive me and fix what I messed up, to cut me a little slack and help me get on the right track. I was twenty-five years old.

I wish I could tell you, "Once I was bad, and now I'm good," but being born again didn't work that way for me. My wife and I visited a few churches, but I found I still didn't like religion.

The lights didn't start coming on for me until a year later when we moved back to our hometown of Greenville, South Carolina. We were visiting the church where we had been married, and I mentioned to someone that I wanted to know more about the Bible (they didn't seem to use it very much at that church). He suggested I join him Friday at 7:00 a.m. with a group he called the Christian Business Men's Committee (CBMC).

My wife thought I had gone completely nuts when I left the house at 6:30 a.m. with my musty old Bible. The group was made up of businessmen from many denominations: Catholic, Episcopal, Methodist, Presbyterian, and a couple of charismatic churches. The purpose of the group was based on 2 Timothy 2:2 that says, "And the things you have heard me say in the presence of many witnesses entrust to reliable men who will also be qualified to teach others" (NIV). We were supposed to train each other and then to share the gospel with other business and professional people.

One of the men offered to take me through a twelve-week Bible study called Operation Timothy. He was a busy businessman and could only meet at 6:30 on Monday mornings. I think my wife began to panic when I started leaving our house with my Bible at 6:00 a.m. on Mondays.

It seemed weird to me too, but God used the Timothy program to finally open my eyes to the truth of the Bible.

I read and memorized verses that gave me confidence in God's love, my salvation in Christ, the assurance I was really forgiven, instructions about how to talk to and listen to God, and encouragement to share my hope in Christ with others. I learned how to find answers for myself in the Bible.

The most amazing part of this whole process was the discovery that the freedom I sought all my life was in the last place I thought I'd find it: Jesus Christ. I always thought religion was about rules, guilt, and boredom. Instead, the more I learned about Jesus, the freer I felt. First it was freedom from sin and guilt. (I didn't know how much I had until I packed them up and handed them over to Jesus.) Then it was the freedom that came with the joy and peace of knowing that, regardless of what happened to me in this world, I had eternal life in heaven. And finally it was the freedom that came from knowing I no longer needed validation from anyone in this world. I am a child of the King and don't need to waste my time trying to impress any of my fellow sinners.

I attended the Friday morning CBMC breakfast for more than twenty years until I was elected to Congress. We had great arguments and discussions, and we forced one another to use the Bible to prove our points.

Nothing was off-limits, and I developed a comfort with the philosophy of "question everything." We dispelled a lot of religious rules and dogma and old wives tales by searching the Scriptures and finding out what God really said. I actually began to sense some stirring of brain activity in my head for the first time in my life.

My ability to question and apply reasoned logic was greatly enhanced over many years as I searched for truth in a book of unchanging facts and principles. My ability to make a reasoned argument about what I believed improved as I shared my faith with others. And my confidence in what I believed grew as my knowledge of the Bible increased and my trust in God became real.

I also found God was using my spiritual development to develop all areas of my life. I discovered principles essential to my marriage and family. My growing confidence in myself and what I believed encouraged me to take leadership positions in my church and community and to eventually start my own business. And finally my freedom in Christ gave me a passion to promote and protect all the freedoms God gave me and my fellow Americans.

Galatians 5:1 became my life verse: "It is for freedom that Christ has set us free" (NIV). My first campaign slogan was "Bring Freedom Home." And now as I see the threat to freedom in America increasing from all sides, I have made it my mission to lead the fight to save freedom for my children and yours.

> Every thinking man, when he thinks, realizes that the teachings of the Bible are so interwoven and entwined with our whole civic and social life that it would be literally—I do not mean figuratively, but literally—impossible for us to figure what that loss would be if these teachings were removed. We would lose almost all the standards by which we now judge both public and private morals.[27] —President Theodore Roosevelt

Principles and Institutions

Accountability to God creates the morality, virtue, self-control, and personal responsibility that make people governable without overt external force. That same accountability to God provides some measure of restraint to leaders who are given the power to govern.

A biblical understanding of human nature underscores the need to disperse political power and avoid the concentration of control under a single authority. An understanding of human nature also demands that democracy be buffered with a representative system that reduces the threat of "mob rule." And to minimize the flaws and ambitions of leaders, a free people must be governed by the "rule of law" not the "rule of men."

All this is not to say atheists and people of other religions cannot participate freely and constructively in an America with a Judeo-Christian foundation. Everyone, regardless of their religious beliefs, will benefit from the freedom, prosperity, and security created when cultural and political institutions are founded on Christian principles.

Secularists will howl that I am suggesting our government promote the Christian faith. *Not at all!* I don't want the government to have anything to do with religion. As the Constitution says, the federal government "will make no law respecting the establishment of religion."

I am suggesting that the biblical principles of individualism, free choice, morality, personal responsibility, private property, traditional marriage and families, temperance, minimizing borrowing, charity, volunteerism, servant leadership, . . . and many more must guide the principles and policies of government and private sector institutions. History makes a strong case that without adherence to Judeo-Christian principles, the foundations of freedom will crumble.

Even in China, the demand for more political, economic, and social freedom is exploding as Christianity spreads across that oppressed land. In an article titled "Jesus in China: Life on the Edge," the *Chicago Tribune* reported the impact of China's growing faith movement:

> Christianity has probably become China's largest non-
> government organization. . . . Their drive for reform has
> proved particularly persistent because many Christians consider
> themselves bound by an authority higher than the government,
> and their beliefs inspire them to demand greater rights of
> expression and organization.[28]

In America, the threat to Christian principles and freedom has come from the growth of a socialistic government intent on purging religious-based values and principles from our culture. As government grows, it displaces faith in God as the source of security and hope. As faith retreats, morality and virtue decline, extinguishing the ability of the people to live without external controls. When virtue is lost, government force is all that remains to control an uncontrollable people. The more external force is used, the less freedom can prevail and the more the people contrive to throw off all restraints. Lawlessness and immorality rule.

> Among the props of order in democratic societies, the chief is religion; and Tocqueville found in his American observations some reassurance on this score. Democratic peoples simplify religion, certainly; but it may remain with them as an abiding force, helping to counteract that materialism which leads to democratic despotism.[29] —Russell Kirk

Religion has come to be widely regarded as irrational, reactionary, and controversial—a baleful, divisive force in society that generates hate and conflict and is best quarantined from public life. . . . There is quite simply no greater sea-change from the world of the American framers to the world of contemporary American intellectuals than the attitude toward faith and its importance to freedom.[1]
—Os Guinness

CHAPTER NINE

The Separation of God and America
Restoring the Wall of Virtue That Protects Freedom

Once two neighboring kingdoms lived in a constant state of war. One kingdom was in a beautiful, fertile valley. The other overlooked the valley kingdom from a high mountain plateau. Each kingdom regularly attacked the other, always fearing their enemy would attack first. The wars went on for generations.

One day as the valley kingdom prepared for an attack from the mountain kingdom, they were attacked from their unguarded side by a new enemy from the south. The surprise attack caught the valley soldiers off guard, and they were in danger of total defeat.

The mountain kingdom quickly came to their aid and fought side-by-side with the valley kingdom. Their combined forces routed the southern attackers and forced them to make a hasty retreat.

After the battle the kings of the mountain and valley kingdoms held a summit with their knights. The mountain king explained he had joined the valley king in the fight because, had he not, the southern kingdom would have defeated the valley and then attacked and defeated the mountain kingdom. Together the two kings were able to defeat their mutual enemy.

The valley king was so thankful for the mountain kingdom's assistance he promised never to attack them again. Both kings agreed to a truce, and they built a large rock wall along the southern border of the valley kingdom to stop future attacks from the south. The mountain king agreed to fight with the valley kingdom if the southern armies ever invaded again. He also said that as long as they could look down from their mountain home and see the rock wall, they would know the valley kingdom would keep its promise not to attack his kingdom and that they would continue to guard against enemies of both their kingdoms.

The truce lasted throughout the lives of both kings. The mountain kingdom kept guards posted on an overlook to make sure the rock wall stayed in place. After both kings died, new kings took the thrones in their kingdoms. The new valley king did not know why the rock wall was built, but the new king and the people of the mountain kingdom had not forgotten. They continued to post guards every day to make sure the promise of peace was kept.

Not knowing of its importance, the new valley king ordered the rock wall be taken down to allow for the expansion of his kingdom. The guards for the mountain kingdom watched from above as all the rocks were removed from the wall below. The day after the removal of the wall was complete, the mountain kingdom attacked and destroyed the valley kingdom.

The rock wall seemed nothing more than an unnecessary obstruction to the new valley king. He did not know its history or meaning. He did not know the wall protected his kingdom for a generation because those before him did not teach his generation its importance. Or maybe he just didn't listen.

The wall in the story was important not only as a physical barrier against potential enemies but also as a visual reminder of the mutual commitments and trust between neighbors. As long as the wall was in place, all the people knew what was expected of them and what they could expect from their neighbors. Once the wall was gone, all trust dissolved and fear returned.

Like a large rock wall, the principles and values derived from religious faith protected Americans for generations from the secular attitudes and behaviors that have destroyed other nations. This "wall of virtue" established moral boundaries Americans knew they shouldn't cross. It created a common expectation of behavior that promoted civility and cooperation among a diverse population. Of course, there have always been those in America who ignored the societal expectations based on religious faith. Yet the "wall" continued to stand, providing guidance and stability for generations.

> Let it simply be asked where is the security for property, for reputation, for life, if the sense of religious obligation deserts the oaths, which are the instruments of investigation in Courts of Justice? And let us with caution indulge the supposition that morality can be maintained without religion. Whatever may be conceded to the influence of refined education on minds of peculiar structure, reason and experience both forbid us to expect that National morality can prevail in exclusion of religious principle. —President George Washington

Today the federal government is systematically removing the rocks from our "wall of virtue" and replacing it with a much different wall, the wall of separation between church and state. This phrase is not in our Constitution, the Declaration of Independence, or any of America's founding documents. It is an idea that has evolved from the First Amendment that was intended to keep the federal government from establishing a national church or interfering with the practice of religion at the state and local levels.

The Supreme Court used a letter written by President Thomas Jefferson to the Danbury Baptist Association in 1802 to devise their justification to purge God from local schools and later most public forums.

Jefferson opposed any federal government sponsorship of a uniform religious exercise. He wrote:

> Believing with you that religion is a matter which lies solely between man and his God, that he owes account to none other for his faith or his worship, that the legitimate powers of government reach actions only, and not opinions, I contemplate with sovereign reverence that act of the whole American people which declared that their legislature should "make no law respecting an establishment of religion, or prohibiting the free exercise thereof," thus building a wall of separation between Church and State.[2]

It is difficult to see how the federal courts have used this letter to justify making laws and court rulings prohibiting the free and autonomous practice of religion in nonfederal schools, businesses, and private associations.

Prior to 1962, the protection by the First Amendment served its purpose for more than 150 years after the adoption of the U.S. Constitution. The federal government allowed states to regulate the interaction of church and state. Some states had churches supported with local taxes. Ministers and religious views were an integral part of public policy debates. For most of America's history, a generally constructive coexistence was in place between religious principles, the operation of government, and the lives of Americans who held many different religious beliefs.

As late as 1947, the Supreme Court continued to defer to the states on religious issues. In *Everson v. Board of Education*,[3] the court ruled that the state of New Jersey could fund the cost of public transportation to school. Although the state money was used to directly assist students attending religious schools, the court ruled this amounted to equal treatment of all students and thus did not impose religion on anyone.

However, in the 1962 *Engel v. Vitale* case,[4] the Supreme Court ruled against a New York school board requiring every class to start each day with the following statement:

The Separation of God and America

"Almighty God, we acknowledge our dependency upon Thee, and we beg Thy blessing upon us, our parents, our teachers and our Country."[5]

New York State officials developed this declaration as part of their "Statement on Moral and Spiritual Training in the Schools." At that time schools commonly accepted their role in character education. The statement did not establish a religion or favor a particular denomination. It was perfectly consistent with the founders' writings, the Declaration of Independence, and numerous court rulings before 1962.

Unfortunately, when the Court banned this statement, it did more than ban God and prayer from public schools. It implicitly banned everything else included in the statement: respect and honor for parents, teachers, and country. When the Supreme Court banned the teaching of respect for God, it effectively rejected the traditionalist worldview and replaced it with a secular-socialist worldview. The *Engel v. Vitale* case began a cascade of court decisions and legislative action at the federal level that have dismantled the "wall of virtue" that has served as the foundation of freedom in America for generations.[6]

As America slides with increasing speed toward a secular-socialistic state, Americans must decide who and what we want to be as a people and a nation. No one can deny that seismic changes have occurred in our culture and our government. Now is the time for Americans to understand the implications of these changes. As Os Guinness writes, "Few things are therefore more in the public interest now than to understand the present significance of faiths in America and to assess their social, national, and international consequences."[7]

> Without God, there could be no American form of Government, nor an American way of life. Recognition of the Supreme Being is the first, the most basic, expression of Americanism.[8] —President Dwight Eisenhower

The Difference between a Secular Government and a Secular Society

On one of my trips to Iraq in 2005, I arrived about a month before their first election. The State Department encouraged my colleagues and I to press the candidates for president and prime minister to form a secular government that promoted religious freedom and capitalism instead of a Muslim theocracy. As I encouraged these Iraqi candidates to adopt a secular government, it occurred to me I was fighting against the destructive forces of secularism back home in America. I became conflicted about the role of religion in government.

This personal conflict encouraged me to think more clearly about the difference between a secular government and a secular society. One is good; the other is destructive. We *do not* want a government that represents a particular religion or forces a particular religion on its people. Our government should be religion-neutral or secular.

But we also *do not* want a government that purges religion from society. We *do not* want a government that prohibits religious-based moral judgments by individuals or private institutions. We *do not* want a government that excludes constructive values and principles from public policy because they may be associated with religious principles. And we *do not* want a government that promotes destructive behaviors opposed to the traditional values of our nation.

The framers . . . knew from history, even early American history, that imposed faith could be disastrous for freedom. . . . Yet the American framers' linking of republicanism and religion was one of their most characteristic, if surprising, emphases. They believed that the self-government of the republic rests on the self-government of the citizens. They recognized that the rule of law constrains the external, whereas an individual's faith is obedience to the unenforceable and an act of freedom. Faith is indispensable to freedom, they claimed—to liberty itself and also to the social vitality and civic harmony that undergird freedom.

The Separation of God and America

Their position can be expressed simply in a kind of eternal triangle of first principles: "Liberty requires virtue, virtue requires religion, and religion requires liberty."[9]

A free nation needs a government that encourages (not forces) the practice of religion and does nothing to diminish its importance in society. America needs a government that guarantees religious freedom and the freedom to practice religion within reasonable legal boundaries. Our faiths will lead us to be tolerant and compassionate toward those with different beliefs, but freedom will demand we have the right to form associations with those who share our religion, values, and principles. This freedom also means that nongovernment, voluntary associations should have the right to exclude those who don't share their faith and values.

For example, if an individual wants to organize a Freedom Club requiring members to believe in God and traditional values, that should be his right. But this arrangement is not acceptable to secular-socialists. They do not want the Freedom Club to have the right to have religious-based standards or the right to exclude people who do not share their values. And they regularly use the force of government to threaten and intimidate individuals and organizations attempting to practice religious freedom.

The distinction here is important: *freedom requires that government not force religious doctrine or morality onto the people, but it must allow the free operation of religion, freedom of association, and the practice of religious-based values throughout society.* If there is to be a "wall of separation," it should be between a secular government and a religious society.

Religion is a threat to socialists because it creates a cultural authority that supersedes government authority. Socialism requires an all-powerful central government to force societal compliance and uniformity. Secular-socialist uniformity is based on the lowest common denominators of values and behaviors because it is based on the minimum standards of external law. A pervasive religious culture creates an internal moral code based on society's highest values and aspirations.

Even a population practicing many diverse faiths will develop a consensus moral code that provides guidance and stability to society. This moral code creates a "wall of virtue" that antagonizes individuals and groups practicing countercultural behavior. They want government protection from religiously informed value judgments.

Freedom depends on guiding values in a culture emanating from the free practice of religion. As a billboard in my hometown expressed it, "When values are present, laws are not needed. Without values, laws are unenforceable."

Because the human spirit is the primary form of democratic capital, the notion of cultural authority is both critical and complementary to freedom. When the cultural authority of beliefs, ideals, and traditions is strong and operative, external laws and coercions are unnecessary. Such beliefs, traditions, and ideals have the power to inspire, discipline, and constrain in a manner that does not contradict personal freedom.[10]

We have no government armed with powers capable of contending with human passions unbridled by morality and religion. Avarice, ambition, revenge, or gallantry would break the strongest cords of our Constitution as a whale goes through a net. Our Constitution was made only for a moral and religious people. It is wholly inadequate to the government of any other.[11] —President John Adams

---

How Government Has Destroyed America's "Wall of Virtue"

For nearly fifty years America's federal government has been aggressively purging religion and religious-based values from our society. How and why has this happened? At its inception the federal government was confined to the executive, legislative, and judicial branches as described in the Constitution. The scope and authority of the federal government was narrowly limited to national functions such as defense, the regulation of interstate commerce, and the maintenance of a standard currency. Religion did not control the federal government, and the federal government did not control religion.

Over the years, as the federal government crept outside its constitutional bounds, it began to fund and regulate local schools, universities, the arts, businesses, and private associations. As the role and scope of the federal government grew, the definition of what was "the government" or "the state" began to expand in the minds of Washington elites, especially in the minds of Supreme Court justices.

This definitional change was codified in 1962 when the Court identified a local school system in New York as being under federal jurisdiction. Until the *Engel v. Vitale* ruling, public schools were a state and local function not under the authority of the federal government.[12] Unfortunately, the expansion of the federal domain did not stop with schools.

Today all aspects of American society are under the authority of the federal government: the air we breathe, the water we drink, the food we eat, the clothes we wear, the homes we live in, the fertilizer we put on our lawns, the phones we talk on, our jobs and businesses, our schools and colleges, the cars we drive, the roads we drive on, the gas we put in our cars, the electricity for our homes, our health care, our investments and retirement plans, how we raise our children, the words we speak . . . even our churches. There is nothing that is not part of "the state."

As the definition of "the state" morphed to include virtually everything that happens in America, the courts also redefined "the church." Early references to "the church" in America were obvious references to organized religious denominations. Our founders did not want the federal government to associate with or to show preference to a particular denomination. But "church" was not "God" or the general concept of religion. The Constitution gave the states the freedom to deal with religion in their own way, but the federal government could "make no law" in regards to the practice of religion.

Beginning with the *Engel v. Vitale* case, the federal courts have completely distorted the definition of the "church." *Engel* banned a statement used by a local school that only referenced God. This statement did not associate the federal government or the local school with any religion or organized denomination. The Court's ruling in this case began the process of separating God from public life in America.

The practical implication of separating God from public life has been to extinguish the cultural authority associated with religious faith for generations. "The separation of church and state" now means "the separation of essential values from the American culture." The results have been devastating.

My concern over the federal government's role in America's cultural deterioration prompted me to coauthor a book in 2008 with Professor J. David Woodard titled *Why We Whisper, Restoring Our Right to Say It's Wrong*. We researched how, through confusing court rulings and legal intimidation, the federal government has been a prime cause of cultural decline in America. We also documented the threats to freedom of speech, freedom of association, and the cost of disappearing values to the American taxpayer.

The Secular-Socialist Crusades against Freedom

There are two destructive dimensions to the federal attempts to separate church and state. One is the elimination of the positive values and constructive behaviors associated with the free practice of religious faith. The other is the cumulative effect of laws and court rulings that actually promote destructive behaviors and violate our national conscience.

The 1962 *Engel* decision unleashed a flood of political attacks, social ostracism, and legal challenges against any and all moral teaching in public schools or tacit support—no matter how minor or tangential—of faith-based groups or activities by any level of government. These challenges to traditional moral standards were exacerbated by welfare legislation encouraging promiscuous sex, unwed births, and dependency on government.

The Separation of God and America

By 1970 America was embroiled in a "sexual revolution," antigovernment demonstrations, an explosion of unwed births, increasing crime, expanding dependency on government, and economic decline. By the 1990s, Americans witnessed moral debauchery in the White House, widespread corporate corruption, serious declines in student achievement, and continuing increases in unwed births and sexually transmitted diseases.

Secular activists found a vehicle in the courts to purge traditional values from the public square and to force compliance to a new secular-socialist agenda. The unelected judicial branch began to overrule existing laws and policy decisions made by the Congress and state legislatures. The federal courts redefined the Constitution as a "living" document that should be interpreted in light of the changing needs of society.

> If everything is endlessly up for question and open for change, then everything is permitted and nothing is forbidden . . . nothing is unthinkable.[13] —Os Guinness

The ACLU and other self-appointed agents of the federal courts attacked traditional organizations like the Boy Scouts and veterans groups, saying their use of the Pledge of Allegiance, traditional standards, and prayers violated the "wall of separation." Federal judges were more than willing to join in the harassment and intimidation. God, prayer, and traditional values were dropped by public schools and many private organizations to avoid expensive lawsuits.

There were no longer common standards to which people appealed in their efforts to measure, judge, or value ideas, opinions, or lifestyle choices. Gone was allegiance to a common sense of authority, or a commonly regarded and respected wielder of legitimate power. Science was elevated as a divine source, as partisans rejected any notion of overarching truth and reduced all ideas to social constructions of class, gender, and ethnicity.[14]

The "living constitution" reached its nadir with a new "right to privacy" discovered by the Supreme Court in 1965. In the *Griswold* case the Court overturned a state law prohibiting the use of any instrument for the purpose of contraception.[15] As one dissenting judge said, "I think this is an uncommonly silly law . . . [that] is obviously unenforceable [but] we are asked to hold that it violates the U.S. Constitution. . . . And that I cannot do."[16]

The *Griswold* decision set loose a score of later decisions based on the dubious theory that an individual in private became a law unto himself. This so-called "right to privacy" was extended to procreative sexual acts and to cover abortion. This "right to privacy" was later stretched to the breaking point when the Court declared sodomy laws unconstitutional and gave presumed legitimacy to gay marriage.[17]

Examples of Attacks on Traditional Institutions

Decentralized, freely operating, and competing religious faiths are a threat to the centralized authority of a socialized democracy. Freedom relies on millions of people making their own political, economic, social, and religious decisions from many competitors and institutions. Freedom is dependent on a decentralized republican form of government in which power is divested to states, local governments, and millions of nongovernment institutions such as families, independent schools, churches, community organizations, and businesses—all of which until the 1960s had the freedom to incorporate faith and religiously informed values without interference from the federal government.

This freedom has been taken away. Secular socialists have used a perverted view of the First Amendment to promote uniformity of beliefs and behavior based on our new national religion: secularism. The federal government has systematically—rock by rock—removed the "wall of virtue" from American life.

Schools and Universities

Since individuals are the foundation of freedom—and character and capabilities are essential for individuals to succeed in a free society—

education must be the top priority of a freedom-loving people. Unfortunately secular socialists understand this better than traditional Americans. Government schools have become the "tip of the spear" for the secular socialist movement in America.

Government schools (K–12) and public universities have become the centralized power behind "values clarification" and secular theology in America. As court rulings at the state and federal level have thrown out traditional values, public schools have quickly adopted new secular values. Parents have little power. When Massachusetts parents protested in 2005 that their kindergartners and first graders were being taught the benefits of the gay lifestyle, they were told, "It's the law in Massachusetts, and we're going to teach it."[18]

> Public schools do not generally teach against traditional views or criticize religion. They just leave it out. Every subject is taught with the assumption that there is no God. There are no moral lessons that draw on the authority of God's laws. "Right" and "wrong" are seldom used as guides for behavior. These omissions are subtle and not evident on every visit to a school. There is certainly nothing about the exclusion of traditional views that would, on the surface, appear harmful to students. But parents should consider what has been lost.[19]

History lessons have been revised to exclude or diminish the impact of religion on civilization and its great leaders. Students don't learn that the great explorers, artists, musicians, and scientists were motivated by their religious convictions. They do not learn of the improbability of accidental creation and evolution, or the credible scientific evidence of a Creator God. And there is little emphasis on the importance of honesty and character.

> Benjamin Franklin promoted public education as a means to develop the public character necessary to sustain political liberty.

He rejected the European model of education that emphasized classical learning and catered to the privileged class. He believed that education should prepare students to be efficient tradesmen and vigilant democratic citizens.

For careers and trade, Franklin promoted basic mathematics and accounting, clear writing, and living rather than dead languages. To develop vigilant democratic citizens, Franklin stressed the historical examples of the advantages of virtue and the disadvantages of vice. He illustrates the importance of public religion and reveals the superiority of Christianity in this role.[20]

We could use a little of Benjamin Franklin's wisdom today. America's government schools are among the worst in the industrialized world, and our students are losing ground every year to our international competitors. The national teachers unions control our local schools through Congress and the courts.

Recently the teachers union in California donated more than $1 million in an attempt to defeat a proposition to ban gay marriage.[21] They were the largest single contributor to the effort to destroy the traditional definition of marriage.[22] Why would teachers invest so heavily in gay marriage? It is all part of the centralization of power and the socialization of our culture. Unions and gays have a common interest in secularism, as do environmental extremists and other groups who support a stronger federal government.

About the same time in South Carolina, a high school principal was forced to resign after he refused to sponsor a gay club. The local school board ordered him to do it because they couldn't afford a threatened lawsuit if they resisted. It is unlikely any of the board members thought it was a good idea to have a school club based on sex of any kind, but they didn't have the courage or the money to fight the ACLU.

The threat of expensive lawsuits is how agents of the court such as the ACLU replace traditional values with secular initiatives such as gay clubs in our public schools. Most schools just comply with ACLU demands rather than face the expense and media criticism that comes with a lawsuit. Colleges and universities face the same secular pressure because they all accept some federal funding.

Community Organizations

Nonprofit community organizations are critically important to creating and maintaining freedom. Civic groups like Rotary, Lions, Jaycees, and Kiwanis clubs provide many charitable services and create networking opportunities for local business owners. Other groups like the YMCA, YWCA, Boy Scouts, and Girl Scouts provide activities and training for youth. Civic groups offer forums for individuals to participate in serving their community and to develop leadership skills.

Many, perhaps most, civic organizations in the United States were formed with a Christian mission. The Salvation Army, Young Men's Christian Association, and Young Women's Christian Association began with a specifically Christian purpose. The Boy Scouts and Girl Scouts were formed to develop character and citizenship skills based on an allegiance to God and country.

Many of these community organizations have been forced to diminish their religious focus because of implicit or explicit threats from the federal government.

Most continue to operate but without the same emphasis on values and character development. Attacks on the Boy Scouts provide a clear picture of how this has happened.

The Boy Scouts have been developing character and patriotism in boys and young men for one hundred years. The majority of America's astronauts, Rhodes scholars, FBI agents, and military academy graduates were Boy Scouts. As an organization that has developed the character and capabilities of millions of individuals, the Boy Scouts have been one of America's most important freedom-creating institutions—all at no taxpayer expense.

Yet the Boy Scouts have been attacked relentlessly by agents of the federal government for three decades. The ACLU continues to threaten and intimidate the Boy Scouts because of their religious mission and values. The ACLU has problems with the Boy Scout oath:

Boy Scout Oath

On my honor I will do my best to do my duty to God and my country, and to obey the Scout Law, to help other people at all times, to keep myself physically strong, mentally awake, and morally straight.[23]

It is difficult to imagine how this pledge of a private organization could violate the Constitution. The fact is it doesn't, as the Boy Scouts have proved in more than thirty lawsuits that they have won since 1975. But this hasn't stopped the constant harassment from the ACLU:

Since 1975, the Boy Scouts have had to defend themselves in more than thirty lawsuits attacking their values. Most of these suits challenged the Boy Scouts' right to set standards for membership: specifically the standards that required members to be male, have a belief in God, and not be openly homosexual. The Boy Scouts won every one of these cases, either at trial or on appeal, but they did not recoup the millions of dollars they had to spend to defend themselves and their values. Neither did they receive any compensation for the millions of dollars in lost contributions and public support due to the hundreds of malicious and misleading news articles that appeared across the country.[24]

Businesses

As a small businessman for many years, I held a regular Bible study at work for those interested in participating. My company was too small to attract the attention of the ACLU, but this simple act of a voluntary Bible study at work could be grounds for a lawsuit today.

You may agree or disagree with an employer who wants to make faith a part of his business practices, but the question is, should he have that freedom? Does the "separation of church and state" include businesses? Most judges, congressmen, and senators would likely say it doesn't but vote that it does.

The Employment Non-Discrimination Act, a bill requiring all businesses and organizations (such as the Boy Scouts) with more than fifteen employees to hire homosexuals and bisexuals, will likely pass a Democrat Congress and be signed into law by President Obama. The law will create a new boon for lawyers looking to see companies deemed insufficiently compliant.

Companies like Wal-Mart, that once had policies against adultery in the workplace, have been forced to drop standards that attract lawsuits for discrimination based on marital status. Wal-Mart, along with many other retailers with pharmacies, refused on moral grounds to sell the Plan B morning after pill until Planned Parenthood and other pro-abortion groups were able to use the government to pressure most into dropping their moral standards.

Chick-fil-A is a successful business operating with a Christian mission. But new guidelines proposed by the federal Equal Employment Opportunity Commission will force the company "to eliminate all references to religion, which would significantly change the culture and morale at Chick-fil-A."[25]

The safest policy for businesses has become a totally secular, religion-free workplace. As Michael K. Whitehead, general counsel to the Southern Baptist Convention's Christian Life Commission notes, "Employers trying to avoid lawsuits want a clear-cut, simple rule which can be understood and obeyed by all employees, whether high school drop-outs or Harvard MBAs. Their primary aim is not to be sensitive to EEOC's intentions or to maximize religious liberty. Their bottom line is to find a policy that will help them stay out of court." Ambiguity in court decisions and regulatory guidelines leave businesses little choice but to adopt secular policies in order to reduce risks.[26]

Churches

The last place you would think the "separation" requirement would apply is church. Yet the federal government has applied pressure to "separate church from church." The "church" is now part of the "state." Pastors, who from colonial days played an important role in guiding America's political process, have been muzzled by legislation that threatens to take away the tax-exempt status of churches. Pastors and churches are prohibited from endorsing candidates who represent their values and principles. If they do, the federal government will levy heavy taxes.[27]

Churches expelling members for violating biblical moral principles have been sued and forced to pay large settlements. The viability and relevance of America's churches are dependent on their freedom to enforce moral standards with members who voluntarily ascent to adhere to these standards. This freedom has been diminished by confusing court rulings that subject churches to expensive lawsuits.

Until the past few decades, churches provided a national conscience, informing and educating Americans about what was right and wrong. The presence of a higher moral standard in society, even for non-members, helped to restrain destructive, immoral behavior in the wider culture. Churches were once a powerful positive influence in the culture. . . . The government, however, has now crippled even this most sacred bastion of faith and constitutional privilege.[28]

The loss of the moral influence of churches on society is immeasurable. For persons involved in immoral behavior, the best thing that could happen to them and the country would be accountability to a church body and subjection to public embarrassment. Nongovernment public discipline creates a deterrent for destructive behavior without the use of legal force. Yet the government has chosen to protect and promote unwed births, abortion, marital infidelity, divorce, homosexuality, gambling, and other behaviors once discouraged by the consensus values of America's churches.

The Separation of God and America

Even Christian schools, organized to provide an alternative to the secular indoctrination of government schools, have been attacked for holding to biblical values. These schools have been sued for dismissing pregnant, unwed teachers and for expelling openly homosexual students. If Christian schools can't enforce biblical standards with students and teachers, they might as well close their doors.

> I have lived, sir, a long time, and the longer I live, the more convincing proofs I see of this truth—that God governs the affairs of men. And if a sparrow cannot fall to the ground without His notice, is it probable an empire can rise without His aid? We have been assured, sir, in the sacred writings that except the Lord build the house, they labor in vain that build it.[29] —Benjamin Franklin

Individuals, Parents, and Families

Secular socialists will contend that—despite the separation of God and faith-based values from schools, businesses, and churches—individuals and families are still free to practice their faith and hold to their personal values. But individuals and families live and work within the framework of government and private institutions that discourage or prohibit the free expression of religious values and principles. Examples of this loss of freedom are plentiful.

One such brave American is Brittany McComb, the 2006 valedictorian of Foothill High School in Nevada. McComb studied hard, earning a 4.7 GPA, the highest grade-point average in the graduating class. In her graduation address she wanted to thank God for her success. In Brittany's written speech, she made two references to the Lord, nine mentions of God, and one mention of Christ. School officials (i.e., government representatives) censored her speech, deleting the reference to Christ and several other references to God and two Bible references. But when Brittany McComb stood up to give her address, she also stood up for her right to freedom of speech. This was her speech, earned as a result of her academic record, and she believed she had the right to use her own words. Unfortunately, school officials were monitoring her speech and cut off her microphone before she could mention the word "Christ."[30]

Individuals and families who choose to fight the secular system are faced with the unlimited power of government and well-funded groups such as the ACLU. Parents who have protested safe-sex programs in public schools such as "Hot, Sexy, and Safer" have been beaten down by the time and expense of lawsuits. And the battle to secularize America's youth extends well beyond public schools.

The ACLU has led the fight to strip parents of their right to protect children from obscenity, even the worst form of pornography—child pornography. "The ACLU has opposed federal legislation that allowed parents to notify the post office if they did not wish to receive sexually oriented advertisements in the mail. It also opposed legislation that would have labeled pornographic mail as such so the post office would know not to deliver it to families who did not wish to receive it."[31] Attacks on parental rights are increasing across America.

> Almost all our contemporary movements showed in their early stages a hostile attitude toward the family, and did all they could to discredit and disrupt it. They did it by undermining the authority of the parents; by facilitating divorce; by taking over the responsibility for feeding, education and entertaining the children; and by encouraging illegitimacy. . . . As one would expect, a disruption of the family, whatever its causes, fosters automatically a collective spirit and creates a responsiveness to the appeal of mass movements.[32]

Individuals and parents have little chance of winning this battle alone. I know because, even as a United States senator, the federal bureaucracy tries to ignore my protests against religious discrimination. I'll give you a few examples.

In September 2007, Andrew Larochelle, a seventeen-year-old boy from Ohio, placed a request through his congressman that a flag be flown over the Capitol in honor of his grandfather. This is a service many congressmen and senators provide for constituents on special occasions. Larochelle requested that the certificate accompanying the flag read, "This flag was flown in honor of Marcel Larochelle, my grandfather, for his dedication and love of God, country, and family."

The architect of the Capitol, who coordinates this service, removed the word "God" from the certificate, citing their Flag Services Rules, which prohibit "any religious or political expression" on flag certificates. This is not a law but a rule made up by federal bureaucrats. Keep in mind that both houses of Congress open every morning with prayer. The Declaration of Independence contains the word "God." The Pledge of Allegiance contains the words "under God." U.S. currency is printed with the words "In God We Trust." Additionally, there are numerous references to God in the U.S. Capitol.

I joined with Larochelle's congressman, Michael Turner, and several other congressmen and senators to protest this violation of free speech. After several national news stories, the architect of the Capitol relented. We held a press conference and invited Larochelle, his grandfather, and family to join us in Washington to celebrate this small victory. In front of cameras from all over the country, Larochelle was able to present the flag and certificate (as he wrote it) to his grandfather. It literally took an act of Congress to save this simple freedom.

The Capitol Visitors Center (CVC), which opened in December 2008, is another example of the subtle purging of America's religious heritage by the federal government. I toured the new gazillion dollar, overbudget, behind-schedule center a few months before it opened. It is really nice—something all Americans can be proud of—except no visitor would leave this facility knowing anything about the essential role religion and faith played in our history.

I found carved in one marble wall, "Our National Motto: E Pluribus Unum" (which means "out of many, one"). But this is not our national motto. "In God We Trust" was adopted as our national motto in 1956. Additionally there were only three references to Rev. Martin Luther King and no mention of the significant role churches played in the civil rights movement.

The CVC includes inconsequential personal items like a senator's watch but does not include religious items of historical significance such as the Aitken Bible of 1782, which was the only Bible ever printed by an act of Congress. There is no mention that the Capitol served as Washington's largest church until 1867.

I was most troubled when I stood in front of the replica of the speaker's chair and platform from the U.S. House of Representatives. It felt like I was standing in front of the real thing, except there was no "In God We Trust" carved above the speaker's chair. I was astonished at the boldness of the Capitol's secular historians.

Again I joined with a number of congressmen and senators to protest this overt revision of American history. We finally achieved some limited success: "In God We Trust" was placed above the speaker's chair and "Our National Motto" will be removed from the carving that says E Pluribus Unum.

> From George Washington to Abraham Lincoln,
> Eisenhower, and beyond, the sense of the sovereignty
> of God above history has been a recurring theme
> in American self-understanding, a genuine point of
> consensus despite obvious dissent.[33] —Os Guinness

Principles and Institutions

In the story about the two kingdoms and the rock wall, the people of the valley kingdom removed the wall because they no longer believed it had any functional value. They didn't understand that its primary function was not as a physical barrier but as physical evidence of a relational truth. It was a tangible reminder of an agreement between neighbors to live together in peace and cooperation.

Religion in America is much like the rock wall. Of course, religion is critically important to individuals as their connection to God and their motivation to live a moral life. But for our nation, religion is more important for what it represents: the consensus values and principles of our people. Religion shouldn't be a motivation for laws and regulations, but values and principles derived from religion must be. When government policies represent the values of the people, they have the moral authority to enlist compliance without the use of force.

A story told by a minister about Thomas Jefferson in the early days of our republic illustrates the point:

> President Jefferson was on his way to church on a Sunday morning with his large red prayer book under his arm. A passing friend asked him where he was going. Jefferson replied, "To Church, Sir." Surprised, the friend chided, "Mr. Jefferson, you don't believe a word of it." To that Jefferson responded, "Sir, no nation has ever yet existed or been governed without religion. Nor will one ever exist. The Christian religion is the best religion that has ever been given to man and I as Chief Magistrate of this nation am bound to give it the sanction of my example. Good morning, Sir."[34]

Jefferson didn't defend his beliefs. That was a personal matter, and he evaded the point. We still don't know exactly what Jefferson believed. But he agreed with all his colleagues in the founding thought; a people cannot maintain liberty without religion.[35]

Most of the examples of the purging of religious content and values from our culture could, taken individually, be viewed as "no big deal." But the cumulative impact of these seemingly insignificant attacks on religious freedom has had an enormous impact on our culture. The quest for unfettered moral freedom enforced by government has come at a high price. This is not a matter of subjective personal opinions about morality or religion. Our government has sacrificed the good of the nation by replacing religiously inspired moral aspirations with the minimum standards of secularism.

> And can the liberties of a nation be thought secure when we have removed their only firm basis, a conviction in the minds of the people that these liberties are the gift of God? That they are not to be violated but with his wrath? Indeed I tremble for my country when I reflect that God is just: that his justice cannot sleep for ever. —President Thomas Jefferson

> We estimate the direct cost [of government sponsored destructive behavior] to be $500 billion annually, with the indirect costs at $2 trillion! Add it up! The cost of diminishing marriage, including sexually transmitted diseases, divorce, cohabitation, unwed births, pornography, same-sex marriages, and abortion, along with the cost of government-sponsored gambling, likely exceeds our total annual federal budget. . . . At a time when our nation is facing the most severe financial crisis in our history, citizens should demand loudly that our elected officials act immediately.[36]

The decentralizing of power in a republican form of government is dependent on the free operation of state and local governments and autonomous societal institutions that help develop individual capabilities and provide outlets for choices and service. The federal government, through legislation and court rulings, has severely restricted the freedom-enhancing institutions in America.

Nonprofit organizations and businesses are not allowed to include overtly religious standards into their operations or to freely participate in the political process. A nonprofit group will lose their tax-exempt status if they endorse political candidates. Corporations are not allowed to advocate for or contribute to candidates for federal office. The federal government has essentially taken power from traditional institutions and given it to special interest political groups who advocate for centralized federal control.

Os Guinness describes the importance and functions of the millions of small institutions sustaining our freedom:

> These are the human-sized institutions, such as the neighborhood, the local church or synagogue, the labor union, the local political organization, the national voluntary agency like Girl Scouts, YMCA, and the Red Cross. They stand midway between the small, private, face-to-face world of the individual and the larger public institutions of society.[37]

> This apparently fragile web of middle-level communities—Edmund Burke's "small platoons," Thomas Jefferson's "small republics," Peter Berger and Richard Neuhaus's "mediating structures"—is deeply important in any society, because these communities provide the matrix of meaning and belonging that is so vital both to individuals and to a genuinely pluralistic society. But in America these middle-level communities are more important still. Free association is one of the secrets of American democracy. It creates a community-based pluralism that avoids the extremes of both individualism and collectivism, statism and laissez-faire, alienation and dependency. From the Puritan-based town meetings in New England and the ethnic communities to the Lions Club, the PTA and the Scouts, America's mediating structures have been a fruitful seedbed for American freedom. To Americans as individuals, the greatest danger in this loss is human impoverishment, just as the danger for American democracy is the loss of the moral and civic foundations on which its own stability and diversity depend.[38]

SAVING FREEDOM

When Alexis de Tocqueville described the miracle of the American experiment, he attributed our success to the autonomous operation of individuals and free, nongovernment institutions. The principles of limited government and individual freedom are totally dependent on the political and religious freedom of America's institutions, beginning with our families and churches. This is America's republican form of government —if we can keep it.

It was a spiritual wind that drove the Americans irresistibly ahead from the beginning. What was behind their compulsion to improve a man's lot was an all-pervading religious sense of duty, the submission to a God-given imperative, to a God-given code of personal behavior, the willing acceptance of all the necessary sacrifices, including death in battle. Few foreigners understand this, even today.[39] —Luigi Barzini

Nothing distinguishes more clearly conditions in a free country from those in a country under arbitrary government than the observance in the former of the great principles known as the Rule of Law. Stripped of all technicalities, this means that government in all its actions is bound by rules fixed and announced beforehand—rules which make it possible to address with fair certainty how the authority will use its coercive affairs on the basis of this knowledge.[1]
—Friedrich Hayek

CHAPTER TEN

Freedom and the Rule of Law
Boundaries That Make Freedom Work

Several years ago when two of my children were still living at home, we got a little schnauzer puppy. Our first dog, a schnauzer named Peppermint, died suddenly, and all of us were still grieving. My oldest daughter, who lived out of town, decided to take matters into her own hands. She bought a new puppy and brought it home to cheer everyone up. We named the puppy Addie because she added back the joy we lost when Peppermint died.

I was determined to "lay down the law" and teach Addie some boundaries so she wouldn't turn our house into a doghouse. We all agreed on the rules: Addie would not go into the living room or get on chairs and sofas. She could stay in the house if she obeyed the rules. Until then she had to stay locked in the laundry room at night and when she was home alone.

I'm no dog whisperer, but I figured this one out. I sat on the floor at the doorway to our living room and held one of Addie's paws. When I touched her paw to the living room carpet, I would correct her by saying "no" in my deepest, meanest voice. Then I would let her go. When she walked into the living room, I would pick her up, and correct her again. I followed the same procedure with the chairs and sofas.

Addie was a quick learner. She soon had the run of the whole house because she stayed off the chairs and sofas, and out of the living room. When the family was sitting in the living room, she would sit at the entrance and look pitiful but wouldn't touch the carpet. My wife and children would often say, "Oh Dad, you're so mean. Let her come in just this once." But I knew that would just confuse her.

The final frontier for Addie was the yard. We kept her in the backyard because it was fenced and she was wild. She had to stay on a leash when we took her outside the fence because, if we didn't, she would just start running like the Gingerbread Man and wouldn't look back. She stayed locked up until I took her out front and repeated the same procedure I did in our living room. I sat at the end of our driveway, touched her paw to the road, and said "no."

Again she learned quickly, and now going to the front yard is her greatest thrill in life. Every morning she and I walk from our back door to the back gate. She beats me to the gate and jumps up and down until I open it. Then she sits as I look down the driveway to make sure its safe. When I say "OK," she takes off. Addie runs wild, barks at our neighbor's dog, but never takes a step out of the yard. No fence, no leash. . . . Addie is free!

One of the great ironies of freedom is that you can only have it if you are willing to obey the rules. Rules restrict your freedom, but real freedom can only exist within a framework of rules. In a free society the rules (laws and regulations) must be knowable and minimally restrictive. The people must also have the willingness and self-control to voluntarily follow the rules without the use of force.

Voluntary compliance to laws requires a respect for the law and a self-disciplined citizenry. Laws will be respected only when they are derived from a fixed set of consensus principles governing the lawmakers. Fixed principles (i.e., a constitution) give the laws a moral authority that elicits respect and voluntary compliance by citizens. Reactive, arbitrary lawmaking undermines constitutional government and the "rule of law."

There is much confusion in America about the meaning of freedom and how the Constitution, laws, and regulations relate to freedom. Elected officials at the federal level swear an oath to "protect and defend" the Constitution but generally ignore its limits once they are in office. Federal, state, and local laws and regulations are so numerous and confusing people feel little obligation to respect or follow them . . . unless they fear they will get caught and punished for ignoring them.

As we develop a better understanding of freedom, we need to revisit the meaning of a constitutional form of government as well as the difference between the "rule of law" and the "rule of men." These concepts were considered essential by our founders, and we ignore them today at our peril.

In professional sports the team owners form a league, appoint a commissioner, and submit themselves to the governance of the league. The owners, in effect, develop a "constitution" that outlines the responsibilities of league officials, including what the league can and cannot do. Team owners agree to adhere to the decisions of the league with the understanding that league officials will adhere to the "constitution."

The league develops the rules of the game (laws and regulations) and hires officials and referees to enforce the rules on the field. The league delegates the responsibilities for enforcing the rules to this semi-independent group of officials. During a game the opinions of owners, players, and fans are irrelevant. Rules are not modified during a game to compensate for extenuating circumstances. The officials must make objective calls based on the "rule of law." The integrity of the game depends on the officials consistently enforcing rules known in advance by the players and coaches.

Coaches are free to design all kinds of plays and to choose the players they want on the field. Owners individually decide how much to pay their own coaches and players. And during a game, the players can do whatever they want, as long as they follow the rules. Fair competition and freedom can only exist within a framework of knowable, minimally restrictive, and consistently enforced rules.

At the risk of overdoing these analogies, I'd like to use one more personal example to make my point. When I joined my local Presbyterian church, I voluntarily took an oath to submit myself to the oversight and discipline of the church elders. In return the church elders agreed to submit themselves to the "constitution"—the Bible.

Later, when I was elected an elder of the church, I took an oath to submit myself to the authority of the Scriptures and to serve the members of the church according to the "rule of law" outlined in the Scriptures. The Bible was, in effect, our constitution and from it we developed the laws and regulations to manage the church and to serve its members. As long as church members believed their elders were holding to Scripture and the guidelines for members were derived from it, voluntary compliance was considered an act of worship to God, and the church was unified around common beliefs and purposes.

> Man is free if he needs to obey no person
> but solely the laws.[2] —Immanuel Kant

Good Intentions without Restraints

People, like governments, need a "constitution" that establishes goals and priorities and focuses our limited time and resources toward activities that move us toward our goals. Unless we limit ourselves to purposeful priorities, we will be pulled in all directions, try to do more than we can do well, waste our time and energy, and ultimately hurt ourselves and those around us.

By the time I reached thirty-five years of age, I had four children, a small business, and no personal constitution. I was ready and willing to serve. My church asked me to be a deacon, then an elder, then a Sunday school teacher, then a scout leader, and then to serve as chairman of the board of the Christian school that was a part of the church. Sure! Sign me up!

The United Way asked me to be on their campaign cabinet; the local Chamber of Commerce asked me to serve on their executive committee;

the Christian Business Men's Committee asked me to be their chairman; the Vocational Rehabilitation Center asked me to be chairman of the board; the Speech, Hearing & Learning Center elected me vice president; the University Center asked me to be on the advisory board; the Greenville Family Partnership wanted me on their board; my Rotary Club wanted more volunteer time . . . yes, yes, yes!

My wife was ready to throw me out, and my staff at work held an intervention. One morning they presented me with a "Just Say No" T-shirt they all signed. I got the message and finally realized "no" is one of the hardest but most important words in life. I began to get some control over my life by setting goals and priorities—developing a constitution of sorts—and by saying "no" . . . every now and then.

When I arrived on Capitol Hill, I found not only 534 other Don Quixotes; I also found hundreds of congressmen and senators who couldn't say "no." They subscribed to no constitution limiting what they could do or how much they could spend. This addiction was made inexorably worse by the fact that, unlike individuals, they were not limited by time or money. More federal programs simply meant more federal workers. More federal spending just meant more borrowed money from a credit line with an unlimited number of blank checks.

Once the Constitution is put away with the Bibles members use to swear to protect and defend it, the restraints on government spending and good intentions are completely eliminated. Saying "yes" becomes the means for personal fulfillment, public praise, and reelection for members of Congress and the president. Judges lose all sense of foundational principles and give their "opinions." The people respond with disrespect and disregard for our laws and the people who make them, even when they are the beneficiaries of government largesse.

> The law has been perverted by the influence of
> two entirely different causes: stupid greed and
> false philanthropy.[3] —Frederic Bastiat

The Basis for Legitimate Government and Law

Frederic Bastiat (1801–1850), a Frenchman who wrote *The Law* in 1848 when France was rapidly turning to complete socialism, explained the fallacies of socialism and how it must inevitably degenerate into communism. These same socialist-leaning ideas and plans have been adopted by many of America's political and academic elites. I will use a number of excerpts from *The Law* because, speaking from more than 150 years in the past, Bastiat provides a clear case for legitimate government and the importance of the rule of law.

> If every person has the right to defend—even by force—his person, his liberty, and his property, then it follows that a group of men have the right to organize and support a common force to protect these rights constantly. Thus the principle of collective right—its reason for existing, its lawfulness—is based on individual right. . . . Since an individual cannot lawfully use force against the person, liberty, or property of another individual, then the common force—for the same reason— cannot lawfully be used to destroy the person, liberty, or property of individuals or groups. . . . If this is true, then nothing can be more evident than this: The law is the organization of the natural right of lawful defense. It is the substitution of a common force for individual forces. And this common force is to do only what the individual forces have a natural and lawful right to do: to protect persons, liberties, and properties; to maintain the right of each, and to cause justice to reign over us all.[4]

People can only satisfy their wants and needs by "ceaseless labor" and by continuously applying all their energies and capabilities toward the development of wealth . . . unless they can live on the wealth created by others.[5] An economic system based on individuals working to increase their own wealth and social standing will continue to grow and progress.

Nations that keep their focus on defense and the development of the capabilities of individual citizens will thrive.

Conversely nations that use government as an instrument to redistribute wealth, or legal plunder as Bastiat described it, cultivate their own economic and moral destruction. When the law is converted into an "instrument of plunder," it becomes arbitrary and loses its moral authority. "When law and morality contradict each other, the citizen has the cruel alternative of either losing his moral sense or losing his respect for the law."[6]

I am not making a case against charity and compassion. Quite the opposite, government redistribution of wealth actually destroys the positive impulses and outcomes of voluntary charity. Instead of every American sharing some responsibility to help those less fortunate, that responsibility is shifted to only the richest citizens who are vilified for their success (they have to be vilified to justify taking their property). Instead of gratitude, the beneficiaries of government charity develop a sense of entitlement. They come to believe they have a right to government beneficence, instead of a responsibility to work for their own sustenance.

Government charity extinguishes the productive incentives and motivations to improve oneself and achieve ones own wealth and standing in society. Despite the trillions of dollars "redistributed" by government since the inception of America's progressive tax code and welfare programs, there are more poor Americans than ever before. Even worse, the cultural deterioration and breakdown of the family caused by perverse "charitable" government incentives have created a large population of Americans who lack many of the values and skills to succeed . . . even when plentiful opportunities exist.

I find it amazing that what Bastiat wrote in France more than 150 years ago is so relevant to America today. He makes a good case that, despite the best intentions of government officials, the law should not be used as an instrument to achieve charitable or social ends. Once the law becomes a flexible tool for social ends, it is no longer respectable or legitimate.

Now, legal plunder can be committed in an infinite number of ways. Thus we have an infinite number of plans for organizing it: tariffs, protection, benefits, subsidies, encouragements, progressive taxation, public schools, guaranteed jobs, guaranteed profits, minimum wages, a right to relief, a right to the tools of labor, free credit, and so on, and so on. All these plans as a whole—with their common aim of legal plunder—constitute socialism.[7]

You say: "There are persons who have no money," and you turn to the law. But the law is not a breast that fills itself with milk. . . . Nothing can enter the public treasury for the benefit of one citizen or one class unless other citizens and other classes have been forced to send it in.[8] —Frederic Bastiat

---

Socialists Use the Law to Shape Society in Their Own Image

We would all like to shape our society to eliminate injustice, suffering, sickness, discrimination, and poverty. Elected officials respond to this innate aspiration in one of two ways. If we believe this perfected society will never exist this side of heaven—but that individuals, families, churches, and voluntary efforts are the best way to move toward these goals—we will support laws that protect and promote freedom. If, however, we believe government can achieve these goals, we will use government and the law to attempt to manage society and force these outcomes.

The question is not which politicians are the most compassionate. The relevant question is which politicians understand what really works and which policies can best achieve the optimal societal conditions for the maximum number of citizens. All the evidence from world and American history confirms that freedom solutions are far superior to government solutions; freedom solutions do not create perfection, but they have proven superior to government alternatives.

Secular socialists attempt to use the law and the process of lawmaking to shape society into their image of justice and equality. They justify themselves when taking freedom from individuals and shifting power to the government with an emotional appeal that "something needs to be done." They assume government is the only means to that end. Theirs is a high moral calling, and those who oppose them are insensitive and intolerant. Their problem is they confuse the roles of government and a free society.

> Socialism, like the ancient ideas from which it springs, confuses the distinction between government and society. As a result of this, every time we object to a thing being done by government, the socialists conclude that we object to its being done at all. . . . We disapprove of state education. Then the socialists say that we are opposed to any education. We object to a state religion. Then the socialists say that we want no religion at all. We object to a state-enforced equality. Then they say that we are against equality. And so on, and so on. It is as if the socialists were to accuse us of not wanting persons to eat because we do not want the state to raise grain.[9]

Socialists also justify themselves with the belief that the legislative and judicial processes legitimize their actions. If Congress debates and passes a law creating another government program, legislators have fulfilled their constitutional duty . . . right? Wrong! Not if the legislation violates constitutional limits. The road to socialism is paved with laws and court rulings. As Bastiat writes:

> But it is upon the law that socialism itself relies. Socialists desire to practice legal plunder, not illegal plunder. Socialists, like all other monopolists, desire to make the law their own weapon.[10]

Since the law organizes justice, socialists assume it should also be used to organize labor, management, economics, education, health care, charity, families, and even religion. They do not understand that government cannot organize societal functions without destroying justice and freedom. In order for them to direct these nongovernment activities, the government must control individuals, personal property, and private institutions. This is not freedom; it's socialism.[11]

Once politicians believe it is their job to help the poor, educate the children, heal the sick, create the jobs, shape the beliefs, and address every problem in society; they cease to use the law as a framework for freedom. They minimize the role of personal responsibility, families, churches, businesses, and community organizations. They cease to develop laws and regulations that encourage freedom-focused solutions to solve problems and advance society. They attempt to make government the solution to problems rather than an instrument of justice.

> When a politician views society from the seclusion of his
> office, he is struck by the spectacle of the inequality that he sees.
> He deplores the deprivations which are the lot of so many of
> our brothers, deprivations which appear to be even sadder when
> contrasted with luxury and wealth.[12]

It is difficult for elected officials to accept the fact government cannot eliminate sorrow, sickness, ignorance, joblessness, bigotry, inequity, and other societal problems. The list of failures and unintended consequences of government's compassionate attempts to manage society could fill several books. Certainly, government must attempt to be a backstop when society fails to keep helpless individuals and families from falling through the cracks. But the first recourse of government must be to make freedom work and to minimize government intrusion into societal functions.

> Since all persons seek well-being and perfection, would
> not a condition of justice be sufficient to cause the greatest

efforts toward progress, and the greatest possible equality that is compatible with individual responsibility? Would not this be in accord with the concept of individual responsibility which God has willed in order that mankind may have the choice between vice and virtue, and the resulting punishment and reward?

But the politician never gives this a thought. His mind turns to organizations, combinations, and arrangements—legal or apparently legal. He attempts to remedy the evil by increasing and perpetuating the very thing that caused the evil in the first place: legal plunder.[13]

Let me be clear; I would also like to heal the sick, educate children, create the best jobs, stop discrimination of all kinds, and create better lives for everyone. As a private citizen, I worked countless hours to do just that. And along with an army of volunteers in my hometown, we helped a lot of people and improved the quality of life for many throughout our community.

But I am fully convinced, as were the framers of the Constitution, that government is wholly incapable of accomplishing these societal aspirations. In fact, virtually all government attempts to organize societal functions for specific outcomes have resulted in more harm than good. That's why America's founders focused on limiting government; believing that maximum societal progress would occur through free, nongovernment institutions.

For example, federal, state, and local tax laws can encourage individual and local assistance to the poor by not taxing money spent to assist the poor. Under the current tax system, this is often accomplished through tax deductions, the elimination of state sales taxes for charitable expenditures, and local property tax waivers.

In this case the government is not attempting to control the outcome but to encourage constructive behavior by lowering the cost of voluntary activities that benefit society as a whole. The people are free to decide what activities work best. I have seen this approach work, resulting in many local partnerships between business groups, churches, community groups, hospitals, and local governments. This is a "freedom solution." The results are almost always good but never perfect.

The socialist-leaning politician needs only to find one person who is not properly served by this voluntary charity model to justify replacing it with a new government program. I have seen a federal government agency set up shop across the street from a community group headquartered in an inner-city church. The agency couldn't work with the established community partnership because it was headquartered in a church and that would be a violation of the "separation of church and state." So they carried on their paperwork alone without accomplishing anything . . . except to salve the consciences of well-intended politicians who voted for the program.

The law cannot force someone to love his neighbor, but it can punish him if he hurts his neighbor. The law must attempt to stop the bad, but it cannot use the force of government to do good without diminishing freedom and justice.

Government should encourage all kinds of constructive voluntary behaviors and organizations throughout society and ensure that safety nets are in place for those who cannot help themselves and are not helped by voluntary efforts. But law is an instrument of force that should be used sparingly. As Bastiat writes:

> Please understand that I do not dispute their right to invent social combinations, to advertise them, to advocate them, and to try them upon themselves, at their own expense and risk. But I do dispute their right to impose these plans upon us by law—by force—and to compel us to pay for them with our taxes. . . . But the organizers desire access to the tax funds and to the power of the law in order to carry out their plans. In addition to being oppressive and unjust, this desire also implies the fatal supposition that the organizer is infallible and mankind is incompetent.[14]

Freedom and the Rule of Law

When law attempts to orchestrate a social good or reshape the nature of mankind, it undertakes a goal proven throughout history to be impossible. Jean-Jacques Rousseau, a Swiss-born Frenchman, was one of the first modern writers to seriously attack the institution of private property and, therefore, is considered a forbearer of modern socialism and communism. Rousseau believed the state should shape the individual and society but admitted it was a difficult task:

> He who would dare to undertake the political creation of
> a people ought to believe that he can, in a manner of speaking,
> transform human nature; transform each individual—who, by
> himself, is a solitary and perfect whole—into a mere part of a
> greater whole from which the individual will henceforth receive
> his life and being. Thus the person who would undertake the
> political creation of a people should believe in his ability to alter
> man's constitution; to strengthen it; to substitute for the physical
> and independent existence received from nature, an existence
> which is partial and moral. In short, the would-be creator of
> political man must remove man's own forces and endow him
> with others that are naturally alien to him.[15]

Rousseau believed the government could do what only God and a free people can do. The substitution of the "state" for God is the foundation of secular socialism. Secularism, for this reason, is central to the socialist agenda; it substitutes external government values for internal, religious-based personal values. Under socialism, government becomes the moral agent to correct injustices caused by the inherent weaknesses and differences in mankind. But "equalizing" millions of different individuals is impossible and attempting to do it is a never-ending process that continuously expands government and leads to the loss of freedom and individuality.

Ultimately Americans must decide, as Hayek writes, "between a system where it is the will of a few persons that decides who is to get what and one where it depends at least partly on the ability and enterprise of the people concerned and partly on unforeseeable circumstances."[16]

> The idea that there is no limit to the powers of the legislator is in part a result of popular sovereignty and democratic government. It has been strengthened by the belief that, so long as all actions of the state are duly authorized by legislation, the Rule of Law will be preserved. But this is completely to misconceive the meaning of the Rule of Law.[17] —Friedrich Hayek

The Constitutional Foundation of Law and Freedom

Government should be a natural extension of individual rights, a collective pact that protects the individual and provides necessary societal services that cannot be accomplished by individuals or private institutions. A police force would seem to be a natural responsibility of government because it is an extension of the individual's right to protect himself and his property. Facilitating the building of roads and bridges might be another legitimate function of government.

But who is to say what are the legitimate functions of government? Who is to say which functions should be the responsibilities of the different levels of government: federal, state, and local? Should this be decided by the legislatures at the state level or by Congress? Should the functions of government constantly change to adapt to the changing needs of society? In America these decisions are determined in advance by the Constitution.

Virtually every doctrine, value, institutional development, and painful lesson gleaned through all the centuries since Magna Carta converged on the Statehouse in Philadelphia in the summer of 1787. Here were combined the notions of the law above the king, the need to impose restraints on power, the wisdom of diffusing authority instead of having it focused in one center, that were the chief political doctrines of the free society, annealed and tested in the fires of battle.[18]

Legitimate government must be restrained by fixed boundaries made clear to citizens and legislators in advance. That is why every congressman, senator, president, Supreme Court justice, all federal officers and military officers swear an oath to defend and protect the Constitution. None of them swear to do what they think is best! They swear to govern within the boundaries of the Constitution. Without adherence to a constitution, laws and lawmaking become completely arbitrary. Our founders referred to arbitrary laws as the "rule of men."

Law is justice. And it is under the law of justice—under the reign of right; under the influence of liberty, safety, stability, and responsibility—that every person will attain his real worth and the true dignity of his being. It is only under this law of justice that mankind will achieve—slowly, no doubt, but certainly—God's design for the orderly and peaceful progress of humanity.[19] —Frederic Bastiat

---

The U.S. Constitution limits the role of the federal government to a few areas: national defense; economic facilitation such as a standard currency, ports and maritime commerce, and the regulation of interstate commerce; federal roads (referred to as postal roads in the Constitution); and a justice system made up of the Supreme Court and lower federal courts. Most Americans would be surprised to find that the Constitution does not prescribe any federal role for education, health care, retirement pensions, disability, unemployment insurance, flood insurance, labor relations, farm assistance, or welfare for the poor . . . or for most current activities of the federal government.

Presidents, congressmen, senators, and the courts have gradually expanded the federal role based on their individual understanding of the "general welfare" phrase used in the Constitution. Almost anything can be argued to be good for the general welfare. A federally funded bridge in my hometown is good for the entire nation. Federal support and regulation of schools throughout the nation is good for everyone (even though state constitutions require them to provide education for their children). Everyone needs health care, so the federal government must guarantee it and prescribe how it is provided. Farmers often need assistance, and helping farmers is good for the nation as a whole. And on and on. Every federal action can be interpreted as being good for the "general welfare."

The Constitution is the only restraint on federal power and control. Most of the organizational principles in the Constitution are still in force. The "process" aspects of the Constitution are generally followed today. These include how the executive, legislative, and judicial branches interact; how elections and appointments are conducted; how legislation is developed and passed; and how the Constitution is amended.

But the most important parts of the Constitution—the limits on federal power—are generally ignored or reinterpreted. I discussed some of the violation of these limits in an earlier chapter, but the issue is of such supreme importance I will revisit it briefly. Article I, Section 8 of the Constitution is referred to as the "enumerated powers" of the federal government. It begins as follows:

> The Congress shall have power to lay and collect taxes,
> duties, imposts and excises, to pay the debts and provide for the
> common defence and general welfare of the United States; but
> all duties, imports and excises shall be uniform throughout the
> United States.

The "taxes" conceived by the framers were transactional taxes, what we would refer to today as sales taxes, tariffs, or usage taxes. Taxes on any property, including income and business taxes, were considered abominable to the men who wrote the Constitution. There were no federal income taxes for more than one hundred years after the Constitution was ratified. As late as 1895, the Supreme Court ruled that a federal income tax was unconstitutional. It took a "financial crisis" (sound familiar?) in 1913 to finally convince Americans to ratify the 16th Amendment that allowed the federal government to tax income and profits.

The first income tax was 1 percent of all income more than $3,000, and politicians assured the people the tax would never exceed a few percentage points. The framers avoided income taxes because they knew taxes on personal property would quickly become discriminatory and a means of confiscating wealth. Transactional taxes are "blind" to any preferences and simplify the tax code by keeping it singularly focused on raising revenues rather than shaping society.

The framers' view of "general welfare" was constrained by their conviction that federal action should show no preference to persons or states. The words of the Constitution make it clear they believed federal laws should be uniform and generally applied throughout the United States. They would be appalled at federal laws and programs today that target specific groups and by Congress's appropriation of funds through thousands of special-interest earmarks that have no federal relevance.

President Barack Obama, like many of today's political leaders, views the Constitution as a flexible document that should be reinterpreted by the courts. In a radio interview in 2001, Obama made it clear he believed the Constitution failed to direct the government to fulfill a social agenda.

> I think we can say that the Constitution reflected an
> enormous blind spot in this culture that carries on until this
> day, and the framers had that same blind spot. . . . The Supreme
> Court never ventured into the issues of redistribution of wealth
> and sort of more basic issues of political and economic justice in
> this society. . . . The Constitution is a chart of negative liberties,
> says what the states can't do to you, says what the federal
> government can't do to you, but it doesn't say what the federal
> government or the state government must do on your behalf.
> And that hasn't shifted.[20]

President Obama obviously understands the intent of the Constitution . . . and he doesn't like it. The Constitution is intended to limit the scope of government, not to spell out a humanitarian and social agenda. Freedom demands that individuals and societies shape their own lives and future. This is not a role the government can or should play.

When politicians ignore constitutional limits and make promises designed to win elections, voters begin to expect more from the government than it can possibly deliver. One statement by a Barack Obama supporter during the 2008 campaign revealed how the siren song of socialism can stupefy people with false promises. In a television interview after a rally, the Obama supporter exclaimed, "It was the most memorable time of my life. It was a touching moment. Because I never thought this day would ever happen. I won't have to worry about putting gas in my car. I won't have to worry about paying my mortgage. You know. If I help him, he's going to help me."[21]

Overpromising by politicians is nothing new, nor is ignoring the Constitution. Congressional spending has ignored the constitutional process for years. More than 90 percent of the billions of dollars spent through earmarks every year are not included in the legislative language of bills. They are listed in what is called "report language" that doesn't follow the constitutionally prescribed legislative process for making law. Section 9 of Article I says:

No Money shall be drawn from the Treasury, but in Consequence of Appropriations made by Law.

President George W. Bush issued an executive order in 2008 directing federal agencies to ignore nonlegislative earmarks. It remains to be seen if President Obama will enforce this directive.

A democracy without a constitution quickly becomes a free-for-all for legislative giveaways. Debt and dysfunction follow. Government cannot efficiently manage a large quantity of complex tasks, and there is never enough money when government injects itself into every national and parochial issue. Out-of-control legislatures are not a new problem.

Louis de Saint-Just, another French philosopher writing in the time of Rousseau, promoted a philosophy that appears to guide most congressmen and senators today:

> The legislator commands the future. It is for him to will the good of mankind. It is for him to make men what he wills them to be.[22]

It is not true that the function of law is to regulate our consciences, our ideas, our wills, our education, our opinions, our work, our trade, our talents, or our pleasures. The function of law is to protect the free exercise of these rights, and to prevent any person from interfering with the free exercise of these rights.[23] —Frederic Bastiat

---

The Rule of Law

The only way to keep lawmaking from becoming completely arbitrary and socialistic is to confine the legislative process within constitutional boundaries. This has proved difficult in all democracies. As Bastiat watched France descend into socialism, he appealed to his countrymen to keep the law focused on its original purpose—justice.

> Can the law—which necessarily requires the use of force—rationally be used for anything except protecting the rights of everyone? . . . Law is organized justice. . . . When justice is organized by law—that is, by force—this excludes the idea of using law (force) to organize any human activity whatever, whether it be labor, charity, agriculture, commerce, industry, education, art, or religion. The organizing by law of any one of these would inevitably destroy the essential organization—justice.[24]

Bastiat might be called a libertarian today. His view of a limited government seems unrealistic given our current state of affairs in America. But his philosophy is almost identical to the constitutional principles that built our great nation. I have no illusions that America can return to these limited government principles quickly. My hope is as Americans come to understand the benefits of a constitutional government and the dangers of a freewheeling, big-spending federal government, we can begin to limit the growth of government in the future.

Legitimate government is based on the goal of justice for all. Legitimate laws are based on an enduring constitution that limits the powers of government. Laws are not legitimate because they are legislated. They are legitimate because they are true to an enduring constitution. When laws are based on constitutional principles, the "rule of law" creates a framework for freedom.

> The Rule of Law thus implies limits to the scope of legislation: it restricts it to the kind of general rules known as formal law and excludes legislation either directly aimed at particular people or at enabling anybody to use the coercive power of the state for the purpose of such discrimination. It means, not that everything is regulated by law, but, on the contrary, that the coercive power of the state can be used only in cases defined in advance by the law and in such a way that it can be foreseen how it will be used.[25]

There must be a bright line between the "rule of law" and the arbitrary "rule of men." The "rule of law" focuses on knowable, predictable rules that allow free people to anticipate how government will respond to private actions. These rules apply equally to all and are not intended to address the wants and needs of particular groups.

> And now that the legislators and do-gooders have so futilely inflicted so many systems upon society, may they finally end where they should have begun: May they reject all systems, and try liberty; for liberty is an acknowledgment of faith in God and His works.[26] —Frederic Bastiat

The Rule of Men

I'm afraid most of the legislation passed during my time in Congress was based on the "rule of men"—designed to achieve a particular outcome for a particular group of people. This is the antithesis of the "rule of law." Consider the series of bailouts and rescues of 2008 and 2009. The federal government handed out money to particular businesses, bought stock in selected companies, created laws regarding salaries and benefits, and arbitrarily changed how taxpayer funds were used after legislation was passed. The justification? . . . "Something had to be done."

The various pieces of that-didn't-work-so-let's-try-this economic rescue legislation began with sending checks to selected Americans in the spring of 2008. Then more bailout money was appropriated for foreclosed homeowners, then home builders, then mortgage lenders, then Wall Street, then the unemployed, then road construction companies, then the American auto companies, then the auto unions. It was hard to keep track of who was benefiting from all the knee-jerk legislation. Congress was just borrowing more money, throwing it at the wall and hoping something would stick. The American people didn't know all the details, but they knew enough to be angry.

This was the "rule of men" on display, a symptom of our slide toward socialism. It was the culmination of more than seventy years of our drift from constitutional government. As we discussed before, America's pivotal shift from a constitutional republic to a social democracy occurred when President Franklin Roosevelt introduced the New Deal in 1933.

Once the constitutional dam was breached with federal government provisions of income for seniors and the poor (Social Security and welfare), and health care (Medicare and Medicaid), there was nothing to hold back the good intentions of legislators and presidents. The federal government expanded its role in education, the environment, transportation, energy, housing, and the financial markets. Nothing is off-limits and little is working. The American people have lost respect for our laws and our lawmakers.

Today not even Congress respects federal laws. This is evident in how we handle issues such as illegal immigration. The Constitution authorizes Congress to establish laws for immigration and citizenship, which we have done. Unfortunately we have not created a workable and enforceable immigration system. Instead of fixing the problem with better border control, worker identification systems, and legal immigration goals that meet America's economic needs, a majority of congressmen and senators are ready to ignore existing laws and grant amnesty and citizenship to illegal immigrants.

I led the effort in the Senate to stop the amnesty legislation for illegal immigrants in 2007. It was painful because I wanted to play a constructive role developing an immigration system that would make all Americans proud, but politics trumped legitimate reform. President Bush wanted to show compassion toward those here illegally, and the Democrats wanted ten million new citizens and voters . . . and union members. Fortunately the American people rose up and demanded that Congress enforce our laws. Unfortunately we were called "bigots" for insisting on the "rule of law."

Americans welcome legal immigrants and naturalized citizens from all over the world. But ignoring the "rule of law" in the name of compassion undermines legitimate government. Demanding that the federal government enforce our laws does not mean Americans are anti-immigrant; it means we want a workable, enforceable immigration system that honors those who follow a legal path when they come to our country. That is how we will save freedom for all Americans, including immigrants.

> Although mankind is not perfect, still, all hope rests upon the free and voluntary actions of persons within the limits of right; law or force is to be used for nothing except the administration of universal justice.[27] —Frederic Bastiat

Principles and Institutions

Let's face it; America's federal government cannot possibly do everything efficiently and effectively. In fact, our government has become completely dysfunctional and dangerously in debt because it is trying to do far more than our founders intended. The Constitution was designed to protect us from a monstrous government consuming our freedom, our wealth, and our hope for the future. We must return to the principles of constitutional government and the "rule of law."

The American people and their government must have a pact—a contract—that prescribes the powers of government and the responsibilities of the people. We have that contract—the Constitution—and to survive and thrive in the future, we must return to its principles.

Congress, the courts, and presidents unbridled by a constitution will expand government until it becomes dysfunctional. A dysfunctional government and a dependent people will eventually lead to public demands for someone to take control and restore order. This is how democracies produce tyrants.

The institutions guaranteeing our freedoms are organized on two sides of the balance scales of power: on one side a constitutionally restrained government; on the other side individuals and active voluntary institutions. Voluntary institutions include the family, churches, businesses, community associations . . . all organized with the purpose to develop and enable individuals to succeed and to serve a purpose greater than themselves. Once government crosses the line and begins to replace and control private voluntary institutions, the balance of power is destroyed along with the freedoms they protect. Freedom can only thrive if there are boundaries constraining the government and the people.

The more the state "plans," the more difficult planning becomes for the individual.[28] —Friedrich Hayek

The fact is that liberty, in any true sense, is a concept that
lies quite beyond the reach of the inferior man's mind.
And no wonder, for genuine liberty demands of its votaries
a quality he lacks completely, and that is courage. The
man who loves it must be willing to fight for it; blood, said
Jefferson, is its natural manure. Liberty means
self-reliance, it means resolution, it means the capacity
for doing without. . . . The average man doesn't want
to be free. He wants to be safe.[1]
—H. L. Mencken

CHAPTER ELEVEN

Personal Responsibility and Freedom
Liberated from Within

One of life's most time-honored traditions is the enrollment of daughters in ballet class. My wife and I did not dishonor this tradition. Before our daughters mastered walking, we signed them up and began to dream of starring roles in Tchaikovsky's Swan Lake.

I will never forget my oldest daughter's first recital after a year of rigorous training. My wife spent weeks planning a costume that included the obligatory leotards, pink ballerina plume, tiara, ballet slippers, hair in a bun, makeup and lipstick. As a dad, I was reminded to show up with roses.

We had to sit through two hours of routines by hundreds of daughters I didn't know . . . cameras flashing and videos running nonstop. Finally, my daughter's troop tiptoed onto the stage. The lights came up, the music started . . . and chaos ensued. There seemed to be only one girl who knew what she was supposed to do. All the other girls were looking at her trying to mimic her steps . . . only with a few seconds of delay and a lot of variance. What had they been doing during all those hours of training? For what had I been paying?

One of my daughters actually stayed with ballet into her teens, and I began to see the dividends from years of practice. In her last recital she and her small troupe of five girls floated onto the stage with grace and confidence. They each had solo routines, which they completed masterfully, and they danced perfectly together as a team . . . without looking at each other to see what to do. They each knew what to do. Their individual knowledge and skills allowed them to dance beautifully alone and in perfect unison.

Like an accomplished ballerina, the characteristics that lead to independence and personal responsibility must be determinately developed over time. Freedom does not work when individuals cannot be responsible for themselves, any more than giving me free rein of a stage could result in an awe-inspiring *attitude en pointe* (for the culturally challenged, that is a ballet term).

Dependency is the opposite of independence and personal responsibility. Government dependency is the enemy of freedom. As Americans become increasingly dependent on the government, we increasingly look to government to solve all our problems. The more the government does, the more dependent we become on it. If we are to save freedom, we must reduce dependency in America.

> Self-reliance is the only road to true freedom,
> and being one's own person is its ultimate
> reward.[2] —Patricia Sampson

I have always prided myself on being a self-reliant, independent person. When I started my business, I was the only employee. I bought the computer, printer, and copier and knew how to use them. I ordered the office supplies and did my own bookkeeping. And I pitied those rich, helpless corporate executives who didn't know how to find the paper clips. I once made a pronouncement that there would never be a piece of equipment in my office that I didn't know how to use.

Fast-forward five years and things had changed. With ten employees I had to delegate a lot of my responsibilities to others. I could still operate my own computer, but my secretary wouldn't let me near the copier. Our phone system was a complete mystery. They kept the checkbook locked up, and I was often heard to say things like, "Daisy, where did you say you kept those paper clips?" I had become like those helpless corporate executives . . . except I wasn't rich.

When you don't do things for yourself, you lose the ability to do them. During my first campaign for Congress, I scoffed at congressmen and senators who had drivers. I was a man of the people and would always drive myself. My mind changed following several near-death experiences while driving home late at night after eighteen-hour days of campaigning. With a staffer driving, I could spend my time in the car making calls and writing speeches. But it wasn't long before I didn't know where I was or how I got there.

After the election I walked to work in D.C. and didn't even have a car. Someone on my staff would drive me to the airport every week when I flew home. One day after nearly six years in Congress and hundreds of trips to the airport, my wife was in town, and I borrowed a car to take her to the airport. After we buckled up, it occurred to me that I didn't have a clue how to get to the airport.

Specialization of skills and delegation of responsibilities are essential to productivity and efficiency. Interdependence among capable people is a healthy part of teamwork. But when dependency is the result of an inability or unwillingness to participate and contribute, the dependent person becomes a detriment to himself, the team and—in the case of America—the cause of freedom.

> A citizenry that reaches a certain tipping point in its dependency on government runs the risk of evolving into a society that demands an ever-expanding state that caters to group self-interests rather than pursuing the public good.[3] —William W. Beach

Dependency in America

More than half of all Americans now receive a significant portion of their income from a government source. This is nearly twice the rate of 1950 when Depression era subsidies and World War II veterans' benefits were at their peak.[4] America's growing dependency on government stands in stark contrast with the legendary rugged individualism and dogged self-reliance of early American settlers.

> One in five Americans hold a government job or a job reliant on federal spending. A similar number receive Social Security or a government pension. About nineteen million others get food stamps, two million get subsidized housing, and five million get education grants.[5]

My concern about American's growing dependence on government was the reason I ran for Congress. Dependency was not your typical "get them on their feet," crowd-pleasing speech material. Eyes glazed over when I spoke about dependency. "He's boring but seems to know what he's talking about," was the highest praise that I received from my less-than-passionate supporters. My sincerity must have eventually overcome my lack of charisma.

During my first term in Congress, I began working with The Heritage Foundation to develop an index that would quantify the trends of dependency in America. Led by Bill Beach, the director of the Center for Data Analysis at Heritage, an "Index of Government Dependency" was developed that tracked dependency rates from 1960 to the present. Every year Heritage publishes an update on dependency trends in America. Beach writes in his 2008 report:

> The year 2008 will likely go down in public-policy history as a singularly important one: the year when the first wave of baby boomers began to retire. Over the next twenty-five years, more than seventy-five million boomers will begin collecting their Social Security checks, drawing down Medicare benefits, and relying on long-term care under Medicaid. No event will financially challenge these important programs over the next two decades more than this movement of the largest generation ever into retirement.[6]

The dependency problem is exacerbated by the fact that fewer Americans are paying the taxes that fund dependency-creating government programs. Nearly a third of all Americans pay no federal income taxes,[7] and more than half pay less than 4 percent of the total taxes (in other words, the other half of Americans pay 96 percent of all federal income taxes). The larger the number of dependent voters grows and the fewer who pay taxes, the less likely politicians will have the political courage to stop the growth of dependency-creating programs. The majority of voters are already more interested in federal spending than tax cuts.

> The growing realization that the flagship entitlement programs and the growing number of taxpayers with no financial stake in the government threaten to bankrupt that government has led to an increasing interest across the political spectrum in the growth of dependency-creating initiatives. Are we closing in on a tipping point that endangers the workings of our democracy? Have we, perhaps, already passed that point? Can our republican form of government withstand the political weight of a massively growing population of Americans who see themselves entitled to government benefits and who contribute little or nothing for them?[8]

The "Index of Government Dependency" measures the extent to which federal social programs have crowded out what were once social obligations and services carried out by families and family networks, churches, community groups, and local governments. Based on the "Index," The Heritage Foundation analysts have found that dependency on government has grown steadily and at an alarming rate in recent decades, from a benchmark of 100 in 1980 to 238 in 2007.[9]

Social Security, Medicare, and Medicaid make up 53 percent of all dependency-related federal spending. These programs will increase to nearly 65 percent over the next two decades as ten thousand new baby boomers retire every day and begin collecting benefits. Together these programs will add eighty million Americans to the list of government dependents. Particularly troubling about these statistics is the fact that millions of middle- to upper-income Americans who do not need assistance will become dependent on the government.[10]

To pay for these middle- and upper-class entitlements in coming years will require unprecedented levels of deficit spending. According to the Government Accountability Office, the amount of debt Americans are facing to pay for these commitments is $53 trillion—$175,000 per American. This will be an unsustainable level of debt that is sure to slow the economy and could force high rates of taxation in the future. The high costs of these programs, which will be shouldered by the children and grandchildren of baby boomers, could lead to further increases in dependency of future generations who would be more likely to rely on welfare in a slow economy, for instance. This snowballing of dependency—caused by Social Security, Medicare, and Medicaid—could send the country past a tipping point of dependency that could endanger democracy itself.[11]

Beach recommends that Congress reform these entitlement programs to refocus them on Americans with real need and to restore their original intent as safety nets for the poor. Unfortunately socialist-leaning congressmen and senators insist that these programs be universal, that they cover everyone regardless of need. Federal programs that were truly based on need would reduce dependency and the power of politicians to manage our lives.

In addition to federal entitlements, the "Index of Government Dependency" includes federal spending on food, housing, income assistance for the poor, and postsecondary education. In America's first century, federal government charity to individuals was strongly opposed because of the disincentives it created for work. Local and state governments often supported poor houses, but they were never the major form of charity. Their existence meant no one would starve, but the stigma associated with going to the "poor house" also meant people would only use them as a last resort. The "worthy poor" continued to receive help through community-based charities, while the government provided a last resort, nonenticing safety net for those who could find no private assistance.[12]

Nothing makes a citizen more selfish than socially equitable communitarianism: once a fellow's enjoying the fruits of government health care and all the rest, he couldn't give a hoot about the general societal interest; he's got his, and if it's going to bankrupt the state a generation hence, well, as long as they can keep the checks coming till he's dead, it's fine by him. "Social democracy" is, it turns out, explicitly anti-social.[13] —Mark Steyn

---

Government Programs That Create Dependency

The word *dependency* elicits images of poverty-stricken Americans who receive a monthly welfare check, use food stamps at the grocery store, and live in government housing. Poverty programs are a significant part of the dependency problem. America's welfare programs, primarily targeted at poor children of unwed mothers, have encouraged a deterioration of the family structure and contributed to millions of Americans becoming chronically dependent on the government. But dependency on government is no longer confined to just the poor and needy.

One of my sons, struggling in graduate school to make ends meet with his wife and child, was disturbed to find that one of his friends in seminary was supporting his wife and child with welfare checks, food stamps, and Medicaid health insurance. One of my daughter's unmarried coworkers, who was from an upper middle-class family, signed up for Medicaid to pay for maternity care rather than pay the co-pay required for the insurance provided by her employer. Several employers have told me it is not unusual for pregnant workers to drop their group insurance coverage and sign up for Medicaid to avoid the co-payments.

Dependency-based social programs always expand and attract more people into dependency. People learn how to beat the system. They learn how long they have to work before they can quit and collect unemployment insurance. They learn how to get signatures from employers to prove they are trying to get another job. Then they go back to work long enough to start the cycle over again.

Seniors are the largest new group of government dependents. Social Security and Medicare have forced America's senior citizens into a dependent relationship with government. Even wealthy seniors get a Social Security check whether they need it or not. And virtually all Americans, regardless of income, are dependent on the government for their health care when they turn sixty-five. Our laws make it very difficult for Americans to buy a health insurance policy they can own and keep in retirement.

Most parents in America are dependent on the government to provide education and day care for their children while they work. This gives the government control over what our children learn and believe. For the children who graduate high school and aspire to higher education, their parents are likely to be at least partially dependent on government scholarships and state universities to assist their children in continuing their education. Government-sponsored student loans are also available to help parents pay for college. Most college students receive some government support.

Personal Responsibility and Freedom

Farmers are heavily dependent on government subsidies. Bankers are dependent on government deposit insurance and Federal Reserve loans. Home builders and realtors depend on a special tax deduction for mortgage interests and affordable housing programs. Road-paving contractors are dependent on the government to pay for road construction. This list of those who are at least partially dependent on government gets longer every year. It would be hard to find a person in America not dependent to some degree on the government now or who will be sometime in the future.

All together about 20 percent of Americans work for the government at some level or receive their income from a company primarily dependent on the government. Another 20 percent are dependent on Social Security or another government pension program. When you add in welfare, Medicaid, and other programs for the poor, you are over 50 percent. Then add parents with children in public schools, farmers, bankers, Wall Street high rollers, American auto companies, doctors and nurses who get most of their income from Medicare and Medicaid, artists who depend on government grants . . . there are not many rugged, self-sufficient Americans left out there on the range where the deer and antelope play!

The notion of a self . . . who exercises self-discipline, postpones gratification, curbs the sexual appetite, stops short of aggression and criminal behavior—a self that can become more intelligent and lift itself to the very peaks of life by its own bootstraps through study, practice, perseverance, and refusal to give up in the face of great odds—this old-fashioned notion . . . of success through enterprise and true grit is slipping away. . . . The peculiarly American faith in the power of the individual to transform himself from a helpless cipher into a giant among men . . . is now as moribund as the god for whom Nietzsche wrote an obituary in 1882.[14] —Tom Wolfe

---

Dangers of Government Dependency

What's the harm with your grandma getting a Social Security check every month from the government? It seems harmless enough, but that check changes the relationship between your grandma and the government. A democracy can only work if the people are watchdogs over their government. People are motivated to restrain the growth of government if there is a direct cost to them in taxes when government grows. Once people are beneficiaries of government largesse and are shielded from taxes, they no longer have any motivation to restrain government growth or spending.

I often speak to senior groups. Those who are older and heavily dependent on Social Security, Medicare, and Medicaid are usually afraid of proposals to cut or even change any government program. The same is true for people who live in government housing or on welfare. They don't like to hear about restraining the growth of government. And when I propose that government spending should not grow any faster than the inflation rate, a lot of farmers, doctors, home builders, road contractors, and other government contractors get worried.

We have plenty of evidence that people dependent on government tend to vote for political candidates who promise more from government. Dependent voters are also more susceptible to manipulation by candidates who use the fear of losing government benefits to win elections. Dependency undermines the concept of "government by the people" because it makes government the master of the people.

> They feel like they are in bondage. Addicts feel out of control, enslaved, stuck, and without hope for freedom or escape. Something or someone other than the living God controls them, and the controlling object tells them how to live, think, and feel.[15] —Edward T. Welch

Dependency also undermines the concept of representative government by transforming elected officials into "codependents." Members of Congress who support programs that create dependency among their "subjects" are drawn into a vicious cycle of codependent behavior mimicking the mental disorder of those who enable drug-addicted behavior by loved ones. Codependency is the psychological mind-set that creates the passionate and sincere motivation of socialists to serve and shape the people.

Perhaps the worst aspect of dependency is what it does to hearts and minds. The symptoms of chronic government dependency follow the same patterns as dependency on drugs and alcohol, "Our bondage is more than the consequence of what we do. It is who we are. It is our nature. . . . It is voluntary slavery."[16]

Today the destructive forces of dependency and secularism have spread beyond the underclass across all socioeconomic lines. The social pathologies long evident among the poor are now entrenched throughout America's culture.

Men are made stronger on realization that
the helping hand they need is at the end of
their own arm.[17] —Sir Philip Sidney

Overcoming Dependency

All the freedoms and rights Americans hold dear can only be preserved by citizens who have the capabilities to be responsible for themselves. There are no "rights" without "responsibilities."

Real rights can be distinguished from false rights simply
in this, that with real rights the same person who carries the
freedom (or the entitlement), carries the responsibility (or the
obligation). With false rights—such as the "right" to be provided
with income, or to behave in a certain way—the balance is

otherwise: one person carries the freedom and another (usually everyone else) carries the responsibility. I have a "right" to an income: you have a responsibility to provide me with it.
I have a "right" to behave as I wish: you have an obligation not to interfere or complain. A real right, by contrast, enforces a restraint on its possessor, requiring him simply to mind his own business, and so to respect the rights of others. The same "fact" which entitles me to my life, liberty and property, obliges me to respect yours.[18]

The ability to be responsible must be developed by a society committed to instilling into every individual the tools to live independently and responsibly. Socialism does the opposite by promoting collectivist solutions leading to dependency on government. As government grows to care for more dependents, it replaces the societal institutions such as the family that develop personal responsibility and individual freedom.

> Without nurture and cultivation in society—starting with nurture in that elemental social unit, the family—the human potentialities that are latent in individuals at birth are doomed to be withered or stunted. Each person undergoes in childhood a development analogous to the evolution of civilization: his upbringing provides him with the cultural inheritance that turns little more than a wild animal into a fully human being with human aspirations and a human conscience.[19]

At a time when other countries have matched America in capital, technology, production efficiency, cost controls, and marketing—human resources are our most underutilized wellspring of advantage.[20] Human resource development must be America's top priority, and this development must begin with motivated individuals.

The American success story was built on the foundation of individuals motivated by the understanding that their future was in their own hands.

Whether their motivation came from faith, ambition, greed, fear, hunger, pride, or honor—regardless of its source—motivated individuals have always been the ones creating wealth and security for themselves and those around them.

Motivated individuals work and struggle to provide for themselves and their families. Work and struggle further develop the values, skills, and wisdom enabling individuals to achieve more and raise their standard of living. The cumulative impact of millions of workers struggling to move up the economic ladder created America's incredible economic machine.

When government diminishes individual motivation by eliminating risk and promising security—and when it seeks to reduce the work and struggle that develops individual capabilities—it undermines America's source of freedom. The good news is, while the damage from dependency will take years to overcome, the principles and institutions that created freedom and prosperity in the past are still in place . . . though greatly diminished. We can rebuild America's freedom-enhancing institutions as we transfer power and control from government back to individuals.

> The reason is that economic independence, honestly come by, is the precondition of all else in a nation where inherited wealth is a rarity, and self-reliance a trait with more than economic implications. The sturdy individualism it fosters is the backbone of the American political system. But this individualism too must be led in the proper direction. It must be wedded to a love of liberty.[21] —Matthew Spalding

Principles and Institutions

I'm afraid our country is beginning to look like my daughter's first ballet recital, too many citizens looking around to get their cues and sustenance from others (who also don't know what they are doing). This is not working well for individuals or the country. An increasing number of Americans are dysfunctional and unable to survive without government assistance. Our nation is hurting and appears near the brink of cultural and economic chaos.

The success of our nation and the value of life itself are closely related to the independence and responsibility of our individual citizens. Government programs promoting dependency should be anathema to every American. Yet the destructive impact of dependency on our citizens and our country has been largely ignored.

The principle of personal responsibility is essential to freedom because it is the counterbalance to central authority and control. Personal responsibility can only be developed by private sector institutions beginning with the family and continuing through life by churches, community organizations, and businesses. Hopefully, more independent schools will one day join the ranks of private institutions promoting personal responsibility and freedom.

The challenge is daunting, but Americans need not be discouraged. The damage done by bad government policy can be corrected with policy changes that reduce dependency. America must end its addiction to programs, subsidies, rescues, and bailouts that lead to debt and dependency. We must constantly remind ourselves that the more we ask of government, the less we have of freedom. The principle of individual responsibility and independence is the foundation of freedom we must protect and defend at all costs. Americans must force the government to be our servant or it will be our master.

Our self-reliant individualists must become public-spirited citizens. Democracy requires a concern for the common good, and an initiative for advancing it, to be diffused throughout the populace.[22] —Matthew Spalding

---

We have officially lost faith in the market. We have lost
faith in the source of our prosperity. We no longer abide
the creative destruction of the market process. We do not
want the suffering that naturally attends real growth. Good
things and only good things are demanded. Losses are
unacceptable, even though these always attend genuine
achievement. Everybody has to be a winner.[1]
—J. R. Nyquist

CHAPTER TWELVE

Capitalism and Freedom
Saving the Goose That Lays the Golden Eggs

There was once a farmer who had a very special goose. Early each morning the farmer would find a solid gold egg in the goose's nest that he promptly took to town and sold for a bag of cash. Over the years the farmer became very rich.

The farmer's wife was very grateful for the goose and took great care that the goose was well fed, groomed, and warm during the winter. But the farmer, who wasted his wealth on many excesses, became increasingly impatient and greedy. He demanded the goose lay more golden eggs, but the goose continued to lay but one egg each day.

Finally the farmer told his wife that he was going to kill the goose, cut her open, and take all her golden eggs. His wife warned him to be patient and wait for the eggs to come one at a time, but the farmer was now heavily in debt and couldn't wait any longer.

The farmer killed the goose and cut her open. To his horror he found that the goose was just like other geese with no golden eggs inside. With the goose

*dead, the daily supply of golden eggs stopped. The farmer was unable to pay his
debts. He lost all he had and spent the rest of his days working as a hired hand
feeding pigs, chickens, and geese.*

America's golden goose is our capitalist economic system. It has made
us wealthy beyond anything the world has ever known. Yet our excesses
and debt are leading us to demand more and more golden eggs. Our taxes,
regulations, and legal liabilities on businesses are now the most onerous in
the world. We haven't yet killed the goose, but we have plucked her clean,
and the socialist axe is at her neck.

In late 2008 the CEOs of the "big three" American auto companies sat
in front of a congressional hearing in Washington like three plucked geese.
For years government mandates and union contracts had changed their
mission from making cars and profits to providing health care, pensions,
and other gold-plated benefits to union workers. Management shared a lot
of the blame, but the fact is the government and the unions essentially run
the American auto companies.

Congress had already granted $25 billion to help the "big three" retool
to satisfy new federal mandates for better gas mileage. Now the CEOs
were back begging for another $25 billion "bridge loan" to continue to
operate for a few more months. Incredibly they sat in front of Congress
and the nation with no plan to return their companies to profitability.
They claimed they cut costs to the bone but then lost all credibility when
it was revealed they had each flown to D.C. on their private corporate jets.
In their defense the hearing was more of a platform for political grand-
standing than a real attempt to find solutions.

The CEOs blamed the bad economy and tight credit for their diffi-
culties, but facts are stubborn things. The American auto companies were
losing money several years before when the economy was at its peak and
credit was cheap and easy. They spent more on health care per car than on
steel. They had more retired employees on health care benefits and pensions than active employees. No amount of federal money could save them
until they restructured their union contracts and employee benefits. It

was my belief that a government bailout would prevent restructuring and ultimately destroy the American auto industry.

I advocated a prepackaged reorganization plan under bankruptcy protection that would allow the "big three" to restructure their entire business model and return to profitability. It is never desirable to declare bankruptcy, but it seemed to be the only way to save these companies and the millions of jobs dependent on them. A compromise was offered by a Republican senator that gave the companies the money they needed but required that their creditors forgive two-thirds of the auto company debt, and their unions restructure worker pay and benefits to match that of Americans working for foreign-owned auto companies in America.

The creditors agreed, but the union bosses said "no." They believed that President Bush would give them a better deal if the Congress didn't do their bidding. They were right! Two weeks after the Senate rejected the "no strings attached" bailout of American auto companies, President Bush circumvented the Congress and the law and gave them money intended only for financial institutions.

There was no denying the fact our economy was in terrible straits and the loss of GM and other American auto companies would be devastating to millions of Americans and thousands of businesses. Something had to be done. The question was whether the federal government should either borrow $25 billion more to prop up the auto companies for a few more months or force them to make the changes needed to succeed in the long term.

The real question was whether to let the market work or have the government intervene. The answer was made more difficult by the fact that the government was already so involved that the market was not operating properly. Federal and state laws allowed labor unions to dominate the manufacturing industry, while government regulations added costs and reduced the competitiveness of American products. These factors contributed significantly to the problems of the American auto industry. Even limited involvement by government in the private sector distorts market checks and balances. As Hayek writes:

We can unfortunately not indefinitely extend the sphere
of common action and still leave the individual free in his own
sphere. Once the communal sector, in which the state controls
all the means, exceeds a certain proportion of the whole, the
effects of its actions dominate the whole system. Although the
state controls directly the use of only a large part of the available
resource, the effects of its decisions on the remaining part of
the economic system become so great that indirectly it controls
almost everything.[2]

As the "communal sector" of unions and government expanded their
control of the American auto industry, decision-making by management
became less and less market focused. American-based foreign car companies in nonunion states (for example, BMW in South Carolina) improved
quality and expanded their market share in the U.S. The poor economy
has been tough on most manufacturers, but those with the flexibility to
respond quickly to changes in market conditions have done significantly
better than manufacturers who are strapped with the third-party decision-
making of union bosses.

We have seen the federal government's "communal sector" replace
local decision-making in public schools, hamstring private sector health-
care services, federalize local banking, socialize farming, nationalize road
construction. We now have federal intrusion into almost every business
sector. Government must provide a consistent and predictable framework
of laws and regulations, but arbitrary intrusion and subjective interpreta-
tions of regulations destroys the operation of the free market. Capitalism
and socialism will not work together.

America cannot have it both ways. We must decide if we want a free-
market economy or socialism. Mixing the central planning principles of
socialism with the decentralized free-market principles of capitalism has
not worked, and it is destroying America's competitive advantage in the
world. Using businesses to collect taxes, provide health care, maintain
pension programs, promote affirmative action, support the unemployed,

absorb the cost of emissions by cars and utilities, and pay for frivolous lawsuits is killing the goose that lays the golden eggs.

All of these functions are important and sometimes necessary, but Americans must understand that putting these costs on the backs of businesses does not save money; it obscures costs and creates inefficiencies that reduce competitiveness. Businesses don't pay for anything; they pass along the costs of taxes, health care, pensions, and all other costs of doing business to their employees and customers. These expenses increase the cost of American workers but reduce their take-home pay. They also increase the cost of products, reduce competitiveness, and hurt profitability.

How Capitalism Works

I started my business with a $10,000 loan from a local bank. With a wife, three children (soon to be four), and a mortgage, this was the riskiest thing I had ever done. My interest payments on that loan contributed in a small way to the success of the bank that loaned me the money. I bought a desk, a computer, a printer, a copier, and other supplies from an office supply store. These purchases contributed to a few retail and manufacturing jobs. I rented some office space, helping the investors in an office building to make a profit.

When I added employees, their income from the business bought clothes, homes, cars, and many other consumer items supporting realtors, home builders, clothing manufacturers and retailers, auto companies, and many other jobs. They used their pay from our little business to get haircuts, go to the movies, take their clothes to the dry cleaners, go to the dentist, buy food, and take vacations, which helped create hundreds of other jobs. We provided health insurance that supported the employees of the insurance company, doctors, nurses, and employees of hospitals . . . and promoted good health in the community.

Our company provided professional services that helped hundreds of other companies grow and prosper. Most of my employees were active volunteers and financial contributors to their churches and local charities. We volunteered along with hundreds of other businessmen and women at the Chamber of Commerce and other organizations to help create a better business environment and improve the quality of life in our community.

During my fifteen years in business, several of my employees developed their expertise and skills to the point where they could start their own businesses. The long-term impact of starting just one small business is immeasurable. Multiply this by hundreds of thousands of entrepreneurs, and you have the dynamic, high-horsepower American capitalist economic machine.

For all the years I was in business, I continued to invest in the business and took as little pay as my family could live on. For this I was rewarded with some of the highest tax rates in the world, a costly frivolous lawsuit, and some crazy regulations. When I built a small office building for our business (creating more jobs), I asked the builder to install a shower in one of the restrooms for our lunchtime joggers. He advised me it would cost an additional $15,000 because the shower had to be wheelchair accessible.

Federal tax laws made it difficult to keep money in the business for future growth. Profits were taxed at more than 30 percent so my accountant advised me every year to spend our profits on equipment, health care, or bonuses. This meant there was never any surplus cash in the business, and all growth or unplanned expenses had to be financed with debt (profits were discouraged with high taxes, and debt was encouraged because interest was deductible).

Federal laws made it impossible for me to help my employees buy their own health insurance. I was only allowed to pay for a group plan I chose and my employees would lose if they took another job. Federal laws also made setting up a pension plan for my employees too complex and expensive for a small business. Fortunately, as a small service business, my company was not faced with the myriad of complex regulations from OSHA, the EPA, FTC, FDA, and other federal agencies that burden larger manufacturing companies and retailers.

My point is this: the high standard of living Americans enjoy comes from successful businesses, not big government. The government produces nothing, and every dollar our government spends comes from profitable businesses. All tax revenues come from income taxes, corporate taxes, sales taxes, excise taxes. Every dime the government spends on education, roads, health care, veterans' benefits, and Social Security comes from successful enterprise. Government cannot create jobs and help our nation by adding to the burden of doing business in America. Elected officials in our country should wake up every day and ask themselves, "How can I make America a better place to operate a business?"

> The uniform, constant, and uninterrupted effort of every man to better his condition, the principle from which public and national, as well as private opulence is originally derived, is frequently powerful enough to maintain the natural progress of things toward improvement, in spite both of the extravagance of government and of the greatest errors of administration.[3] —Adam Smith

Adam Smith and The Wealth of Nations

Adam Smith published *The Wealth of Nations* in Britain in 1776, the same year of America's Declaration of Independence. Smith established a positive moral standing for individuals like me who pursue personal gain through business activity. He made a strong case that individuals involved in free-market competition would benefit society as a whole—whether they meant to or not.

> *The Wealth of Nations* seemed to lend a certain sanctity to the self-interested pursuit of gain, by showing that such activity was productive of benefit to society at large; by demonstrating that the enterprise of individuals was capable, when left free of regulation, of carrying the standard of material well-being to heights hitherto impossible and scarcely calculable.[4]

Smith also argued that successful enterprise and the progress of the entire social order was dependent on individuals who possessed the virtue to restrain themselves, "unfolding at least part of a Divine Plan; a Plan which is given substantial expression by virtue of the activities of individuals who are unconscious of the end which these activities help to promote."[5] Smith's suggestion that profitable business enterprise was part of God's plan to improve the state of humanity stood in direct contrast with the sentiments of anticapitalist socialists and social reformers who blamed greedy businessmen for societal ills.

Smith popularized the notion that under a free-market system, an "Invisible Hand" guided the actions of those in pursuit of selfish gain to serve the good of others. My own business experience confirms this point. I started my business to do the work I loved, to make money, and to support my family. In the process my business created a platform to serve God and my fellowman.

Because of strong competition, my success was dependent on my ability to deliver high-quality services at competitive prices to my clients. Because I had to compete for the best employees, I had to treat my employees fairly and pay them well. Serving the community was also a good way to network with potential clients. I'd like to think that I would have done these good things without competition, but the free market held me accountable and made sure I did.

> It is not from the benevolence of the butcher, the brewer, or the baker that we expect our dinner, but from their regard to their own interest.[6] —Adam Smith

Smith isolated three means of production (the goose): land, labor and capital. He also isolated three forms of rewards (the golden eggs): rent, wages, and profits. The Rule of Law must protect the means of production and not diminish the rewards resulting from individual risk and work. The government doesn't need to punish or reward business activity. The potential rewards of enterprise provide ample incentive to encourage individuals to pursue their own advancement and the progress of society.

In this context it makes no sense for government to tax and over-regulate property, labor, or capital—the means of production. This is the equivalent of cutting open the goose to get more golden eggs. It also makes no sense for government to take the fruits of labor and investment by taxing income and profit. When you tax something, you get less of it. Why would America want less production, income, and profit? Why would we want fewer golden eggs?

> The role of the State must be minimal in a system which
> depends wholly on the self-regarding actions of individuals.
> Within the framework of the competitive model, or the system
> of "perfect liberty" as Smith described it, the sovereign is
> expected to refrain from interfering with individual enterprise,
> and discharged from the "duty of superintending the industry of
> private people, and of directing it towards the employments most
> suitable to the interest of the society."[7]

Smith maintained that the limited role of government should include the administration of justice, the common defense, and public works to facilitate economic activity such as roads, bridges, canals, and harbors. He argued that those who use these public works projects should pay for them, suggesting he would support usage fees and tolls rather than large government budgets for infrastructure. Smith believed usage fees would ensure that infrastructure projects were only built when there was a need for them (as opposed to "the bridge to nowhere"). The limited role of government prescribed by Smith was similar to the enumerated powers of government listed in the U.S. Constitution.

We have progressively abandoned that freedom in economic affairs without which personal and political freedom has never existed in the past. Although we had been warned . . . that socialism means slavery, we have steadily moved in the direction of socialism. And now that we have seen a new form of slavery arise before our eyes, we have so completely forgotten the warning that it scarcely occurs to us that the two things may be connected.[8] —Friedrich Hayek

---

SAVING FREEDOM

Friedrich Hayek and The Road to Serfdom

Friedrich Hayek (1899–1992) was born in Austria, taught economics at the University of London, the University of Chicago, and the University of Freiburg in Germany. He watched the progression of secularism, socialism, and totalitarianism sweep across Europe and published *The Road to Serfdom* in 1944 to warn the world of the impending dangers of socialism. As with Adam Smith, Hayek viewed the individual as the foundation of freedom.

> Individualism has a bad name today, and the term has come to be connected with egotism and selfishness. . . . But the essential features of that individualism which, from elements provided by Christianity and the philosophy of classical antiquity, was first fully developed during the Renaissance and has since grown and spread into what we know as Western civilization—are the respect for the individual man qua man, that is, the recognition of his own views and tastes as supreme in his own sphere, however narrowly that may be circumscribed, and the belief that it is desirable and men should develop their own individual gifts and bents.[9]

Hayek emphasized that the spontaneous and uncontrolled efforts of individuals were capable of producing a complex order of economic activities that could not be managed by a central authority. Socialists argue that this spontaneous economic system produces inequities and, consequently, must be managed by government. Their argument belies historical evidence that central economic planning inevitably leads to economic stagnation and wide-scale human suffering.

Hayek documented how economic freedom stimulated the use of new knowledge and scientific breakthroughs. He contended that individuals backing new technologies at their own risk cultivated more learning and knowledge than education managed by the central governing authorities. But he lamented that, despite the obvious superiority of economic and social freedom, society was "tending more and more to regulate the whole of social life."[10] Quoting De Tocqueville he argued that democracy and societal management by government (socialism) were incompatible.

> Nobody saw more clearly than De Tocqueville that democracy as an essentially individualist institution stood in an irreconcilable conflict with socialism: "Democracy extends the sphere of individual freedom," he said in 1848; "socialism restricts it. Democracy attaches all possible value to each man; socialism makes each man a mere agent, a mere number. Democracy and socialism have nothing in common but one word: equality. But notice the difference: while democracy seeks equality in liberty, socialism seeks equality in restraint and servitude."[11]

One of Hayek's most persuasive cases against socialism was that, not only does government management wreck economies, government attempts to manage economic and social affairs wreck the government. Legislative bodies cannot effectively manage the "detailed administration of the economic affairs of a nation."[12] When government attempts to manage a large quantity of complex economic and social issues, it becomes completely dysfunctional.

> They are not asked to act where they can agree, but to produce agreement on everything—the whole direction of the resources of the nation. For such a task the system of majority decision is, however, not suited.[13]

If you've ever wondered why your federal government is so dysfunctional, wasteful, and corrupt, this is the reason. Our government is attempting to make decisions that can only be made by individuals and our civil society. We are trying to do too much. This is why you see bitter fighting, partisanship, and billions of dollars invested in winning elections at the federal level. There can be no agreement when legislation is directed by specific groups and special interests.

There can also be no agreement when there is so much at stake with almost every piece of legislation. Congress is always picking winners and losers, deciding who will receive money and who will pay, who will be advantaged and who will be disadvantaged. Power and money have been transferred from the people to the government and now the people are looking to government to solve our problems. Too many Americans now believe it is the government that lays the golden eggs, but government has no golden eggs unless it steals them from the goose.

Hayek made a distinction between the legitimate role of government—"advancing general and formal rules which prevent arbitrariness"—and arbitrary government that provides "for the actual needs of people as they arise and then choose deliberately between them."[14] Government must not attempt to meet the particular needs of individuals or groups. When it does, it destroys the principles of democracy. Hayek insisted that government operate within predetermined limits that keep it focused on the common good.

> It is the price of democracy that the possibilities of conscious control are restricted to the fields where true agreement exists and that in some fields must be left to chance. But in a society which for its functioning depends on central planning this control cannot be made dependent on a majority's being able to agree; it will often be necessary that the will of a small minority be imposed upon the people, because this minority will be the largest group able to agree among themselves on the question at issue.
>
> Democratic government has worked successfully where, and so long as, the functions of government were, by a widely accepted creed, restricted to fields where agreement among a majority could be achieved by free discussions; and it is the great merit of the liberal creed that it reduced the range of subjects on which agreement was necessary to one on which it was likely to exist in a society of free men.

It is now often said that democracy will not tolerate "capitalism." If "capitalism" means here a competitive system based on free disposal over private property, it is far more important to realize that only within this system is democracy possible. When it becomes dominated by a collectivist creed, democracy will inevitably destroy itself.[15]

> Political leaders in capitalist countries who cheer the collapse of socialism in other countries continue to favor socialist solutions in their own. They know the words, but they have not learned the tune.[16] —Milton and Rose Friedman

Milton and Rose Friedman and Free to Choose

Milton Friedman (1912–2006), winner of the Nobel Prize in Economics, was one of the twentieth century's most passionate advocates of free-market capitalism. He wrote *Capitalism and Freedom* in 1962, and, together with his wife Rose, published the best seller *Free to Choose* in 1980.

Friedman describes the United States as an economic and political miracle made possible by two sets of ideas formulated in two documents published thousands of miles apart in the same year—1776. One set of ideas was embodied in *The Wealth of Nations* by Adam Smith. The second set of ideas was proclaimed in the Declaration of Independence.

Adam Smith popularized the notion that individuals, acting in their own interest and restrained by fixed laws and internal morality, would serve the public good . . . even when they intended to serve only themselves. The Declaration of Independence launched the first nation in history "established on the principle that every person is entitled to pursue his own values." An individual making his own choices based on his own values, according to Friedman, was the essence of freedom.

Friedman also argued that the free operation of the economy provides a backstop to the centralization of power in the government sector.

When economic and social decisions are made in the private sector and wealth is held by individuals, the size and scope of government power is restricted.

The combination of economic and political freedom produced a golden age in both Great Britain and the United States in the nineteenth century. The economic miracle began in agriculture. In 1776 nineteen out of twenty workers were required just to feed Americans. Today it takes less than one out of twenty workers to feed Americans and to make the U.S. the largest exporter of food in the world.[17] Millions of workers freed from agriculture evolved into a specialized workforce that created a diversified and dynamic economy.

Friedman makes the point that during this period of rapid growth in productivity in agriculture the government played a negligible role. Progress was the result of millions of Americans pursuing their own best interests. Innovations exploded in all areas of commerce. America became the world's greatest economy, with government acting "as an umpire, not a participant."[18]

Bad monetary policy and protectionist trade policies by the government, according to Friedman, caused the Great Depression. The public, however, believed that the economic breakdown was a failure of free market capitalism. This led to a loss of confidence in freedom and an increase in confidence in government. "Emphasis on the responsibility of the individual for his own fate was replaced by emphasis on the individual as a pawn buffeted by forces beyond his control."[19]

Friedman writes that Americans still have time to make the choice between freedom and socialism. "We have not yet reached the point of no return."[20] He challenges all Americans to make their choice wisely.

> Will our golden age come to an end in a relapse into the tyranny and misery that has always been, and remains today, the state of most mankind? Or shall we have the wisdom, the foresight, and the courage to change our course, to learn from experience, and to benefit from a "rebirth of freedom"?

If we are to make that choice wisely, we must understand the fundamental principles of our system, both the economic principles of Adam Smith, which explain how it is that a complex, organized, smoothly running system can develop and flourish without central direction, how coordination can be achieved without coercion; and the political principles expressed by Thomas Jefferson. We must understand why it is that attempts to replace cooperation by central direction are capable of doing so much harm. We must understand also the intimate connection between political freedom and economic freedom.[21]

Liberty forced on a people unfit for it is a curse, bringing anarchy. Not all people are equally entitled to liberty, which is "the noblest and highest reward for the development of our faculties, moral and intellectual."[22] —Russell Kirk

---

Principles and Institutions

The most foundational principle of freedom—spiritual, economic, and political freedom—is built on the voluntary actions of capable, morally guided individuals. Freedom is indivisible in the sense you can't have political freedom (i.e., democracy) unless you first have spiritual and economic freedom. Freedom becomes possible when voluntary institutions of faith establish the value, autonomy, and responsibility of individuals. Capitalism further develops individualism and extends freedom.

Free-market capitalism is the institution serving as the catalyst for the development of individual motivation, skills, and material advancement. Capitalism can only succeed if there is a moral consensus among the people derived from religious faith. The disciplines of capitalism, in turn, reinforce faith-based morality; the "invisible hand" of capitalism causes the individual to serve the common good as he pursues his own gain.

Democratic governments can only succeed with well-developed voluntary institutions of faith and a decentralized free-market economic system. Without the counterbalances of power from capable individuals and free markets, democratic governments grow increasingly oppressive, dysfunctional, and socialistic. Socialism ultimately destroys freedom by diminishing the faith and the prosperity of the people.

> It is becoming an increasingly obvious fact of economic history that the development of economic systems which concentrate on the common good depends on a determinate ethical system, which in turn can be born and sustained only by strong religious convictions. Conversely, it has also become obvious that the decline of such discipline can actually cause the laws of the market to collapse.[23] —Pope Benedict XVI

Part III

ACTION PLANS

Commit your activities to the Lord and
your plans will be achieved.
PROVERBS 16:3

God who gave us life gave us liberty. And can the liberties
of a nation be thought secure when we have removed their
only firm basis, a conviction in the minds of the people
that these liberties are the gift of God? That they are
not to be violated but with His wrath? Indeed, I tremble
for my country when I reflect that God is just; that
His justice cannot sleep forever.[1]
—President Thomas Jefferson

CHAPTER THIRTEEN

The Plan to Save Freedom

Change Begins with Us

One of the most popular and enduring movies of all time is It's a
Wonderful Life. *Produced in 1946, it continues to be a must-watch Christmas
time favorite for millions of American families. George Bailey, the lead character played by legendary actor Jimmy Stewart, is a small-town banker and
genteel family man. Bailey's trust and generosity with his neighbors ultimately
bring his bank to the brink of failure on Christmas Eve and a lost deposit by his
uncle who had too much Christmas cheer put Bailey in trouble with the law.*

*Despondent, Bailey decides it would be better for everyone if he had never
been born. He runs through the falling snow to a bridge over an icy river. As
he climbs over the rail to throw himself into the cold river, Bailey spots a man
drowning in the water below. True to his character, Bailey jumps in to save a
man he doesn't know.*

*The stranger turns out to be a clumsy, disheveled man named Clarence,
who is actually an angel in training sent to save Bailey. When the two emerge*

from the water, the entire town of Bedford Falls has changed. Clarence shows Bailey what Bedford Falls would have been like had he never been born. Instead of a quiet middle-class family town, it had become a red-light district with loud bars and gambling. None of Bailey's friends knew him because he had never been born.

Friends to whom Bailey lent money to buy homes and start businesses were homeless bums and bartenders. His wife was an old maid librarian, and, of course, his children had never been born. His house was a dilapidated, unoccupied "haunted house." Bedford Falls was owned and controlled by the "richest and meanest man in town."

When Bailey saw what his life really meant to others, he finally realized his was a wonderful life. He "woke up" on the bridge where he intended to end his life and found things as they were before his encounter with Clarence. Bailey ran back through the snow yelling "Merry Christmas" to every person and business he passed, even Mr. Potter. Bursting through the door of his home, he cried as he hugged his children and wife Mary.

The townspeople heard Bailey was in trouble. Dozens arrived at his house and sang "Auld Lang Syne," the song that celebrates old friends coming together. Bailey's friends filled a basket with enough money to save his building and loan business, his brother arrived home from the war, and a bell on the Christmas tree rang to signify that Clarence the angel had done his job and received his wings.

We all change the world in ways we may never know. Every life makes a difference. The more we understand the value of every human being, the more we will understand the value of freedom. The fight to save freedom begins with us as individuals.

I sometimes find myself sitting in church listening to the pastor and thinking to myself, *I hope she (my wife) is listening because she really needs to hear this one.* Of course, it doesn't take long to realize the pastor is looking straight at me, not her. Our tendency is, as the Bible says, to find the "speck" in someone else's eye and forget about the "log" in our own eye (see Matt. 7:3).

As we survey the many challenges facing our country today, our first response might be to say, "Someone ought to do something." It's easy to blame the president, the Congress, the Republicans, the Democrats, or some stupid senator like me. But in a free society the best solutions are always "bottom up" not "top down." Freedom is built one person at a time.

We must *be* what we want others to be and *do* what we want our neighbors to do. If freedom depends on a foundation that begins with faith, then that's where we need to begin as individuals and families. We can't control what others do, but each of us in our own way can develop a close, personal relationship with the God who created and loves us.

Faith . . . Values . . . Principles . . .

Plans . . . Policies . . . Actions . . .

Accountability = Freedom

If freedom is based on values derived from faith, then we need to know God's constitution, the Bible, and learn to value the things He values. We need to know our moral limits because freedom can only exist within limits. We must make our plans and live by fixed principles that guide our actions based on the things we value. Our actions must be consistent with these principles, and associating with like-minded people will hold us accountable to what we believe. The values and principles of our citizens will ultimately shape our government and determine whether we will live free.

> It is essential, my son, in order that you may go through life with comfort to yourself, and usefulness to your fellow-creatures, that you should form and adopt certain rules or principles, for the government of your own conduct and temper. . . . It is in the Bible, you must learn them, and from the Bible how to practice them. Those duties are to God, to your fellow-creatures, and to yourself.
> "Thou shalt love the Lord thy God, with all thy heart, and with all thy soul, and with all thy mind, and with all thy strength, and thy neighbor as thy self." On these two commands, Jesus Christ expressly says, "hang all the law and the prophets."[2] —President John Quincy Adams

SAVING FREEDOM

The most important biblical principles are to love God and to love others as much as we love ourselves (see Matt. 22:37–39). This is not an admonition for government to love people; it is a command for us to love people. Love is not a responsibility we can delegate to government, though by working with others through churches and charitable organizations we can multiply the ways we help others. When people love one another, they create a unity that displays the love of God (see John 17:27) and builds a sense of community.

Freedom that begins in the heart and soul of individuals can thrive even in the most oppressive environments. Spiritual freedom leads to a sense of thankfulness, forgiveness, and a release from guilt. It frees us to forgive and love others. It lifts us to serve a cause greater than ourselves. It inspires us to seek social, economic, and political freedom for ourselves and others. As Jesus said, "If you continue in My word, you really are My disciples. You will know the truth, and the truth will set you free" (John 8:31–32).

It is not enough to talk about family values; we've got to live them. This means fighting to keep our marriages and families together and doing everything we can to instill biblical truth and personal responsibility into our children. It means giving time and money to our churches, synagogues, and community organizations . . . and asking less from our government.

We promote freedom when we take responsibility for ourselves and share in the responsibilities that come with being part of families and communities. We can do a lot as individuals to help our country. For example, poor health is one of our nation's greatest challenges. Are we doing everything we can to keep our families and ourselves healthy and fit? Let's not complain about the high cost of health care in America if we are not willing to live healthy lives ourselves.

Protecting the environment is another great challenge for our nation. As individuals and families, we need to conserve gas, electricity, and water. Debt is threatening to destroy our nation. Are we doing everything we can as individuals to reduce our personal debt and save for the future? Personal debt and low savings rates by Americans are among our most serious economic problems. America also needs better educated, higher skilled workers. Are we doing everything we can as individuals to continue to learn and develop our skills? Are we the best we can be?

It doesn't take a majority to change America or the world. The biblical metaphors describing individual believers as salt and light (see Matt. 5:13 and Acts 13:47) are good reminders that it takes only a few people to make a big difference. A few grains of salt can improve the flavor of a whole plate of food, and a small candle flame will light an entire room. The challenges before us appear overwhelming, but we should never be discouraged. We can make a difference.

You get the idea; let's not sit in the audience and criticize the ballerinas. We need to figure out how to make ourselves and our children the kind of citizens who can build a great country. *It's a Wonderful Life* provides an inspiring example of how one average life can make a big difference. People who labor in obscurity to overcome the rigors of life do more to build a better world than those who achieve greatness for themselves.

> Liberty has never come from government.
> Liberty has always come from the subjects of
> government. The history of liberty is the history
> of resistance.[3] —President Woodrow Wilson

A Government of, by, and for the People

As we try to get our acts together as individuals, we need to embrace our most important responsibility as citizens—to be vigilant over our government. It is not the federal government's responsibility to run our lives; it is our responsibility to run the federal government. Despite what some Americans may believe, our rights, prosperity, and freedom do not come from the federal government. They come from God. And our Constitution establishes that "We the People" are in charge of this country.

The Declaration of Independence proclaims that all people are "endowed by their Creator with certain unalienable rights." This governmental philosophy is uniquely American and is based on the Judeo-Christian belief that people are creations of God and ultimately accountable only to Him. Our rights are "unalienable" or inseparable from us as individuals because they are of divine origin. Government has no right to take these "natural" rights granted to every human being.

As Americans, it is our responsibility to shape our government and to force it to act within the terms of the agreement—the Constitution—between the people and the government. We cannot allow the government to shape our beliefs, our children, our economy, or our future. We must decide for ourselves whether to live as passive spectators or as active participants in the fight to save freedom.

> Government is not the solution to our problem, government is the problem.[4] —President Ronald Reagan

Government Policies That Reflect the Principles of Freedom

Anyone who believes the federal government is currently operating according to constitutional principles and the "rule of law" is delusional. Almost everything that comes out of Washington today is reactionary and arbitrary. We have bankruptcy laws that allow financially troubled companies to reorganize, but we ignore these laws and develop new ones based on "special circumstances." The president proposes a budget every year; the Congress debates it, then ignores any budget at all.

Businesses don't know what their federal tax rate will be next year or five years from now. Investors don't know what the capital gains tax will be when they sell their assets. Doctors and hospitals don't know what they'll be paid to treat Medicare and Medicaid patients next year, but they know it won't be enough to cover their costs. Parents don't know how to plan their estates because they don't know what the "death tax" will be when they die. Electric utilities don't know how to plan new generating capacity because they don't know what their "carbon taxes" will be in the future.

The Plan to Save Freedom

The whole concept of fixed, predictable laws is passé in Washington today. The constitutional principle of limited government is largely ignored. Laws are created based on whose opinions can get enough votes to pass Congress. Congressional leaders pack bills with special interest favors and parochial pork to guarantee their bills pass and their opinions prevail.

Our government has never been further from the principles of freedom, but we can begin to change the direction of our country if a vocal minority of Americans speak out and fight for the cause of freedom. It starts with individual Americans understanding the difference between policies that promote freedom and those that advance socialism. These are the people who can make a difference by calling their elected representatives, writing letters to the editors of local newspapers, or even by creating a Web site or blog to let their opinions be known. Some of these informed individuals will be leaders in the media, national organizations, and businesses who will challenge politicians when they propose socialistic policies.

Freedom fighters must be equipped with freedom solutions for the major problems facing America. We cannot just be naysayers. And we cannot expect to return to constitutional government quickly. Our strategy must be to develop policies that slowly wean Americans from government dependency and devolve power from the federal government one step at a time.

There are many freedom-oriented policy ideas, but I will focus here on just a few major policy initiatives that could be accomplished in the current political environment if voters rallied behind them. I am not ignoring the fight to keep the federal government within the bounds of the Constitution, or the need to force the Congress to operate under a balanced budget, or the need to pressure federal courts to protect the rights of traditional Americans. There are many other priorities such as securing our borders and energy independence that we must continue to demand.

The policy ideas presented here will support many of these goals by promoting individual freedom and by cutting federal spending and debt. The next chapter in this book lists many sources that will provide freedom fighters with the resources to get involved.

Education Choice

Because all the principles of freedom revolve around the values and capabilities of individuals, the development and education of children are the most fundamental goals of a free society. Education is not a responsibility that can or should be delegated to the government.

Faith, virtue, and morality are essential elements of the character of individuals. Our government cannot instill these characteristics into our children. Americans should, therefore, demand the freedom to teach religious concepts and to apply the values derived from faith in non-government schools, private businesses, voluntary organizations, and churches. Freedom of speech must include teaching and saying that some things are right and some things are wrong based on religious convictions and common sense. We cannot allow our government to promote immoral destructive behavior or to classify religion-based moral opinions as "hate speech."

The development of faith and values begins at home, but with so many broken homes in America, parents should be able to send their children to schools that reinforce their worldviews. Churches should consider how they could expand their ministry vision to include education and citizenship training. Faith without application is meaningless, just as "faith without works is dead" (James 2:26).

Charles Finney (1792–1875) was one of the greatest American preachers of the early nineteenth century, an educator, author, and the president of Oberlin College in Ohio. He believed every human life was valuable and strongly supported giving freedom to the slaves. Oberlin College was the first university in America to award college degrees to women and to blacks, as well as being a busy station on the Underground Railroad that brought slaves to freedom.[5] He insisted churches take a more active role in government and politics.

> The church must take a right ground in regards to
> politics. . . . The time has come for Christians to vote for
> honest men, and take consistent ground in politics or the Lord
> will curse them. . . . God cannot sustain this free and blessed

country, which we love and pray for, unless the church will take right ground. Politics are a part of a religion in such a country as this, and Christians must do their duty to their country as a part of their duty to God. . . . God will bless or curse this nation according to the course Christians take in politics.[6]

Because faith and values are foundational to the principles of freedom, the most important public policy change in America today would be to facilitate more choices in education, choices including various forms of nonsecular education and more faith-based schools teaching a Judeo-Christian worldview. To accomplish this goal, Americans must distinguish between publicly funded education and government schools. Our commitment to publicly funded education for all children is a good thing, but not if this means a commitment only to government-run schools.

American taxpayers spend approximately $550 billion a year on K–12 education; more than any other government program . . . and more per child than any other country spends on education. Taxpayers also fund another $373 billion for higher education every year.[7] Yet American graduates are losing ground to students in almost every industrialized nation.

Publicly funded education should be a priority of local and state governments. In 2005, 83 cents out of every dollar spent on education came from local and state governments. Most states are now required by their state constitutions to provide education services for their children.

The federal government provides approximately 8.3 percent of the total funding for public education in America today,[8] but federal program requirements cause more than half of all the administrative costs in public schools. Federal funding is divided into dozens of duplicative programs, and the federal government pays for only a part of these programs. States and local schools must match federal funding with local funds and then administer the programs, which always requires massive amounts of paperwork. After public schools spend all of their local and state money to fully fund federal programs, there is little money left in their budgets to address local priorities.

How can we reduce the federal role in education and increase choices for parents?

> A general State education is a mere contrivance for molding people to be exactly like one another; and as the mold in which it casts them is that which pleases the dominant power in the government, whether this be a monarch, an aristocracy, or a majority of the existing generation; in proportion as it is efficient and successful, it establishes a despotism over the mind, leading by a natural tendency to one over the body.[9] —John Stuart Mill

The "A-PLUS" Education Act

I am one of the sponsors of the A-PLUS Act (the Academic Partnerships Lead Us to Success Act) that has been offered in both houses of Congress. It would give states more flexibility to improve their schools without federal interference. This legislation would allow states to operate much like a charter school operates within a local public school system. Under this legislation states would agree to meet certain standards but have the freedom to reach these standards in their own way. Federal money now divided into multiple programs would be block-granted to states. If states do not meet the standards established in their charter, they have to return to the federal regimen.

This legislation could represent an important step away from federal control, and it could result in a fifty-state competition to create the best schools in the world. Schools in one state could learn from the "best practices" in another state. Better schools would attract better teachers, and teachers would have many more choices for professional opportunities. Meanwhile, states could use their funds to allow children to attend any school of their choice: public or private, secular or religious.

The teachers' unions, most Democrats, and a few Republicans who want to expand federal control of education have consistently opposed this idea. Central control of education is essential to their goals of central control of our culture. Those who want to decentralize the control of education support the A-PLUS Act as a simple and logical step toward creating a better education system through innovation, competition, and choice.

A-PLUS will require congressional action, but we do not have to wait for federal legislation or court rulings to expand education choices. The 2002 Supreme Court decision, *Zelman v. Simmons-Harris,* confirmed that states have the right to provide vouchers for students to attend non-government schools. This landmark decision makes a clear distinction between "public education" and "government schools." Public education does not have to mean government-run, politically managed schools.

The Zelman decision means governors and state legislators now have the freedom to provide vouchers or tax credits for children to attend any school their parents choose—government, private, or religious. Considering most states now spend more than $10,000 per year for every child in government schools, even a $5,000 scholarship to independent schools would stimulate the development of a wide range of new school choices. Innovation would flourish as investors, entrepreneurs, and churches rushed to win market share from parents seeking better education opportunities for their children.

Vouchers would encourage massive private-sector investments in America's education system. New schools would be built at no cost to tax-payers because, with millions of education "consumers" empowered with thousands of dollars a year to shop for the best schools, education would become a profitable enterprise for the best operators. America's best minds would turn to creating the best education technology and services in the world. Rather than hurt public education, school choice would increase the number and quality of schools available to the public.

School choice is the most important public policy goal in our effort to save freedom. It's just that simple. We need a few governors who will be the champions of education freedom. Once a few states demonstrate the power of freedom in education, all Americans will demand their children and grandchildren have access to the best schools in the world.

> This Road Map is built on a fundamental conviction
> that America's greatest strengths lie in Americans
> themselves—in their creativity, their productive capacities
> and their personal initiative. . . . Therefore this plan,
> to the greatest extent possible, builds on the initiative
> of individual Americans, exercised responsibly in a free
> economy and a democratic political system. Strengthening
> the role of the individual is the key to invigorating the
> society and the economy.[10] —Congressman Paul Ryan

Reforming the Tax Code, Social Security, Medicare, Medicaid, and All Health Care

Most congressmen and senators—Republican and Democrat—campaign on simplifying the tax code, fixing Medicare and Social Security, and making health care available to everyone. Yet once in office, few take the time to develop and propose legislation to accomplish any of these reforms.

A notable exception to this hypocrisy is Representative Paul Ryan of Wisconsin. Ryan is one of the brightest and hardest working congressmen on Capitol Hill. He came to Congress when I did in 1998, and he has been working on major reforms of our tax code and entitlement programs for more than ten years. Realizing Social Security, Medicare, Medicaid, and private health insurance are all entwined with our tax code, Ryan spent two years working with dozens of staff and experts to develop a comprehensive reform proposal that encompasses all of these important domestic issues. His plan is called A Road Map for America's Future.[11] In his introduction to the plan, Ryan writes:

> Currently, we are on a path of unsustainable Federal
> Government spending. The main problem, and greatest
> threat to our nation's economic future, is the looming crisis of
> entitlement spending. The well-intentioned social insurance

strategies of the past century—particularly Social Security, Medicare, and Medicaid—are headed toward financial collapse . . . compounding this problem is a tax code that discourages work, saving, and investment—and puts American companies at a significant competitive disadvantage with business overseas.[12]

It is important to recognize the difference between general campaign promises and specific legislation. As long as politicians talk in generalities like "we must simplify our tax code" or "we will save Social Security for our seniors," everyone is clapping. But once you actually write the legislation, you are open to criticism and misrepresentation. That's why congressmen like Paul Ryan or senators like Tom Coburn from Oklahoma are rare; they have brains and courage. I will summarize each aspect of Ryan's plan.

The Road Map for Tax Reform

The Road Map plan simplifies both the personal and corporate tax code. As individuals, we could choose between the current tax code and a simplified two-level flat tax. The simplified plan would tax the first $50,000 of individual income at 10 percent ($100,000 for joint filers). All income above $50,000 for individuals and $100,000 for joint filers would be taxed at 25 percent. There are no taxes on interest, capital gains, dividends, and no "death taxes" on personal estates. There is also no Alternative Minimum Tax.

The new, simplified tax code eliminates nearly all existing tax deductions and exclusions, but it allows generous standard deductions and personal exemptions. Individuals receive a $12,500 deduction, and joint filers receive $25,000. Personal exemptions allow $3,500 for each family member. This means a family of four would have $39,000 in total deductions. If that family had a total income of $80,000, they would pay a 10 percent tax on $41,000, a total income tax of $4,100 for the year. Their tax return could be done on a post card.

The Road Map plan would not require major changes in the current income tax system now collected by employers. People who don't like the simplified tax alternative could stay with the current tax system. This gives people a choice, and the total tax revenue to the government would be the same. Who could complain about that?

The Road Map plan for business and corporate taxes is also simple and fair. Instead of taxing profits as we do now, the new plan would only tax what a business "consumes" to make a product or provide a service. It's called a Business Consumption Tax that would be, in effect, a sales tax of 8.5 percent on everything a business buys. Under this plan, every business would have ample incentive to maximize profits and minimize expenses (which is the opposite of our current tax code).

Perhaps the best news for our economy and American jobs is that this plan would not tax American exports. Imported products from other countries will pay an 8.5 percent tax. This means our tax code would finally tax foreign and domestic manufacturing the same. Our current tax code taxes American exports but not imports. This is killing American manufacturing and jobs and hurting our entire economy. We couldn't be more stupid!

The Road Map for Individual Health Plans

Every American should have a health insurance plan he can afford and keep from job to job. Health insurance should not depend on employment, health status, or income level. No one should face bankruptcy because of catastrophic illness; people should not be denied health coverage because they are branded "uninsurable."[13]

Currently employers can deduct from their taxes the cost of health insurance for their employees. This is great for those who work for employers with good insurance—until they change jobs. Then they lose their insurance and have to start over with another company. Workers are not allowed the same deduction if they buy health insurance outside of their employers.

If your employer doesn't offer health insurance, you are out of luck. This is obviously unfair. Health insurance should not be controlled by employers. Every American should have access to affordable and portable health plans, and health insurance should be owned by the individuals who use it.

If the total value of the employer tax "exclusion" was added up and shared equally among all Americans, every family in America could receive $5,000 to buy their own health insurance ($2,500 for individuals). This is the Road Map proposal for health insurance. Employees could continue to receive health insurance through their employer, and the employer could still deduct the cost of health insurance from their taxes if they so choose.

Under this plan employers and associations will begin to offer portable health insurance plans employees can keep when they change jobs (you get the $5,000 even when you are unemployed). Individuals who work for companies not offering health plans can shop for their own insurance. States could partner with the federal government to ensure high-risk individuals have access to affordable insurance.

This plan includes a provision originally authored by Representative John Shadegg from Arizona (another guy with brains and courage) that would allow individuals to buy health insurance from any state in the country. Currently individuals can only buy plans certified in their state. This limits competition and increases prices.

In summary: without spending one additional nickel of taxpayer money, every American family could receive $5,000 a year to buy a health insurance policy they could own and keep, or they could use the money to pay the taxes on an employer-sponsored health plan. Every American could have health insurance, which means the cost of health insurance and health care would decrease. This is a freedom solution because it puts individuals in charge of their health insurance and their health care. It also gives every American hundreds of choices between competing health plans from all over the country.

The Road Map for Medicaid

The federal-state Medicaid program for low-income and indigent individuals is outdated and financially unsustainable. It encourages irresponsible behavior and dependency, and it is fraught with waste and fraud.

Under the Road Map plan, states can choose to allow low-income individuals to buy private health insurance plans by participating in the $5,000 ($2,500 for individuals) health voucher available to every American family. States can supplement the voucher with federal funds currently provided through the Medicaid program.

States assisting low-income citizens in purchasing their own health insurance would be developing the capabilities of these individuals, reducing their dependency, and promoting freedom—all without spending any more federal or state money than they are spending today. In fact, the cost of Medicaid for states would likely decrease significantly as the cost of health insurance and health care declines and more individuals take responsibility for their own health. This is a freedom solution!

The Road Map for Medicare

Under the Road Map plan for Medicare, there would be no changes for current retirees and those who are fifty-five and older. Those younger than fifty-five, upon reaching the age of sixty-five, would receive a standard payment of $9,500 a year to pay for their private health insurance plan. This is the average amount Medicare currently spends per beneficiary. The amount would be inflation adjusted, and high-risk seniors could apply for additional risk-adjusted payments. Low-income seniors can also establish a Medical Savings Account to pay for other medical expenses. This is a freedom solution because future retirees would be free to own and control their health insurance.

The Road Map for Social Security

Under the current system the federal government will not be able to pay promised benefits in the future without significant tax increases or benefit cuts. Neither will be necessary if the Road Map plan for Social Security is adopted.

The plan makes no changes in Social Security for current retirees or those over fifty-five years old. But Americans who are fifty-five and younger will have a choice to contribute part of their current payroll taxes into a personal savings account they own and the government can't spend.

Initially younger workers will be allowed to invest only 2 percent of their first $10,000 of annual income into their personal accounts and 1 percent of all income above $10,000. Eventually (by the time my children retire), workers will be able to invest 5.1 percentage points (nearly half) of the 12.4 percent that they and their employers now contribute to Social Security.

The Road Map plan guarantees no worker will ever receive less from Social Security than is now promised under the current system. There will be no risk to workers who choose to save for their own future rather than retire as dependents of the government. This is a freedom solution because it empowers seniors with their own retirement income that cannot be controlled or spent by politicians.

The Road Map Will Reduce Federal Spending

The Road Map for America's Future will not only make individual Americans freer; it will significantly reduce federal spending. The chart below[14] shows how the Road Map will change America's fiscal course.

Government Spending as a Percent of GDP

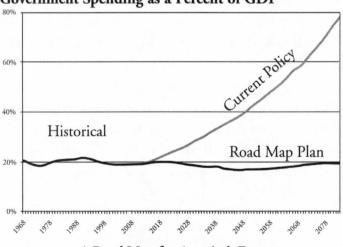

A Road Map for America's Future

Source: Committee on the Budget/Congressional Budget Office/Office of Management and Budget

Expanded school choice and the implementation of Paul Ryan's Road Map for America's Future would significantly expand freedom in America. There are many other important policy improvement ideas, but it is important that freedom fighters focus on a few bold, feasible ideas in the current political environment. Reducing government spending and individual dependency are two of the most important ways to save freedom.

One Nation under God, Indivisible, with Liberty and Justice for All

The socialists will demagogue, misrepresent, and frighten Americans with claims the changes recommended here will hurt the poor and benefit the rich. They will tell seniors that giving younger workers more ownership and control of their own Social Security accounts will threaten current benefits, even though the legislation guarantees it won't.

They will tell Americans that owning their own health insurance is somehow "risky." They will tell the poor we will take away their Medicaid, even though we are just giving them another choice.

Few politicians will have the courage to lead the way with these changes. They will wait to see how the media and the public respond. I will lead, as will a few others in Congress, but we will need thousands of other leaders outside of Washington to stand with us. We need Americans who understand freedom and are willing to speak out for the values, principles, and policies that will allow freedom to work.

We have every reason to be optimistic about America's future because if we show Americans the target, they'll shoot. The readers of this book now know what the target of freedom looks like. Please lift it up for everyone to see! Future generations will thank you for saving freedom.

Heavenly Father, we come before you today to ask forgiveness and to seek your direction and guidance. We know Your Word says, "Woe to those who call evil good," but that is exactly what we have done. We have lost our spiritual equilibrium and reversed our values. We have exploited the poor and called it the lottery. We have rewarded laziness and called it welfare. We have killed our unborn and called it choice. We have shot abortionists and called it justifiable. We have neglected to discipline our children and called it building self-esteem. We have abused power and called it politics. We have coveted our neighbor's possessions and called it ambition. We have polluted the air with profanity and pornography and called it freedom of expression. We have ridiculed the time-honored values of our forefathers and called it enlightenment. Search us, oh God, and know our hearts today; cleanse us from every sin and set us free. Amen![15] —The Reverend Joe Wright

The value of government to the people it serves is in direct relationship to the interest citizens themselves display in the affairs of state.[1]
—William Scranton

CHAPTER FOURTEEN

Citizenship 101
How You Can Make a Difference

Freedom is under assault from every direction. You might be tempted to throw up your hands in despair and say, "I'm just one person; what can I really do to help?" But you can make a big difference if you know how to stay informed and get involved.

While the mainstream media has become more and more blatant with their liberal bias and promotion of socialist policies, many groups and alternative media sources have been created to offer a more balanced and freedom-oriented message for Americans. On the following pages I have listed some sources of information I have found helpful and some ideas about how to get more involved to save freedom.

None of these sources of information are perfect, and I don't always agree with their views, but I have found their opinions and perspectives are usually based on a belief in freedom, free people, and free markets. You should have at least two or three trusted sources of information to make sure you are getting a balanced view of every issue.

This list of sources and ideas is certainly not exhaustive (I apologize to the many good sources not included in this list). Good sources of information will also change over time. That's why B&H Publishing Group, the publisher of *Saving Freedom*, will maintain and update Citizenship 101 on

251

its Web site (www.savingfreedombook.com). This site will allow you to rate media and information sources and offer you ideas on how to improve this citizenship guide.

Citizenship 101 is a challenging course: homework is required. **Step 1** is all about staying informed. **Step 2** is about getting more involved with shaping your government. It's hard work, but nothing less than freedom is on the line, and nothing less than an informed citizenry can save freedom. Please join me: let's roll up our sleeves and get to work!

Step 1: Get Informed

Television

The major broadcast networks have become increasingly liberal over the past decade. FOX News has become the most reliable news source on television.

- **Fox News:** www.FOXnews.com
- **Fox Business:** www.FOXbusiness.com
- **Kudlow & Company** on CNBC: www.kudlow.com
- **John Stosselon** on ABC's 20/20: abcnews.go.com/2020
- **Morning Joe** on MSNBC: www.msnbc.msn.com

National/Regional Radio

Almost every city has a local radio talk show. Many are conservative, but they vary in the quality of their analysis. Compare their views with those of the following national/regional talk show hosts who consistently offer a freedom-oriented perspective. See their Web sites for the stations in your broadcast area. Sirius XM satellite also provides new conservative talk show alternatives.

- **Andrew Wilkow:** www.sirius.com/andrewwilkow
- **Bill Bennett:** www.bennettmornings.com
- **Brian and the Judge:** www.foxnews.com/radio/brianandthejudge
- **Dave Ramsey:** www.daveramsey.com
- **Dennis Prager:** www.dennisprager.com

- Focus on the Family: www.focusonthefamily.com
- Glenn Beck: www.glennbeck.com
- Hugh Hewitt: hughhewitt.townhall.com/blog
- Jerry Doyle: www.jerrydoyle.com
- John Gambling: www.wor710.com
- John Gibson: www.foxnews.com/johngibsonradio
- Lars Larsen: www.larslarsen.com
- Laura Ingraham: www.lauraingraham.com
- Mark Levin: www. marklevinshow.com
- Mike Gallagher: www.mikeonline.com
- Michael Medved: www.michaelmedved.com
- Michael Reagan: www.reagan.com
- Neal Boortz: www.boortz.com
- Radio America: www.radioamerica.org
- Rush Limbaugh: www.rushlimbaugh.com
- Sean Hannity: www.hannity.com
- Salem Radio Network: www.srnonline.com

Magazines/Newspapers

Local newspapers vary in their news quality, and most lean liberal/socialist. I have found several local papers in South Carolina, however, that employ well-informed, balanced editorial writers. Compare the views of your local paper with those of the following national newspapers/magazines.

- American Spectator: www.spectator.org
- Forbes Magazine: www.forbes.com
- Human Events: www.humanevents.com
- Investor's Business Daily: www.investors.com
- National Review: www.nationalreview.com
- Wall Street Journal: www.wsj.com
- Washington Examiner: www.washingtonexaminer.com
- Washington Times: www.washingtontimes.com
- Weekly Standard: www.weeklystandard.com
- WORLD Magazine: www.worldmag.com

Blogs/Online

Some of the best new sources of information are now available on the Internet. Blogs collectively have millions of readers, and they have been instrumental in helping conservatives in Congress defeat the amnesty immigration legislation, reduce wasteful earmarks, end the oil and natural gas drilling moratorium, and defeat the auto bailout (until the President went around Congress and did it anyway). Blogs and online sources are a dynamic and rapidly changing media, so you'll have to stay vigilant to make sure the sources you use are reliable.

- **The Corner at National Review Online:** corner.national review.com
- **Drudge Report:** www.drudgereport.com
- **Free Republic:** www.freerepublic.com
- **HotAir:** www.hotair.com
- **Instapundit:** www.instapundit.com
- **Little Green Footballs:** www.littlegreenfootballs.com
- **Lucianne:** www.lucianne.com
- **Mark Steyn:** www.steynonline.com
- **Media Research Center:** www.mediaresearch.org
- **Michael Yon:** www.michaelyon-online.com
- **Michelle Malkin:** www.michellemalkin.com
- **Newsbusters:** www.newsbusters.org
- **Newsmax:** www.newsmax.com
- **Porkbusters:** www.porkbusters.org
- **Powerline:** www.powerlineblog.com
- **Real Clear Politics:** www.realclearpolitics.com
- **Red State:** www.redstate.com
- **Right Wing News:** www.rightwingnews.com
- **Say Anything:** www.sayanythingblog.com
- **Townhall:** www.townhall.com
- **World Net Daily:** www.worldnetdaily.com

Think Tanks/Grassroots Organizations

My staff and I rely heavily on several groups that research and publish information based on a conservative, freedom-oriented point of view. The following have provided insightful analyses of many important issues.

- **Accuracy in Media:** www.aim.org
- **American Conservative Union:** www.conservative.org
- **American Enterprise Institute:** www.aei.org
- **American Legislative Exchange Council:** www.alec.org
- **American Solutions:** www.americansolutions.com
- **Cato Institute:** www.cato.org
- **Center for Freedom and Prosperity:** http://www.freedomandpros perity.org
- **Center for Security Policy:** www.centerforsecuritypolicy.org
- **Competitive Enterprise Institute:** www.cei.org
- **Eagle Forum:** www.eagleforum.org
- **Family Policy Council:** www.citizenlink.org/fpc
- **Federalist Society:** www.fed-soc.org
- **Freedom's Watch:** www.freedomswatch.org
- **Gun Owners of America:** www.gunowners.org
- **Heritage Foundation:** www.heritage.org
- **Hoover Institution:** www.hoover.org
- **Independent Women's Forum:** www.iwf.org
- **Leadership Institute:** www.leadershipinstitute.org
- **National Federation of Independent Business (NFIB):** www.nfib.com
- **National Journalism Center:** www.nationaljournalismcenter.org
- **National Rifle Association:** www.nra.org
- **National Right to Work Committee (NRTW):** www.right-to-work.org
- **Reagan Ranch Center:** www.reaganranch.org
- **Young America's Foundation:** www.yaf.org

Business Groups

- National Federation of Independent Business (NFIB): www.nfib.com
- National Right to Work Committee (NRTW): www.right-to-work.org

Fiscal Responsibility

- Americans for Prosperity (AFP): www.americansforprosperity.org
- Americans for Tax Reform (ATR): www.atr.org
- Citizens Against Government Waste (CAGW): www.cagw.org
- Freedom Works: www.freedomworks.org
- National Taxpayers Union (NTU): www.ntu.org
- Taxpayers for Common Sense: www.taxpayer.net

School Choice

- Alliance for School Choice: www.allianceforschoolchoice.org
- Home School Legal Defense Association: www.hslda.org
- ParentalRights.org: www.parentalrights.org
- Students for Academic Freedom: www.studentsforacademicfreedom.org

Social Issues

- Alliance Defense Fund: www.alliancedefensefund.org
- American Center for Law and Justice (ACLJ): www.aclj.org
- Concerned Women for America (CWA): www.cwfa.org
- Family Research Council: www.frc.org
- Focus on the Family: www.focusonthefamily.com
- National Right to Life: www.nrlc.org

Immigration Reform

- Center for Immigration Studies (CIS): www.cis.org
- Federation for American Immigration Reform (FAIR): www.fairus.org
- Numbers USA: www.numbersusa.org

Step 2: Get Involved

If all you ever do is work hard at your regular job, raise a family, set a good example for others, stay informed, and vote for good candidates, you would have helped to save freedom. But if you want to take a more active role in the political process and help us reshape our government and take back our country, the following are a few ways to get more involved.

Start Writing!

The best way to crystallize your thinking and ideas is to start writing them down. I can trace my political birth to a poorly written, verbose analysis of freedom that I wrote five years before I ran for Congress. It was never published, but it helped me begin to organize my ideas. I then wrote a speech about freedom that I gave to a Rotary club (it may have put them to sleep, but it woke me up to the opportunities to shape opinions).

Write a Letter to the Editor

My first "publication" was a letter to the editor in my local paper about a controversial hospital merger in my hometown. Fortunately, I had learned by then that I needed some editorial help, so I asked a few people at my office to give me their opinions. Their criticism and laughs were painful, but they helped me write a better article. After it was published, I received dozens of calls and personal thank-you notes for "telling it like it is." A local TV station saw my letter and asked me to join a televised panel discussion of the issue. Suddenly, I was a public figure.

When my position on the hospital issue prevailed, I believed that my involvement had made a difference. This helped me see how being informed, taking a position, getting involved, speaking out, and writing about an issue could make a difference.

Write an Opinion Editorial (OP/ED)

Bolstered by the success of my letter to the editor, I began writing a longer "op/ed" about how freedom works. It took several months of doodling and then editing down a ten-page epistle. I called the editor of my local paper to ask how long it should be. She said no longer than eight hundred words but encouraged me to send it. It helped that she was a member of my local Rotary club, so we at least knew each other.

When *Freedom Is in Our Hands* was published one Sunday morning in the *Greenville News*, I must have read it ten times. It even had my picture. I received dozens of calls congratulating me. Friends cut it out and mailed it to me with nice notes. One average person can make a difference!

Create a Blog

There were no such things as blogs when I first got involved with politics, but today personal blogs are a great way to express yourself and let your opinion be heard . . . at least by a few members of your family and some friends. The process of regularly researching, writing about, and posting your opinion of issues will sharpen your views and help you find out how others respond to what you think. It's easy to set up your own blog; just use any search engine on the Web to find "how to set up a blog site."

Communicate with Elected Officials

You would be surprised how few people actually contact their elected officials, but those "squeaky wheels usually get the grease." Every letter, e-mail, or phone call makes a difference because elected officials know that for every one person who contacts us about an issue there are at least a hundred and maybe a thousand who feel the same way.

If you know the name of your local, state, or federal elected officials, you can just "google" their name to find their contact information. There are national Web sites such as www.usa.gov that can help you find the names of your congressmen and senators.

Direct contacts to representatives from the American people can stop the Congress and the federal government from continuing to push our country toward socialism.

Support Political Candidates

One of the best ways to shape our government is to actively support candidates who will stand for the principles of freedom. If you don't already know the candidate, call his or her campaign office and ask a few questions. Research candidates positions on the Internet. Don't support candidates because they are friends or go to the same church as you. Make sure they stand for freedom.

Make a contribution to their campaigns (even a small contribution will get you on their mailing list) and sign up to volunteer for phone calls or whatever they need. It doesn't take a lot of time to be recognized as an important asset to any campaign. And there's an important side benefit to you personally: the best way to learn how to be a candidate is to help another candidate. I knew nothing about politics when I first volunteered to help someone run for Congress, but I learned much of what I needed to know to be a candidate myself.

Be a Candidate

The only reason to run for office is to serve others by building a better community, state, and nation. Some run for public office because they like to manage other people's lives; some do it to allow freedom to work for everyone. I hope your love for freedom will lead you to consider running for elected office.

Being a candidate is both fun and miserable. It can be rewarding and humiliating. People will love you and people will hate you. Some will encourage you and others will try to ruin your day . . . and your life. Politics takes a thick skin and a passion to make a difference. And more today than ever before it takes a love of freedom and the courage to stand against the forces of socialism.

The Constitution of the United States

We the People of the United States, in Order to form a more perfect Union, establish Justice, insure domestic Tranquility, provide for the common defence, promote the general Welfare, and secure the Blessings of Liberty to ourselves and our Posterity, do ordain and establish this Constitution for the United States of America.

Article. I.
Section. 1.
All legislative Powers herein granted shall be vested in a Congress of the United States, which shall consist of a Senate and House of Representatives.

Section. 2.
The House of Representatives shall be composed of Members chosen every second Year by the People of the several States, and the Electors in each State shall have the Qualifications requisite for Electors of the most numerous Branch of the State Legislature.

No Person shall be a Representative who shall not have attained to the Age of twenty five Years, and been seven Years a Citizen of the United States, and who shall not, when elected, be an Inhabitant of that State in which he shall be chosen.

Representatives and direct Taxes shall be apportioned among the several States which may be included within this Union, according to their respective Numbers, which shall be determined by adding to the whole Number of free Persons, including those bound to Service for a Term of Years, and excluding Indians not taxed, three fifths of all other Persons. The actual Enumeration shall be made within three Years after the first Meeting of the Congress of the United States, and within every subsequent Term of ten Years, in such Manner as they shall by Law direct. The Number of Representatives shall not exceed one for every thirty Thousand, but each State shall have at Least one Representative; and until such enumeration shall be made, the State of New Hampshire shall be entitled to chuse three, Massachusetts eight, Rhode-Island and Providence Plantations one, Connecticut five, New-York six, New Jersey four, Pennsylvania eight, Delaware one, Maryland six, Virginia ten, North Carolina five, South Carolina five, and Georgia three.

When vacancies happen in the Representation from any State, the Executive Authority thereof shall issue Writs of Election to fill such Vacancies.

The House of Representatives shall chuse their Speaker and other Officers; and shall have the sole Power of Impeachment.

Section. 3.

The Senate of the United States shall be composed of two Senators from each State, chosen by the Legislature thereof for six Years; and each Senator shall have one Vote.

Immediately after they shall be assembled in Consequence of the first Election, they shall be divided as equally as may be into three Classes. The Seats of the Senators of the first Class shall be vacated at the Expiration of the second Year, of the second Class at the Expiration of the fourth Year, and of the third Class at the Expiration of the sixth Year, so that one third may be chosen every second Year; and if Vacancies happen by Resignation, or otherwise, during the Recess of the Legislature of any State, the Executive thereof may make temporary Appointments until the next Meeting of the Legislature, which shall then fill such Vacancies.

No Person shall be a Senator who shall not have attained to the Age of thirty Years, and been nine Years a Citizen of the United States, and who shall not, when elected, be an Inhabitant of that State for which he shall be chosen.

The Vice President of the United States shall be President of the Senate, but shall have no Vote, unless they be equally divided.

The Senate shall chuse their other Officers, and also a President pro tempore, in the Absence of the Vice President, or when he shall exercise the Office of President of the United States.

The Senate shall have the sole Power to try all Impeachments. When sitting for that Purpose, they shall be on Oath or Affirmation. When the President of the United States is tried, the Chief Justice shall preside: And no Person shall be convicted without the Concurrence of two thirds of the Members present.

Judgment in Cases of Impeachment shall not extend further than to removal from Office, and disqualification to hold and enjoy any Office of honor, Trust or Profit under the United States: but the Party convicted shall nevertheless be liable and subject to Indictment, Trial, Judgment and Punishment, according to Law.

Section. 4.

The Times, Places and Manner of holding Elections for Senators and Representatives, shall be prescribed in each State by the Legislature thereof; but the Congress may at any time by Law make or alter such Regulations, except as to the Places of chusing Senators.

The Congress shall assemble at least once in every Year, and such Meeting shall be on the first Monday in December, unless they shall by Law appoint a different Day.

Section. 5.

Each House shall be the Judge of the Elections, Returns and Qualifications of its own Members, and a Majority of each shall constitute a Quorum to do Business; but a smaller Number may adjourn from day to day, and may be authorized to compel the Attendance of absent Members, in such Manner, and under such Penalties as each House may provide.

Each House may determine the Rules of its Proceedings, punish its Members for disorderly Behaviour, and, with the Concurrence of two thirds, expel a Member.

Each House shall keep a Journal of its Proceedings, and from time to time publish the same, excepting such Parts as may in their Judgment require Secrecy; and the Yeas and Nays of the Members of either House on any question shall, at the Desire of one fifth of those Present, be entered on the Journal.

Neither House, during the Session of Congress, shall, without the Consent of the other, adjourn for more than three days, nor to any other Place than that in which the two Houses shall be sitting.

Section. 6.

The Senators and Representatives shall receive a Compensation for their Services, to be ascertained by Law, and paid out of the Treasury of the United States. They shall in all Cases, except Treason, Felony and Breach of the Peace, be privileged from Arrest during their Attendance at the Session of their respective Houses, and in going to and returning from the same; and for any Speech or Debate in either House, they shall not be questioned in any other Place.

No Senator or Representative shall, during the Time for which he was elected, be appointed to any civil Office under the Authority of the United States, which shall have been created, or the Emoluments whereof shall have been encreased during such time; and no Person holding any Office under the United States, shall be a Member of either House during his Continuance in Office.

Section. 7.

All Bills for raising Revenue shall originate in the House of Representatives; but the Senate may propose or concur with Amendments as on other Bills.

Every Bill which shall have passed the House of Representatives and the Senate, shall, before it become a Law, be presented to the President of the United States: If he approve he shall sign it, but if not he shall return it, with his Objections to that House in which it shall have originated, who shall enter the Objections at large on their Journal, and proceed to reconsider it. If after such Reconsideration two thirds of that House shall agree to pass the Bill, it shall be sent, together with the Objections, to the other House, by which it shall likewise be reconsidered, and if approved by two thirds of that House, it shall become a Law. But in all such Cases the Votes of both Houses shall be determined by yeas and Nays, and the Names of the Persons voting for and against the Bill shall be entered on the Journal of each House respectively. If any Bill shall not be returned by the President within ten Days (Sundays excepted) after it shall have been presented to him, the Same shall be a Law, in like Manner as if he had signed it, unless the Congress by their Adjournment prevent its Return, in which Case it shall not be a Law.

Every Order, Resolution, or Vote to which the Concurrence of the Senate and House of Representatives may be necessary (except on a question of Adjournment) shall be presented to the President of the United States; and before the Same shall take Effect, shall be approved by him, or being disapproved by him, shall be repassed by two thirds of the Senate and House of Representatives, according to the Rules and Limitations prescribed in the Case of a Bill.

Section. 8.

The Congress shall have Power To lay and collect Taxes, Duties, Imposts and Excises, to pay the Debts and provide for the common Defence and general Welfare of the United States; but all Duties, Imposts and Excises shall be uniform throughout the United States;

To borrow Money on the credit of the United States;

To regulate Commerce with foreign Nations, and among the several States, and with the Indian Tribes;

To establish an uniform Rule of Naturalization, and uniform Laws on the subject of Bankruptcies throughout the United States;

To coin Money, regulate the Value thereof, and of foreign Coin, and fix the Standard of Weights and Measures;

To provide for the Punishment of counterfeiting the Securities and current Coin of the United States;

To establish Post Offices and post Roads;

To promote the Progress of Science and useful Arts, by securing for limited Times to Authors and Inventors the exclusive Right to their respective Writings and Discoveries;

To constitute Tribunals inferior to the supreme Court;

To define and punish Piracies and Felonies committed on the high Seas, and Offences against the Law of Nations;

To declare War, grant Letters of Marque and Reprisal, and make Rules concerning Captures on Land and Water;

To raise and support Armies, but no Appropriation of Money to that Use shall be for a longer Term than two Years;

To provide and maintain a Navy;

To make Rules for the Government and Regulation of the land and naval Forces;

To provide for calling forth the Militia to execute the Laws of the Union, suppress Insurrections and repel Invasions;

To provide for organizing, arming, and disciplining, the Militia, and for governing such Part of them as may be employed in the Service of the United States, reserving to the States respectively, the Appointment of the Officers, and the Authority of training the Militia according to the discipline prescribed by Congress;

To exercise exclusive Legislation in all Cases whatsoever, over such District (not exceeding ten Miles square) as may, by Cession of particular States, and the Acceptance of Congress, become the Seat of the Government of the United States, and to exercise like Authority over all Places purchased by the Consent of the Legislature of the State in which the Same shall be, for the Erection of Forts, Magazines, Arsenals, dock-Yards, and other needful Buildings;—And

To make all Laws which shall be necessary and proper for carrying into Execution the foregoing Powers, and all other Powers vested by this Constitution in the Government of the United States, or in any Department or Officer thereof.

Section. 9.

The Migration or Importation of such Persons as any of the States now existing shall think proper to admit, shall not be prohibited by the Congress prior to the Year one thousand eight hundred and eight, but a Tax or duty may be imposed on such Importation, not exceeding ten dollars for each Person.

The Constitution of the United States

The Privilege of the Writ of Habeas Corpus shall not be suspended, unless when in Cases of Rebellion or Invasion the public Safety may require it.

No Bill of Attainder or ex post facto Law shall be passed.

No Capitation, or other direct, Tax shall be laid, unless in Proportion to the Census or enumeration herein before directed to be taken.

No Tax or Duty shall be laid on Articles exported from any State.

No Preference shall be given by any Regulation of Commerce or Revenue to the Ports of one State over those of another; nor shall Vessels bound to, or from, one State, be obliged to enter, clear, or pay Duties in another.

No Money shall be drawn from the Treasury, but in Consequence of Appropriations made by Law; and a regular Statement and Account of the Receipts and Expenditures of all public Money shall be published from time to time.

No Title of Nobility shall be granted by the United States: And no Person holding any Office of Profit or Trust under them, shall, without the Consent of the Congress, accept of any present, Emolument, Office, or Title, of any kind whatever, from any King, Prince, or foreign State.

Section. 10.

No State shall enter into any Treaty, Alliance, or Confederation; grant Letters of Marque and Reprisal; coin Money; emit Bills of Credit; make any Thing but gold and silver Coin a Tender in Payment of Debts; pass any Bill of Attainder, ex post facto Law, or Law impairing the Obligation of Contracts, or grant any Title of Nobility.

No State shall, without the Consent of the Congress, lay any Imposts or Duties on Imports or Exports, except what may be absolutely necessary for executing it's inspection Laws: and the net Produce of all Duties and Imposts, laid by any State on Imports or Exports, shall be for the Use of the Treasury of the United States; and all such Laws shall be subject to the Revision and Controul of the Congress.

No State shall, without the Consent of Congress, lay any Duty of Tonnage, keep Troops, or Ships of War in time of Peace, enter into any Agreement or Compact with another State, or with a foreign Power, or engage in War, unless actually invaded, or in such imminent Danger as will not admit of delay.

Article. II.
Section. 1.

The executive Power shall be vested in a President of the United States of America. He shall hold his Office during the Term of four Years, and, together with the Vice President, chosen for the same Term, be elected, as follows:

Each State shall appoint, in such Manner as the Legislature thereof may direct, a Number of Electors, equal to the whole Number of Senators and Representatives to which the State may be entitled in the Congress: but no Senator or Representative, or Person holding an Office of Trust or Profit under the United States, shall be appointed an Elector.

The Electors shall meet in their respective States, and vote by Ballot for two Persons, of whom one at least shall not be an Inhabitant of the same State with themselves. And they shall make a List of all the Persons voted for, and of the Number of Votes for each; which List they shall sign and certify, and transmit sealed to the Seat of the Government of the United States, directed to the President of the Senate. The President of the Senate shall, in the Presence of the Senate and House of Representatives, open all the Certificates, and the Votes shall then be counted. The Person having the greatest Number of Votes shall be the President, if such Number be a Majority of the whole Number of Electors appointed; and if there be more than one who have such Majority, and have an equal Number of Votes, then the House of Representatives shall immediately chuse by Ballot one of them for President; and if no Person have a Majority, then from the five highest on the List the said House shall in like Manner chuse the President. But in chusing the President, the Votes shall be taken by States, the Representation from each State having one Vote; A quorum for this purpose shall consist of a Member or Members from two thirds of the States, and a Majority of all the States shall be necessary to a Choice. In every Case, after the Choice of the President, the Person having the greatest Number of Votes of the Electors shall be the Vice President. But if there should remain two or more who have equal Votes, the Senate shall chuse from them by Ballot the Vice President.

The Congress may determine the Time of chusing the Electors, and the Day on which they shall give their Votes; which Day shall be the same throughout the United States.

No Person except a natural born Citizen, or a Citizen of the United States, at the time of the Adoption of this Constitution, shall be eligible to the Office of President; neither shall any Person be eligible to that Office who shall not have attained to the Age of thirty five Years, and been fourteen Years a Resident within the United States.

In Case of the Removal of the President from Office, or of his Death, Resignation, or Inability to discharge the Powers and Duties of the said Office, the Same shall devolve on the Vice President, and the Congress may by Law provide for the Case of Removal, Death, Resignation or Inability, both of the President and Vice President, declaring what Officer shall then act as President, and such Officer shall act accordingly, until the Disability be removed, or a President shall be elected.

The President shall, at stated Times, receive for his Services, a Compensation, which shall neither be increased nor diminished during the Period for which he shall have been elected, and he shall not receive within that Period any other Emolument from the United States, or any of them.

Before he enter on the Execution of his Office, he shall take the following Oath or Affirmation:—"I do solemnly swear (or affirm) that I will faithfully execute the Office of President of the United States, and will to the best of my Ability, preserve, protect and defend the Constitution of the United States."

Section. 2.
The President shall be Commander in Chief of the Army and Navy of the United States, and of the Militia of the several States, when called into the actual Service of the United States; he may require the Opinion, in writing, of the principal Officer in each of the executive Departments, upon any Subject relating to the Duties of their respective Offices, and he shall have Power to grant Reprieves and Pardons for Offences against the United States, except in Cases of Impeachment.

He shall have Power, by and with the Advice and Consent of the Senate, to make Treaties, provided two thirds of the Senators present concur; and he shall nominate, and by and with the Advice and Consent of the Senate, shall appoint Ambassadors, other public Ministers and Consuls, Judges of the supreme Court, and all other Officers of the United States, whose Appointments are not herein otherwise provided for, and which shall be established by Law: but the Congress may by Law vest the Appointment of such inferior Officers, as they think proper, in the President alone, in the Courts of Law, or in the Heads of Departments.

The President shall have Power to fill up all Vacancies that may happen during the Recess of the Senate, by granting Commissions which shall expire at the End of their next Session.

Section. 3.
He shall from time to time give to the Congress Information of the State of the Union, and recommend to their Consideration such Measures as he shall judge necessary and expedient; he may, on extraordinary Occasions, convene both Houses, or either of them, and in Case of Disagreement between them, with Respect to the Time of Adjournment, he may adjourn them to such Time as he shall think proper; he shall receive Ambassadors and other public Ministers; he shall take Care that the Laws be faithfully executed, and shall Commission all the Officers of the United States.

Section. 4.
The President, Vice President and all civil Officers of the United States, shall be removed from Office on Impeachment for, and Conviction of, Treason, Bribery, or other high Crimes and Misdemeanors.

Article III.
Section. 1.
The judicial Power of the United States shall be vested in one supreme Court, and in such inferior Courts as the Congress may from time to time ordain and establish. The Judges, both of the supreme and inferior Courts, shall hold their Offices during good Behaviour, and shall, at stated Times, receive for their Services a Compensation, which shall not be diminished during their Continuance in Office.

Section. 2.
The judicial Power shall extend to all Cases, in Law and Equity, arising under this Constitution, the Laws of the United States, and Treaties made, or which shall be made, under their Authority;—to all Cases affecting Ambassadors, other public Ministers and Consuls;—to all Cases of admiralty and maritime Jurisdiction;—to Controversies to which the United States shall be a Party;—to Controversies between two or more States;—between a State and Citizens of another State,—between Citizens of different States,—between Citizens of the same State claiming Lands under Grants of different States, and between a State, or the Citizens thereof, and foreign States, Citizens or Subjects.

In all Cases affecting Ambassadors, other public Ministers and Consuls, and those in which a State shall be Party, the supreme Court shall have original Jurisdiction. In all the other Cases before mentioned, the supreme Court shall have appellate Jurisdiction, both as to Law and Fact, with such Exceptions, and under such Regulations as the Congress shall make.

The Trial of all Crimes, except in Cases of Impeachment, shall be by Jury; and such Trial shall be held in the State where the said Crimes shall have been committed; but when not committed within any State, the Trial shall be at such Place or Places as the Congress may by Law have directed.

Section. 3.

Treason against the United States, shall consist only in levying War against them, or in adhering to their Enemies, giving them Aid and Comfort. No Person shall be convicted of Treason unless on the Testimony of two Witnesses to the same overt Act, or on Confession in open Court.

The Congress shall have Power to declare the Punishment of Treason, but no Attainder of Treason shall work Corruption of Blood, or Forfeiture except during the Life of the Person attainted.

Article. IV.
Section. 1.

Full Faith and Credit shall be given in each State to the public Acts, Records, and judicial Proceedings of every other State. And the Congress may by general Laws prescribe the Manner in which such Acts, Records and Proceedings shall be proved, and the Effect thereof.

Section. 2.

The Citizens of each State shall be entitled to all Privileges and Immunities of Citizens in the several States.

A Person charged in any State with Treason, Felony, or other Crime, who shall flee from Justice, and be found in another State, shall on Demand of the executive Authority of the State from which he fled, be delivered up, to be removed to the State having Jurisdiction of the Crime.

No Person held to Service or Labour in one State, under the Laws thereof, escaping into another, shall, in Consequence of any Law or Regulation therein, be discharged from such Service or Labour, but shall be delivered up on Claim of the Party to whom such Service or Labour may be due.

Section. 3.

New States may be admitted by the Congress into this Union; but no new State shall be formed or erected within the Jurisdiction of any other State; nor any State be formed by the Junction of two or more States, or Parts of States, without the Consent of the Legislatures of the States concerned as well as of the Congress.

The Congress shall have Power to dispose of and make all needful Rules and Regulations respecting the Territory or other Property belonging to the United States; and nothing in this Constitution shall be so construed as to Prejudice any Claims of the United States, or of any particular State.

Section. 4.

The United States shall guarantee to every State in this Union a Republican Form of Government, and shall protect each of them against Invasion; and on Application of the Legislature, or of the Executive (when the Legislature cannot be convened), against domestic Violence.

The Constitution of the United States

Article. V.

The Congress, whenever two thirds of both Houses shall deem it necessary, shall propose Amendments to this Constitution, or, on the Application of the Legislatures of two thirds of the several States, shall call a Convention for proposing Amendments, which, in either Case, shall be valid to all Intents and Purposes, as Part of this Constitution, when ratified by the Legislatures of three fourths of the several States, or by Conventions in three fourths thereof, as the one or the other Mode of Ratification may be proposed by the Congress; Provided that no Amendment which may be made prior to the Year One thousand eight hundred and eight shall in any Manner affect the first and fourth Clauses in the Ninth Section of the first Article; and that no State, without its Consent, shall be deprived of its equal Suffrage in the Senate.

Article. VI.

All Debts contracted and Engagements entered into, before the Adoption of this Constitution, shall be as valid against the United States under this Constitution, as under the Confederation.

This Constitution, and the Laws of the United States which shall be made in Pursuance thereof; and all Treaties made, or which shall be made, under the Authority of the United States, shall be the supreme Law of the Land; and the Judges in every State shall be bound thereby, any Thing in the Constitution or Laws of any State to the Contrary notwithstanding.

The Senators and Representatives before mentioned, and the Members of the several State Legislatures, and all executive and judicial Officers, both of the United States and of the several States, shall be bound by Oath or Affirmation, to support this Constitution; but no religious Test shall ever be required as a Qualification to any Office or public Trust under the United States.

Article. VII.

The Ratification of the Conventions of nine States, shall be sufficient for the Establishment of this Constitution between the States so ratifying the Same.

The Word, "the," being interlined between the seventh and eighth Lines of the first Page, the Word "Thirty" being partly written on an Erazure in the fifteenth Line of the first Page, The Words "is tried" being interlined between the thirty second and thirty third Lines of the first Page and the Word "the" being interlined between the forty third and forty fourth Lines of the second Page.

Attest William Jackson Secretary

Done in Convention by the Unanimous Consent of the States present the Seventeenth Day of September in the Year of our Lord one thousand seven hundred and Eighty seven and of the Independence of the United States of America the Twelfth In witness whereof We have hereunto subscribed our Names.

Notes

Introduction

1. Reverend Robert A. Sirico, "How Will Freedom Succeed?" from a Heritage Foundation lecture series delivered on April 24, 2008. The Hayek quote was excerpted from Sirico's lecture.
2. Daniel Yankelovich and Sidney Harman, *Starting with the People* (Boston: Houghton Mifflin Company, 1988), 1.
3. Andrew J. Bacevich, *The Limits of Power: The End of American Exceptionalism* (New York: Metropolitan Books, Henry Holt and Company, 2009), 39.
4. Ibid., 172–73.
5. Ronald Reagan, "A Time for Choosing," from a speech in 1964.
6. Ronald Reagan, from a national radio address on April 13, 1977.
7. *The Greatest Winston Churchill Quotes,* available at jpetrie.myweb.uga.edu/bulldog. html.
8. Alan Maass, *The Case for Socialism*, The International Socialist Organization, available at www.internationalsocialist.org/caseforsocialism.html, adapted from Alan Maass, *Why You Should Be A Socialist* (Chicago: International Socialist Organization, 2000).
9. Reagan, "A Time for Choosing."

Chapter One

1. John F. Kennedy, 35th President of the United States: www.hkweaponsystems.com/ cgibin/quote.pl?john_kennedy.

Chapter Two

1. Friedrich Hayek, Austrian economist and philosopher: http://thinkexist.com/search/ searchquotation.asp?search=millions+voting.
2. John Stossel, *The Public Trough Is Bigger Than Ever, Real Clear Politics,* May 9, 2007, available at http://www.realclearpolitics.com.
3. Eric Hoffer, American social writer and philosopher: www.worldofquotes.com/author/ Eric-Hoffer/1/index.html.
4. Baron Geoffrey Lane, Lord Chief Justice of England from 1980 to 1992: www.answers. com/topic/lane-baron.
5. Theda Skocpol, *Protecting Soldiers and Mothers, The Political Origins of Social Policy in the United States* (Cambridge, MA: The Belknap Press of Harvard University Press, 1992), 83.
6. Ibid., 83, 86.
7. Ibid., 87–88.
8. Ibid., 90.
9. Ibid., 120–21.
10. Ibid., 131.
11. Isaac Max Rubinow, *Social Insurance*, Harvard University (1916), 11.
12. Theda Skocpol, *Protecting Soldiers and Mothers, The Political Origins of Social Policy in the United States,* 174.
13. Milton and Rose Friedman, *Free to Choose* (New York: Harcourt Brace & Company, 1980), 94.
14. Andrew J. Bacevich, *The Limits of Power: The End of American Exceptionalism* (New York: Metropolitan Books, Henry Holt and Company, 2009), 67.
15. Ibid., 24–25.
16. President George Washington, Washington's Farewell Address to the People of the United States, delivered September 17, 1796 (New York: D. Appleton & Co., 1861), 24.
17. Mark Trumbull, "As U.S. Tax Rates Drop, Government's Reach Grows," *Christian Science Monitor,* April 16, 2007, available at www.csmonitor.com.
18. Bacevich, *The Limits of Power, The End of American Exceptionalism*, 32.
19. Ibid., 28–29.
20. President Jimmy Carter, "Crisis of Confidence," delivered July 15, 1979, www.cartercenter.org.
21. Ibid.
22. President Ronald Reagan, "Inaugural Address," January 29, 1981, www.reaganlibrary. com.
23. Ibid.
24. Andrew J. Bacevich, *The Limits of Power: The End of American Exceptionalism,* 39.

Chapter Three

1. Friedrich A. von Hayek, *The Road to Serfdom* (Chicago: The University of Chicago Press, 1944), 15.
2. Will Dunham, "Study Reveals 'Robin Hood' Impulse in Human Nature," April 11, 2007, Reuters, news.yahoo.com.
3. Friedrich A. von Hayek, *The Road to Serfdom,* 15–16.
4. Ibid., 30.
5. Ibid., 173, taken from Peter Drucker's *The End of Economic Man,* (Edison, NJ: Transaction Publishers, 1995), 74.
6. Ibid., 133.
7. J. A. Leo Lemay, *The Life of Benjamin Franklin, Vol. 3, Soldier, Scientist, and Politician* (2008), 625.
8. Peter Drucker, *The End of Economic Man,* 189.
9. Myron Magnet, *The Dream and the Nightmare: The Sixties' Legacy to the Underclass* (New York: William Morrow and Company, 1993), 19.
10. Ibid., 19.
11. Ibid., 19–20.
12. Eric Hoffer, *The True Believer, Thoughts on the Nature of Mass Movements* (New York, Harper & Row, Publishers, Inc., 1951), 100.
13. From Milton Friedman Quotes at www.quotationcollection.com/author/Milton_Friedman/quotes.
14. U.S. Bureau of Labor Statistics, Union Members Survey, 2008.
15. John Stossel, "The Public Trough Is Bigger Than Ever, Real Clear Politics," May 9, 2007, available at www.realclearpolitics.com.
16. U.S. Bureau of Labor Statistics.
17. Kate O'Beirne, "Cash Bar—How Trial Lawyers Bankroll the Democratic Party," *National Review,* August 20, 2001.
18. Ibid.
19. John Stossel, "The Public Trough Is Bigger Than Ever."
20. Ibid.
21. Alan Maass, *The Case for Socialism,* International Socialist Organization, adapted from *Why You Should Be a Socialist* (Chicago, International Socialist Organization, 2000).
22. Thomas Sowell, American economist and social commentator: www.brainyquote.com/quotes/quotes/t/thomassowe371250.html.

Chapter Four

1. Russell Kirk, *The Conservative Mind, From Burke to Eliot* (Washington, D.C.: Regnery Publishing, 1986), 162 (Kirk is quoting John Randolph).
2. Amartya Sen, *Development as Freedom* (Anchor Books, A Division of Random House, 1999), 18.
3. Daniel Webster, U.S. diplomat, lawyer, orator, and politian: www.quotationspage.com/quote/36327.html.
4. Russell Kirk, *The Conservative Mind, from Burke to Eliot,* 162.
5. George Weigel, "A Better Concept of Freedom," from *First Things, the Journal of Religion and Public Life,* 121 Edition, March 2002, 3.
6. Fareed Zakaria, *The Future of Freedom* (New York: W.W. Norton & Company, 2007), 17.
7. Ibid., 98.
8. Ibid., 106.
9. Ibid., 99.
10. Ayn Rand, Russian born, American writer and novelist: http://thinkexist.com/quotation/the_smallest_minority_on_earth_is_the_individual/222861.html.
11. Amartya Sen, *Development as Freedom,* 37.
12. Milton and Rose Friedman, *Free to Choose* (New York: Harcourt Brace & Company, 1980), 2–3.
13. Amartya Sen, *Development as Freedom,* 37.
14. *Psychological Self-Tools-Online Self-Help Book* from www.mentalhelp.net/poc/view_doc.php?type=doc&id=9841&cn=353.
15. Ibid.
16 Jim DeMint, Heritage Foundation Lecture.
17. Frank Herbert, "The Dosadi Experiment" from *Quotes from the Dosadi Experiment* at www.geocities.com.

Notes

Chapter Five

1. Salvador de Madariaga y Rojo, Spanish diplomat, writer, historian, and pacifist: www.quotesdaddy.com/author/Salvador+De+Madariaga.
2. Amartya Sen, *Development as Freedom*, 290, from Peter Bauer, *Economic Analysis and Policy in Underdeveloped Countries* (Durham, NC: Duke University Press, 1957), 113–14. See also *Dissent on Development* (London: Weidenfeld & Nicolson, 1971).
3. Peter Bauer, *Economic Analysis and Policy in Underdeveloped Countries* (Durham, NC: Duke University Press, 1957).
4. George Weigel, "A Better Concept of Freedom," from *First Things, the Journal of Religion and Public Life*, 121 Edition, March 2002, 4.
5. Amartya Sen, *Development as Freedom*, 291
6. Milton and Rose Friedman, *Free to Choose* (New York: Harcourt Brace & Company, 1980), 138.
7. See www.worldofquotes.com/author/Brian-S.-Wesbury/1/index.html.
8. James Baldwin, *Nobody Knows My Name* (Vintage Publishers, 1961/1992), quote from www.anvari.org/fortune/Quotations.
9. George Weigel, "A Better Concept of Freedom," 4.

Chapter Six

1. Meese, Spaulding, and Forte, *The Heritage Guide to the Constitution* (Washington, D.C.: Regnery Publishing, 2006).
2. J. R. Nyquist, "High Finance and Bolshevik Principles," *Global Analysis*, July 18, 2008, available at www.financialsense.com.
3. Ibid.
4. Representative Paul D. Ryan, "A Roadmap for America's Future, a Plan to Solve America's Long-Term Economic and Fiscal Crisis," May 2008, www.AmericanRoadMap.org.
5. David M. Walker (comptroller general of the U.S.), "Saving Our Future Requires Tough Choices Today," from the U.S. Government Accountability Office, January 14, 2008, GAO-08-465CG.
6. Ibid. All data in this section is taken from Mr. Walker's presentation.
7. Myron Magnet *The Dream and the Nightmare, The Sixties' Legacy to the Underclass* (New York: William Morrow and Company, 1993), 19.
8. Dennis Callchon, "Taxpayers' Bill Leaps by Trillons," *USA Today*, May 19, 2008, www.usatoday.com.
9. John Tamny, "Ben Bernanke Still Misses the Point," October 21, 2008, *Real Clear Markets* (Tamny is a senior economist with H. C. Wainwright Economics).
10. Representative Paul D. Ryan, "A Roadmap for America's Future."

Chapter Seven

1. Friedrich A. von Hayek, *The Road to Serfdom* (Chicago, IL: University of Chicago Press, 1944), 118.
2. Alexis de Tocqueville, *Democracy in America* (New York: D. Appleton & Co.: 1904), 290 (first published in 1835).
3. Newt Gingrich, "Get the Politicians Out of the Economy: A Recipe for Sound Economic Growth," September 21, 2008, www.solutionsday2008.com.
4. U.S. Department of Transportation Inspector General Report, Review of Congressional Earmarks within Department of Transportation Programs, Rept. No. AV-2007-066 (issued September 7, 2007), 1.
5. Ibid., 4.
6. Ibid., 11.
7. Ibid.
8. Ibid., 12
9. Ibid.
10. Ibid., 13.
11. "A Disgraceful Farm Bill," Editorial, *The New York Times*, May 16, 2008.
12. "Farm Bill Chestnuts," Editorial, *The Washington Post*, May 16, 2008, A-18.
13. "Our View on Agriculture Payments: On Good Times and Bad, Farmers Get Their Subsidies," Editorial, *USA Today*, May 8, 2008.
14. "Pork, Not Policy," Opinion, *The Los Angeles Times*, May 15, 2008.
15. "Pork Farm," Editorial, *National Review Online*, May 15, 2008, www.nationalreview.com.
16. Dave Williams, "Oops They Did It Again—Earmarks in the Farm Bill," Citizens Against Government Waste, May 15, 2008, http://swineline.org.

17. Ken Dilanian, "Farm Payments Benefited Legislators," *USA Today*, November 13, 2007, www.usatoday.com.
18. "Harvesting Cash: A Year Long Investigation by *The Washington Post*," *The Washington Post*, 2007, www.washingtonpost.com.
19. Jeff Patch, "Last Minute Farm Bill Earmarks," The Cato Institute, May 21, 2008, www.cato-at-liberty.org.
20. Secretary Mary Peters, "Refocus. Reform. Renew, a New Transportation Approach for America," 2008 (U.S. Department of Transportation), 9.
21. Milton Friedman, from Milton Friedman Quotes at www.quotationcollection.com.
22. Ronald Reagan, "Time for Choosing," from an address on behalf of Senator Barry Goldwater, October 27, 1964, www.reaganlibrary.com.
23. Michael J. Boskin, "Our Next President and the Perfect Economic Storm," October 23, 2008, *The Wall Street Journal*.
24. "Another Bubble Bursts, Subprime Mortgages Were Just the Beginning," October 24, 2008, *The Wall Street Journal*.
25. Public Law 110–343, enacted October 3, 2008.
26. "The Federal Bailout: Porky's Revenge," Editorial, *The Seattle Times*, October 4, 2008.
27. "Bailout Bummer," *The N.Y. Daily News*, October 5, 2008.
28. Gingrich, "Get the Politicians Out of the Economy."
29. Mark R. Levin, "Thank You, House Republicans," from letter to U.S. House members of the Republican Study Committee on September 30, 2008.

Chapter Eight

1. Rodney Stark, *The Victory of Reason, How Christianity Led to Freedom, Capitalism, and Western Success* (New York: Random House, 2005), 76.
2. Paraphrased, abridged from the Bible, Judges 13–16.
3. Stark, *The Victory of Reason*, 233.
4. Robert Welch, "Republics and Democrates," from a speech delivered in Chicago on September 17, 1961, 4, from http://serendipity/jsmill/welch.html.
5. Ibid.
6. Ibid., 5.
7. Stark, *The Victory of Reason*, x–xi.
8. Ibid., xiv.
9. Ibid.
10. Ibid., 7.
11. Ibid.
12. Ibid., 12.
13. Ibid., 17.
14. Ibid., 20.
15. Timothy Keesee and Mark Sidwell, *United States History for Christian Scholars* (Greenville, SC: Bob Jones University Press, 1991), 8.
16. Ibid.
17. Ibid., 9.
18. George F. Will, *The Morning After, American Successes and Excesses 1981–1986* (New York: The Free Press, 1986), 223–24.
19. Timothy Keesee, *American Government* (Greenville, SC: Bob Jones University Press, 1989), 4.
20. Stark, *The Victory of Reason*, 14.
21. Ibid., 16.
22. Ibid.
23. Ibid., 18.
24. Ibid.
25. Alexis de Tocqueville, *Tocqueville: Democracy of America,* translated by Arthur Goldhammer (New York: Library of America, 2004).
26. Os Guinness, *The Great Experiment, Faith and Freedom in America* (Colorado Springs, CO: NavPRESS, 2001), 13 (excerpts from Tocqueville's *Democracy in America*).
27. Timothy Keesee and Mark Sidwell, *United States History for Christian Scholars*, 110.
28. Ibid.
29. Timothy Keesee, *American Government* (Greenville, SC: Bob Jones University Press, 1989), 12.
30. Evan Osnos, "Jesus in China: Life on the Edge," June 24, 2008, chicagotribune.com.
31. Russell Kirk, *The Conservative Mind, from Burke to Eliot* (Washington, D.C.: Regnery Publishing, 1995), 218–19.

Notes

Chapter Nine

1. Os Guinness, *The Great Experiment, Faith and Freedom in America* (Colorado Springs: NavPRESS, 2001), 22.
2. Matthew Spalding, *The Founders' Almanac* (Washington, D.C.: The Heritage Foundation, 2002), 84.
3. *Everson*, 330 U.S. 1 (1947).
4. *Engel*, 370 U.S. 421 (1962).
5. Ibid., 422.
6. Ibid., 421.
7. Os Guinness, *The American Hour, a Time of Reckoning and the Once and Future Role of Faith* (New York: The Free Press, 1993), 20.
8. Ibid., 46.
9. Os Guinness, *The Great Experiment*, 25–26.
10. Os Guinness, *The American Hour*, 28.
11. Os Guinness, *The Great Experiment*, 146.
12. *Engel*, 370 U.S. 421 (1962).
13. Os Guinness, *The Great Experiment*, 16.
14. Jim DeMint and J. David Woodard, *Why We Whisper, Restoring Our Right to Say It's Wrong* (Lanham, MA: Rowman & Littlefield Publishers, 2008), 39.
15. *Griswold v. Connecticut*, 381 U.S. 479 (1965).
16. Jim DeMint and J. David Woodard, *Why We Whisper*, 41.
17. *Lawrence v. Texas*, 539 U.S. 558 (2003).
18. Jim DeMint and J. David Woodard, *Why We Whisper*, 79.
19. Ibid., 81.
20. Matthew Spalding, *The Founders' Almanac*, 55.
21. "Big Labor Does Gay Marriage," *The Wall Street Journal*, October 24, 2008.
22. Ibid.
23. Boy Scout Oath, www.scouting.org.
24. Jim DeMint and J. David Woodard, *Why We Whisper*, 73.
25. Ibid., 123.
26. Ibid., 123–24.
27. Ibid., 119.
28. Ibid., 121.
29. Rousas J. Rushdoony, *This Independent Republic* (Fairfax, VA: Thoburn Press, 1978), 5.
30. Jim DeMint and J. David Woodard, *Why We Whisper*, 115.
31. Ibid., 118.
32. Eric Hoffer, *The True Believer, Thoughts on the Nature of Mass Movements* (New York: Harper & Row Publishers, 1951), 36–37.
33. Os Guinness, *The American Hour*, 46.
34. Michael Novak, "Faith and the American Founding: Illustrating Religion's Influence" (First Principles Series #7 by The Heritage Foundation), 2.
35. Ibid.
36. Jim DeMint and J. David Woodard, *Why We Whisper*, 148.
37. Os Guinness, *The American Hour*, 75.
38. Ibid.
39. Ibid., 58.

Chapter Ten

1. Friedrich A. von Hayek, *The Road to Serfdom* (Chicago: University of Chicago Press, 1944), 80.
2. Ibid., 90.
3. Frederic Bastiat, *The Law* (New York: The Foundation for Economic Education, 1996), 9.
4. Ibid., 6.
5. Ibid., 10.
6. Ibid., 12.
7. Ibid., 22.
8. Ibid., 30–31.
9. Ibid., 32–33.
10. Ibid., 22–23.
11. Ibid., 28.
12. Ibid., 29.
13. Ibid., 29–30.
14. Ibid., 63–64.

15. Ibid., 46.
16. Friedrich A. von Hayek, *The Road to Serfdom*, 115–16.
17. Ibid., 90–91.
18. M. Stanton Evans, *The Theme Is Freedom, Religion, Politics, and the American Tradition* (Washington, D.C.: Regnery Publishing, 1994), 248.
19. Frederic Bastiat, *The Law*, 72.
20. Quotes from 2001 interviews on Chicago's WBEZ-FM, October 30, 2008.
21. Sarasota, Florida, from NBC Channel 6, www.youtube.com/watch?v=Bg98BvqUvCc.
22. Frederic Bastiat, *The Law*, 52.
23. Ibid., 67.
24. Ibid., 24.
25. Friedrich A. von Hayek, *The Road to Serfdom*, 92.
26. Frederic Bastiat, *The Law*, 75.
27. Ibid., 73.
28. Friedrich A. von Hayek, *The Road to Serfdom*, 84.

Chapter Eleven

1. H. L. Mencken, from *In Character Magazine*, vol. 3, no. 2, Winter 2007, 9.
2. Patricia Sampson, from *In Character Magazine*, vol. 3, no. 2, Winter 2007, 11.
3. William W. Beach, "The 2008 Index of Government Dependency," October 23, 2008, The Heritage Foundation, Center for Data Analysis Report #08-08, 1.
4. Mark Trumbull, "As U.S. Tax Rates Drop, Government's Reach Grows," April 16, 2007, *The Christian Science Monitor*.
5. William W. Beach, "The 2008 Index of Government Dependency," 1.
6. Ibid.
7. Ibid.
8. Ibid.
9. Ibid.
10. Ibid.
11. Ibid.
12. Marvin Olasky, *The Tragedy of American Compassion* (Washington, D.C.: Regnery Publishing, 1992), 45.
13. Mark Steyn, *America Alone, the End of the World as We Know It* (Washington, D.C.: Regnery Publishing, 2006), 44.
14. Tom Wolfe, quoted from article by George Scialabba, "The American Virtue," *In Character Magazine*, vol. 3, no. 2, Winter 2007, 16.
15. Edward T. Welch, *Addictions, a Banquet in the Grave* (New Jersey: P & R Publishing, 2001), 12.
16. Ibid., 46.
17. Sir Philip Sidney, *In Character Magazine*, 10.
18. Danny Kruger, "On Fraternity, Politics Beyond Liberty and Equality" (Civitas Institute, 2007), 26–27.
19. Myron Magnet, *The Dream and the Nightmare, The Sixties' Legacy to the Underclass* (New York: William Morrow and Company, 1993), 28.
20. Daniel Yankelovich and Sidney Harman, *Starting with the People* (Boston: Houghton Mifflin Company, 1988), 12.
21. Matthew Spalding, *The Founders Almanac* (Washington, D.C.: The Heritage Foundation, 2002), 58.
22. Ibid., 59.

Chapter Twelve

1. J. R. Nyquist (paraphrasing Joshua Rosner), "High Finance and Bolshevik Principle," Geopolitical Global Analysis, July 18, 2008, at www.financialsense.com.
2. Friedrich A. von Hayek, *The Road to Serfdom* (Chicago: The University of Chicago Press, 1944), 68.
3. Adam Smith, *The Wealth of Nations* (London: Penguin Books, 1986), 443.
4. Ibid., 11.
5. Ibid., 17.
6. Ibid., 119.
7. Ibid., 77.
8. Friedrich A. von Hayek, *The Road to Serfdom*, 15.
9. Ibid., 15.
10. Ibid., 24–25.
11. Ibid., 29.
12. Ibid., 71.

13. Ibid.
14. Ibid., 81.
15. Ibid., 77.
16. Milton and Rose Friedman, *Free to Choose* (New York: Harcourt Brace & Company, 1990), ix.
17. Ibid., 3.
18. Ibid., 4.
19. Ibid., 5.
20. Ibid., 6.
21. Ibid., 7.
22. Russell Kirk, *The Conservative Mind, from Burke to Eliot* (Washington, D.C.: Regnery Publishing, 1985), 178.
23. Joseph Cardinal Ratzinger (Pope Benedict XVI), "Market Economy and Ethics," presented to a 1985 symposium in Rome titled "Church and Economy in Dialogue."

Chapter Thirteen

1. William J. Federer, *America's God and Country* (Coppell, TX: FAME Publishing, 1994), 323.
2. Ibid., 16.
3. Quotes About Liberty, Liberty Education Fund, at www.libertyed.org/quotes.html.
4. Ronald Reagan, First Inaugural Address, January 20, 1981, at www.reaganlibrary.com.
5. William J. Federer, *America's God and Country*, 234.
6. Ibid., 235.
7. "10 Facts about K-12 Education Funding," U.S. Department of Education, 2005, at www.ed.edu.
8. Ibid.
9. John Stuart Mill, 1859, available at http://quotes.liberty-tree.ca.
10. See www.heritage.org/Research/Education/denotes58.cfm.
11. Paul Ryan, see www.AmericanRoadmap.org.
12. Ibid.
13. Dr. Benjamin Rush, 1787, available at www.medicalchoiceforaz.com.
14. The Congressional Budget Office and Office of Management and Budget.
15. Billy Graham's "Prayer for Our Nation" recited by The Reverend Joe Wright, www.snopes.com/politics/soapbox/prayernation.asp.

Chapter Fourteen

1. See www.quotesdaddy.com/author/William+Scranton.